2-

FLORIDA FIREARMS

LAW, USE & OWNERSHIP

Sixth Edition – 2009

By: Jon H. Gutmacher, Esq.

Copyright 2009 by jon h. gutmacher

D0094244

WARLORD PUBLISHING
-- a division of --
Jon H. Gutmacher, P.A.
200 N. Thornton Ave.
Orlando, Florida 32801
Phone: (407) 650-0770

www.FloridaFirearmsLaw.com

Author: *Jon H. Gutmacher*

First Publication: November 1993
Fifth Edition: December 2003
Sixth Edition: 11/05; 7/06; 3/08; 12/08; 4/09
Copyright 1993 thru 2009
by jon h. gutmacher

Warnings & Disclaimer:

ISBN   978-0-9641958-4-4 $29.95

The author wishes to thank, and gratefully
acknowledge Kahr Arms for supplying for testing its Model PM-9, polymer, semi-auto 9mm pistol. This is a 14 oz. (unloaded), DAO (double action only)) pistol with excellent accuracy and recoil. The manufacturer is situated in New York state, and has an outstanding reputation. My testing of the firearm was flawless in every respect, and in the author's opinion is an excellent concealed carry gun in this caliber.

Cover photo: KAHR Model PM-9

TABLE OF CONTENTS

FORWARD

I was assisting a Sergeant on a local police department range about four years ago while we were teaching a firearms safety course. During a break he handed me a book he had recently acquired, and told me it was the only up-to-date, viable work of its kind, and that it covered everything anybody would want to know about the law concerning firearms, weapons, and self-defense. He told me I should read it. I thought I didn't need to, but when I took it home, I found myself reading it three times straight, cover-to-cover. The book was an earlier version of the one you are holding: "FLORIDA FIREARMS — Law, Use & Ownership".

While reading it, I became convinced that it was the very best work of its kind I have ever seen, anywhere. The author, who I've since had the pleasure to meet, and call a friend, has relentlessly researched his data, and is considered in the trade as not just an expert on the subject, but is also known as "the man who wrote the book". But, it's not just a book about the law — it's a serious reality check on how the law actually works, and how to unravel the confusion. More importantly, it wasn't written for lawyers, it was written for you and me — and not only is it understandable, but it has humor, and is a quick read. That's really something when you realize that this is one of the most over-regulated areas of the law there is!

When I teach a course in firearms tactics for the average citizen, the fear they express isn't so much of criminal attack, instead, it's the fear of what happens afterwards. "Will the police arrest me?" "How will I pay for my defense?" "What if I get sued? Will I lose everything I own just because I defended my life, and the lives of my family?"

These are serious concerns — but most firearms instructors, including police officers, are not equipped to handle any but the most basic answers — and many times, the answers they give are dead wrong. We're not lawyers, and never will be. Why kid yourself? Even most lawyers don't deal with this stuff regularly enough to know all the nuances. So, where do we get the advice? How do we keep ourselves, and our students out of trouble?

Common sense is a good starting place, but if you don't know the rules — it's kind of tough to play the game. So, like I said before, I advise my students, my instructors, and my friends that there is only one "reliable" place to do that — and that starts and ends with reading this book.

Take the author's advice. This is the man professionals call for legal and practical guidance. This is the man I want to defend me if I ever get in a jam. Read it! Not once, not twice — but on a regular basis, because every time you pick it up you'll find something you missed the last time you looked at it. I've put a protective cover on mine, and I still wear books out on a regular basis.

There's not much more I can tell you. I've been doing this all my lifetime, and I know a good thing when I see it. If you want to stay out of jail, and keep from paying serious attorney fees on a mistake that could have been prevented — this book is the best answer you'll ever find. Tell your friends about it if they really are your friends. I do.

Gary W. Belson
Firearms Instructor

INTRODUCTION

You're now reading the fifth printing of the Sixth edition. The first printing came out in November 2005. This latest revision was completed in April 2009. It is a <u>substantial</u> rewrite of all prior printings of this edition, and involved quite a bit of new research. If you had the earlier December 2008 release – you'd hardly recognize some parts of the book. If you had the November 2005 version, or earlier – you wouldn't recognize it at all.

The book has now sold over 110.000 copies since inception, and continues to be the leading book of its kind in the country. We're used in over eighty law enforcement agencies, in numerous circuit courts, and we're in every appellate court in the state. It's no longer a hard sell – it's a "must have". For many instructors, making sure students purchase the book is mandatory – not because they need the money – but because owning a firearm without this book is just legally dangerous.

As usual, I've tried to update everything that's been happening in the law, with a few exceptions. Plus, as time passes, sometimes my thinking modifies on various issues, and often it gives me new insight which I try to pass on. Firearms and self-defense are constantly evolving areas – if you want to stay on top of it, you're always learning, and always open to what's happening in the field.

If you're interested in why the book was first written – that happened back in 1993. After I left the State Attorney's Office, I used to go to gun shows, and give out free information on self-defense issues. It seemed like a good way to meet prospective clients, and was fun, besides. While I was doing this – people would ask me lots of questions about other firearm, weapon, and self-defense issues I hadn't come across before. I therefore gave the individual an answer based on common sense and my legal experience – but I also had the intelligence to tell them to come back the following day, or the next gun show – and I'd look it up, and give them the "researched" answer.

The amazing thing that happened was – even with numerous years of experience – I was wrong at least half the time, especially if it involved federal law. What I learned from that is that in the area of firearms, weapons, and self-defense – you either know "exactly" what the law says – or you're probably wrong. Common sense doesn't count that much – knowing the law does! Moreover, to understand the statutes – especially the federal ones – you have to chart them, then read the regulations – and then read the case law that explains it. If you don't – your answer is more likely wrong than right. And that, my friends – can mean the difference between a jail sentence, or not getting in trouble in the first place.

Well, that's how it all started. Eventually people asked me where they could get all the answers I was giving them – and quite frankly, there was no other place except me! That's when people started asking me to write a book. It took a couple of years before that started to make sense – but in 1993 it finally did – and after 3000 hours of research and writing – the first edition of Florida Firearms came off the press.

Times change. I don't give out free information at gun shows anymore. Instead, I get lots and lots of emails from citizens asking questions in this complex area. Most of the questions come thru my website where I have an email link. Some I use for the book, some I use for my column in Rods N Guns magazine, some I use for my blog. However, I try to answer all the emails as long as they're not looking for advice that really requires extensive time – and that keeps abreast of new issues, and what people want to know about.

To make sure the book stays up-to-date, I place free updates on my website twice yearly. Check the update policy in the last chapter. However, please understand that no matter what you do – even if you faithfully update your book – your book has an average "effective" life span of two years. After that – if you're serious about staying out of jail – purchase a new one.

Why?

Because the law is constantly changing, and so is the book. It gets rewritten at least once a year – sometimes twice a year. And, although the updates will keep you current on all major changes in the law, the book will always go into more detail, and will many times go into areas that are not "major changes", but are still real important.

As with all books about the law, there is a warning that it carries. That warning is that no matter what you do, there is no guarantee that the responding police officer knows the law, or that the law will be interpreted in your favor, even when it seems clear to you. There are a number of issues that are in flux, or have not been decided on by the courts. Likewise, there was a certain amount of information that was left to my interpretation, and interpretations can be changed when an appellate court gets hold of the issue – especially when the attorneys and judges don't know or understand the area. Moreover, firearms law is a field of mountainous regulations that are always changing, and when you talk about the area of self-defense, your actions will often be judged after-the-fact, by persons far removed from the actual circumstances. Common sense rarely seems to apply, and you must know what the law says in order to legally survive.

While this book is not written as legal advice, it's been found to be authorative by an awful lot of very knowledgeable people including the NRA, Florida Sheriffs Association, Florida Association of State Troopers, Gun Owners of America, and the American Firearms Industry. It will clarify most of your questions about some very complicated areas, and will point out the areas of law that appear to remain in controversy. While it's not perfect -- many people – including those in the industry, law enforcement, and the courts – think it's about as good as it can get.

I plan to keep it that way. Hope you enjoy it, and more so, I hope it does what it was designed for: to keep you out of trouble.

Jon H. Gutmacher, Esq.

CHAPTER ONE

THE RIGHT TO BEAR ARMS
AND CONSTITUTIONAL ASPECTS

On December 15, 1791, the Congress of the United States ratified the first ten amendments to the Constitution. These Amendments have been become known to us as the "Bill of Rights". Foremost among them, from the standpoint of this book, is the Second Amendment.

In a historical context, the Second Amendment covers two clearly distinct concerns of the framers of our Constitution. One was to insure the rights of the People to keep and bear arms. The other was to insure the existence of the popular militia. I will discuss both.

THE BILL OF RIGHTS
THE SECOND AMENDMENT

"A well regulated militia, being necessary to the security of a free State, the right of the people to keep and bear arms, shall not be infringed."

A WELL REGULATED MILITIA:

At the time of the Constitutional Convention, a loose confederation of thirteen individual colonies had just defeated King George of England in what was basically a citizen's revolution. For the most part, the American Revolution was won by a collection of locally organized militia which had been banded together into larger groups and armies to fight the common enemy, the British. These militia were comprised of freemen from all walks of life, who were locally organized, self-armed, and who trained and drilled under locally elected leaders. This was the choice method of defense -- as regular, or "standing armies" were thought by many of the free populace to be instruments of tyranny -- the means by which despots and kings were able to control their subjects by force, and thereby rule. Thus, the definition of "well regulated militia", was simply a well understood reference to an independent group of self-armed freemen, under self-elected leadership, who regularly or occasionally drilled, and were not under government control. In more general terms, it was clearly understood that the phrase "well regulated militia" referred to the "body of the people", ie: the free citizens of the land, as a whole.[1]

There was much argument during the Constitutional Convention whether the creation of a central government would tend to foster tyranny, and much of this discussion revolved around the argument as to whether a standing army for this central government should be permitted at all. Many enlightened thinkers of the time believed in the concept that "power tends to corrupt", thus they had a basic fear of any centralized government, and its eventual ability to oppress.

The only counter to this fear was that a well organized militia comprised of the free people of the several states would always be more powerful than any standing army -- and thus the People could overthrow any corruption of government by force of numbers. Moreover, the thinking that also pervaded the times was clearly that the local militia would always be necessary to the national and local defense -- as there was no desire to allow a centralized government to gain such power as to obviate this need. Of course, to guarantee these beliefs, the right for a people's militia had to be ensured. The result of this thinking lies in the first part of the wording in the Second Amendment: "being necessary to a free state".

Somehow, the well regulated militia has passed-away over time, and has been replaced by the professional soldier, the National Guard, and an organized police force. The National Guard has little to do with what the Framers of the Constitution envisioned as "a well regulated militia" as it lacks the localization, freedom from government control, and freedom from government purse strings that would be necessary to this concept. In fact, the National Guard would have been defined as a "select militia" in the late 1700's, that term meaning a militia armed and maintained by the government, and obviously subject to its discipline.

So, don't get thrown off track by media misinformation. A "well organized militia" historically referred to the body of the free citizens of this country, locally organized, and free of government control. While we probably don't need such active militias now, the right to have them is historic, and is guaranteed in the Constitution.

THE RIGHT TO KEEP AND BEAR ARMS:

What phrasing could be any more clear than that of "the right of the people to keep and bear arms, shall not be infringed." Yet, until 2008 hardly anyone except historians, and the Fifth Circuit Court of Appeals[2] understood that it meant exactly what it said. However, on June 26, 2008, the United States Supreme Court, decided the case of District of Columbia v. Heller, 128 S.Ct. 2783 (2008), which changed that forever. Let me tell you in very succinct fashion exactly what the Opinion said:

First – the Second Amendment protects an individual right of firearms ownership for purposes of self defense unconnected with any militia or military purpose. The Court held that the historical purpose of the Amendment was to make sure the federal government would not seize firearms from citizens, and thereby be able to rule over them in a tyrannical fashion. Moreover, it made clear that at the time of its passage the right of free citizens to own and possess firearms for self defense was sacrosanct.   Still, the Court recognized that the right to own and possess firearms is not without limitations, and that unusually dangerous weapons, and those used primarily by criminals could be regulated - just as they were in Colonial times.   However, since handguns are the primary defensive weapon of choice in the modern era – these weapons are protected under the Second Amendment.

That's the entire essence of the Opinion.   There are lots of historical quotes, lots of cases quoted, and lots of facts and figures – but – in the end, it's all that simple. Now true, four Justices weren't real happy with that analysis. Their main argument was that the Second Amendment has outlived its usefulness - so we should just ignore it!

The majority opinion responded to this argument by stating:

"A constitutional guarantee subject to future judges' assessments of its usefulness is no constitutional guarantee at all. Constitutional rights are enshrined with the scope they were understood to have when the people adopted them, whether or not future legislatures or (yes) even future judges think that scope too broad."[3]

A WARNING ABOUT CONSTITUTIONAL INTERPRETATION:

People should be wary about constitutional changes. Every time the State or Federal Constitution is amended -- you, the ordinary citizen, are giving-up more and more of your "retained", and supposedly "inalienable" rights.

Why?

Because in our country, government derives <u>all</u> of its power from the People. This is in the form of those grants of power embodied in the Constitution. What the Constitution says the government can do -- is all it is authorized to do, nothing more! If it wasn't given to the government in the Constitution -- it is "retained" by the People -- and the government cannot legally interfere with any of these "retained" rights.

So, why do we have a "Bill of Rights"? Aren't these rights retained, anyway?

Basically, whenever a Bill of Rights is adopted, it is a precautionary statement of those rights which the People want to make especially sure the government realizes are off limits to legislative or judicial erosion! In other words, it's a statement by a bunch of real nervous people that don't trust the government, in the first place. Or, like Thomas Jefferson said:

"Government is a necessary evil"

In Florida we've gotten into some bad habits, because we tend to randomly amend the State Constitution on fairly regular basis, instead of recognizing it for what it is. Since a constitution is supposed to be a basic framework for government -- it's not a good idea to go amending it every year. That's what the legislature is for. They pass laws, amend laws, repeal laws -- all within the framework the constitution has set forth.

It may seem like a good idea to amend the Constitution in the heat of the moment, but most of the time, we realize we'd have been better off if we just left it alone, and let the courts or the legislature deal with it. An example of this are the additions recently made to the Florida Constitution regarding the right to keep and bear arms. Here it is:

FLORIDA'S RIGHT TO KEEP AND BEAR ARMS:

Florida Constitution, Article I, Section 8:

(a)   The right of the people to keep and bear arms in defense of themselves and of the lawful authority of the state shall not be infringed, except that the manner of bearing arms may be regulated by law.

(b)   There shall be a mandatory period of three days, excluding weekends and legal holidays, between the purchase and delivery at retail of any handgun. For the purposes of this section, "purchase" means the transfer of money or other valuable consideration to the retailer and "handgun" means a firearm capable of being carried and used by one hand, such as a pistol or revolver. Holders of a concealed weapon permit as prescribed in Florida law shall not be subject to the provision of this paragraph.

(c)   The legislature shall enact legislation implementing subsection (b) of this section, effective no later than December 31, 1991, which shall provide that anyone violating the provisions of subsection (b) shall be guilty of a felony.

(d)   This restriction shall not apply to a trade in of another handgun.

The restrictions set forth in this section of the Constitution cannot be changed by the Legislature, the Governor, or the Judiciary. The People voted for it, and made it part of the "unchangeable" portion of our basic law. For better or worse, it's there forever -- unless the citizens vote to change the Constitution, again.

PREEMPTION LAW:

Florida is a "preemption" state. That means that the legislature has decided to keep local government out of firearms regulation, unless it specifically authorizes an exemption. The reason we have a preemption law is because of all the problems we had before this law was enacted. Every local government had its own version of the law, and nobody knew what the heck the law was from city-to-city, or county-to-county. In essence, it was politics at its worst — and the citizens paid the price.

F.S. 790.33 sets forth the preemption law as follows:

"Except as expressly provided by general law, the legislature hereby declares that it is occupying the whole field of regulation of firearms and ammunition, including the purchase, sale, transfer, taxation, manufacture, ownership, possession, and transportation thereof, to the exclusion of all existing and future county, city, town, or municipal ordinances or regulations relating thereto. Any such existing ordinances are hereby declared null and void. This subsection shall not affect zoning ordinances which encompass firearms businesses along with other businesses. Zoning ordinances which are designed for the purpose of restricting or prohibiting the sale, purchase, transfer, or manufacture of firearms or ammunition as a method of regulating firearms or ammunition are in conflict with this subsection and are prohibited."

"It is the policy and intent of this section to provide uniform firearms laws in the state; to declare all ordinances and regulations null and void which have been enacted by any jurisdiction other than state and federal, which regulate firearms, ammunition, or components thereof unless specifically authorized by this section or general law; and to require local jurisdictions to enforce state firearms laws."

You might note that the preemption statute does not apply to weapons other than firearms and ammunition. F.S. 790.33 This was a serious oversight by the legislature. However, pursuant to Florida constitutional law, local government is still restricted from regulating other weapons if they pass laws that conflict with Chapter 790 of the Florida Statutes. [4]

STATISTICAL DATA ON USE OF FIREARMS:

In recent years there has been a serious attempt to discredit the private ownership of firearms, and to minimize and distort the meaning of the Second Amendment. Media has taken an increasingly active part in this conspiracy, and seems to be a leading proponent in the battle to despoil your right of self-defense. The classic argument is that if by banning firearms we can "save one life" -- it will be worth it all.[5] Of course, that means giving up more of your fast disappearing personal liberty. But more importantly, it distorts the actual truth.

Statistics compiled by the government show that firearm accidents have significantly declined over the years, not just percentage wise -- but also numerically. In fact, according to a 1990 study by the Florida Office of Vital Statistics -- Floridians are more likely to die from an accident involving medical malpractice (126), a fall (620), a drowning (453), or electrocution (45), rather than from a firearm's accident (36). Statistics thru 2007 show the average is now down to 21 deaths per year with only 17 in 2007 out of a population of 18,396,828 Floridians.

Moreover, research done by Florida State University professor Gary Kleck has established that 800,000 to 2.5 million people a year use a firearm throughout the United States in lawful self-defense, and in stopping the commission of serious felonies.[6] How many lives are saved by firearms? Plenty! But, don't ask the media to tell you about that. That's not what they're in business for.

In an ideal society, there would be no criminals, no terrorists, no foreign enemies, and no need for self-defense. But that society is a dream, and the reality is that law-abiding citizens need a method to defend themselves, their property, and their families. A firearm furnishes that method, and if a person learns gun safety, and has a basic knowledge of what he or she can lawfully do, all of society benefits by their being armed. That is one of the basic pillars upon which this Great Nation was founded. The media be damned.

THE EXTENSION OF THE POWERS OF CONGRESS:
Earlier in this chapter I briefly mentioned why you need to be cautious about giving away your "retained rights", by constitutional amendment. Let me show you how this has run amuck in the federal system -- so you can understand where all these federal regulations are coming from, at least, from a legal standpoint.

Article 1, section 1, of the United States Constitution states that "all legislative powers *herein granted* shall be vested in a Congress of the United States . . . ." That literally means that if the Constitution doesn't grant them the power -- they don't have the power. The Bill of Rights, in the Tenth Amendment, states that "the powers not delegated to the United States by the Constitution, nor prohibited by it to the States, are reserved to the States respectively, or to the people." That section basically means the same thing, but more forcefully. Literally, it means that the powers not granted to Congress, and not withheld from the states (such as the right to make treaties, formulate currency, etc.) are reserved to the several states, or their citizens.

Last but not least, we have the Ninth Amendment to the United States Constitution. This states that "the enumeration in the Constitution of certain rights, shall not be construed to deny or disparage others retained by the people". This means that those rights which were thought by the framers of the Constitutional to be the "natural" or "inalienable" rights of free citizens -- cannot be infringed upon by the government.

Well, it all sounds good, but in actuality it hasn't been working too well since the time the Civil War began. Let me show you why, by giving you a brief lesson in Constitutional law:

A BRIEF LESSON IN CONSTITUTIONAL LAW:

The Tenth Amendment to the United States Constitution reserves all powers not otherwise delegated to Congress, to the individual States, or to the People. However, Congress, with the apathetic assistance of the federal judiciary, has managed to completely usurp the purpose of this Amendment. In essence, the federal judicial system has generally failed in its responsibilities, and lets Congress run amuck by not policing it. Let me give you an example:

An extremely important federal appellate decision, United States v. Lopez, invalidated a portion of the 1990 "Gun-Free School Zones Act". This remarkably dumb federal law made it a federal felony to possess a firearm within 1000 feet of a school zone. It was dumb because if you happened to be driving within 999.9 feet of a one room wooden kindergarten, even if the kids were home on vacation, even if you didn't know it was there until you went around that blind curve in the road that suddenly revealed it, and even if there's a raging river between the road you're on and the school -- you're in deep buffalo chips with the law unless you have a CWP.

Now, you ask: "How can Congress legislate such a law? Isn't this a purely an area of state concern, reserved to the state legislatures?"

Excellent question! I see I've gotten you thinking!

However, and unfortunately, the answer, according to your wonderful federal government, is "no" -- and that's because Congress can presumably pass any law they want, under the power of the "Commerce Clause", because Congress has the Constitutionally granted power to regulate anything that "substantially affects interstate or foreign commerce", and in such instances, the Tenth Amendment doesn't apply. In other words, the Tenth Amendment would restrict the exercise of federal lawmaking jurisdiction only when there are no other clauses in the Constitution under which the Congress has power to act! In essence, this would require a process of elimination.   Thus, if Congress can't pass legislation under the Commerce Clause -- is there another clause they could still pass it under? If not -- the law would be outside of its power to act, and therefore "reserved" to the States.

"Is this really the law," you ask?

The unfortunate answer is "yes"   -- but that's not the most unfortunate part.   You see -- the courts are supposed to have the authority to make sure that any power exercised by Congress is exercised legitimately. That's what our Founding Fathers meant by "a system of checks and balances". In other words, if the Congress wants to legislate something under the Commerce Clause, then the problem it's attempting to address and rectify should, in actuality, "substantially affect interstate or foreign commerce". If it doesn't -- then it's an illegitimate use of power that's supposed to be reserved to the individual state legislatures, or the People.

The problem here is that the federal courts normally don't do that kind of policing. In actuality, they routinely "defer" to any factual findings made by Congress, no matter how unsupported, or outlandish these findings may be! All you need is some Senator or Congressman saying: "We're passing this legislation because gun possession around a school affects interstate commerce" -- and Whoop-de-Doo -- the court usually says: "Fine -- sounds good to us!"

That's basically what United States v. Lopez said. In fact, the Opinion of the Court actually said that it was not really its job to second guess Congress -- but, it was *up to the People* to elect representatives who would not pass unconstitutional laws under the guise of constitutional ones. To put it another way: if you elect representatives who don't understand or care about the Constitution, and your rights -- you get what you deserve.

So much for the system of "checks and balances" that our Founding Fathers envisioned. Let one part fail, and the result is that Liberty pays the price!

However, the Lopez court still invalidated the law because the federalists in Congress actually forgot to include any statement that commerce "was affected" by guns near schools when they passed the Act -- and thus the court was free to determine from a standpoint of common sense (something little used in government) -- that this stupid law really had nothing to do with interstate commerce in the first place, didn't affect it one iota -- and was therefore unconstitutional.

So, for a short time, the citizens lucked out -- only because of a simple oversight. If not, the magic words, "affecting commerce" would have been uttered at the right moment in Congress, and another oppressive law would have stayed on the books, unchecked by the one branch of government that the Founding Fathers thought would stop such abuses.

It seems that the federal courts are too political, and too "politically correct". If the Constitution must suffer -- it usually does. However, there is some rare good news in this rather one-sided area. In the last few years we've started to see changes in the cases coming out of the United States Supreme Court. It appears that a small majority of the Supreme Court is beginning to interpret legislation in a more traditional manner, consistent with our basic constitutional precepts. This is a very welcome change. In fact, in the <u>Lopez</u>[7] case that I just discussed, the Supreme Court, by a very narrow margin, sustained the decision of the federal appellate court, and agreed that the "1000 foot law" had no substantial affect on interstate commerce, and was therefore beyond the power of Congress to enact.

Of course, Congress was not to be deterred, and after the Supreme Court made it clear that the law was an unconstitutional intrusion into an area of purely state concern — Congress reenacted the law, once again, with the following findings:

> "The Congress finds and declares that crime, particularly crime involving drugs and guns, is a pervasive, nationwide problem; crime at the local level is exacerbated by the interstate movement of drugs, guns, and criminal gangs; firearms and ammunition move easily in interstate commerce and have been found in increasing numbers in and around schools, as documented in numerous hearings in both the Committee on the Judiciary of the House of Representatives and the Committee on the Judiciary of the Senate; in fact, even before the sale of a firearm, the gun, its component parts, ammunition, and the raw materials from which they are made have considerably moved in interstate commerce; while criminals freely move from State to State, ordinary citizens and foreign visitors may fear to travel to or through certain parts of the country due to concern about violent crime and gun violence, and parents may decline to send their children to school for the same reason; the occurrence of violent crime in school zones has resulted in a decline in the quality of education in our country; this decline in the quality of education has an adverse impact on interstate commerce and the foreign commerce of the United States; States, localities, and school systems find it almost impossible to handle gun-related crime by themselves--even States, localities, and school systems that have made strong efforts to prevent, detect, and punish gun-related crime find their efforts unavailing due in part to the failure or inability of other States or localities to take strong measures; and the Congress has the power, under the interstate commerce clause and other provisions of the Constitution, to enact measures to ensure the integrity and safety of the nation's schools by enactment of this subsection.

So, we're back where we started — and we've proven what we knew all along -- that many of our representatives don't care about the Constitution when it comes to guns. The question that remains now is what will the Supreme Court do if the issue gets back to them, again? At least two appellate decisions have held the amended statute as constitutional. <u>Danks</u>, 221 F.3d 1037 (8th Cir. 1999); <u>Pierson</u>, 139

F.3d 501 (5th Cir. 1998). But, a recent Supreme Court decision seems to reassert the invalidity. U.S. v. Morrison, 146 L.ed.2d 658 (2000).[8] From a practical standpoint, it's likely the lower appellate decisions will stand, because the Supreme Court rarely accepts jurisdiction, even when a decision is wrong. Just remember, if you have a concealed permit, you don't have a problem with this law because that's one of the law's few exceptions. So — get the permit!

Obviously, only the Supreme Court should be able to change that interpretation of unconstitutionality. However, federal courts tend to rule in favor of the government almost all the time. They rarely interpret the law to protect the People — instead, they interpret the law to protect the government. Again, a concept that the Founding Fathers might have trouble with. Only time will tell.

Some other recent decisions of the Supreme Court have also been promising. The Court invalidated portions of the Brady law [9], and in another case required the government to prove "willful" violations of certain firearm laws before a conviction could be obtained.[10] Still, these decisions have been won by a one vote majority -- and are being made by a very divided Court. The tide is beginning to change, but it sure has a long way to go.

Interesting, huh?

So, now that you've gotten your first lesson in Constitutional Law, maybe you'll see the reality of how important it is in voting the right people in (or out) of office. And maybe, when next you hear someone complain, you can tell them that if things go badly, it's probably their own damn fault for not electing patriots.

WAITING PERIODS ON FIREARMS SALES:
Florida has multiple laws and constitutional provisions regarding gun sales. The provisions, and statutes overlap – and only cause confusion. Why we need all of them is beyond me, but since we have them – here's your explanation in a nutshell – no pun intended.

First, Florida Constitution, Article 1, section 8, requires a three (3) day waiting period between the purchase and delivery at retail of any handgun, except as to Concealed Weapon Permit holders. The provision does not apply to a trade of a handgun for another handgun with no cash involved. Weekends and legal holidays are not counted in the waiting period, and you begin counting days on the day following the sale. (ie: sale is Monday – delivery can't be until Friday. Sale is on Sunday – delivery can't be until Thursday).

Fla. Const., Article 8, section 5(b), is a more recent provision that grants each county the right to pass ordinances that require a criminal history records check, and/or a 3-5 day waiting period (excluding weekends and legal holidays) on the sale of **any** type firearm when any part of the transaction is conducted on property "*to which the public has a right of access*". Holders of a Concealed Weapons Permit are again exempted from this provision. The phrase "to which the public has a right of access", has not been defined. However, since the entire purpose of the provision was to curb alleged (but almost non-existent) "gun show abuses" at municipally owned facilities – the phrase should mean it applies to non-private property, or, to put it another way – "government owned property". That's because on private property – the general public has no "right" to enter, although they usually have a limited "license" to enter, which may be revoked at will by the owner. However, since the amendment failed to define the phrase regarding "right of access" some counties have been interpreting this as anywhere the public is allowed to go. A test case waiting to happen.

There are also a couple of statutes that cover waiting periods and criminal history checks. The first, Florida Statute 790.33(2), allows a county to adopt up to a three (3) working day waiting period for any gun sales from a retail establishment, but exempts sales at gun shows, exhibits, and sales by private collectors. Thus, it does not apply to private sales not made at a retail establishment. On the other hand, Florida Statute 790.0655 imposes a mandatory three (3) day waiting period on the sale of any handgun at retail - anywhere. Almost an exact duplicate of Florida Constitution, Art. 1, section 8, which was discussed earlier.

So – like I keep telling people – instead of trying to remember all this stuff – just get a concealed weapons permit, and relax.

(this page reserved)

CHAPTER TWO

QUALIFICATIONS FOR PURCHASING, OR POSSESSION OF FIREARMS

Did you notice the title of this chapter? Did it seem a little unusual? Qualifications for purchasing -- or possession of firearms? Surely, it should say qualifications for purchasing, and possession of firearms?

However, the answer is a definite no. Anytime a person seeks to purchase, borrow, own, or possess a firearm, a different set of rules probably applies. Moreover, these rules are governed by both State and Federal law. You must comply with both sets of law to be legal.

In fact, there are certain qualifications for ownership of a firearm, that are dramatically different from those required to purchase a firearm. This chapter will outline those requirements for you, at least as required by Florida and federal law. In another state, different rules could apply.

DEFINITION OF A "FIREARM":
Before we get into the guts of this chapter, you need to know what is, and what is not -- a firearm. So, let me tell you what the definitions and non-definition of a firearm are.

In its most basic form, a firearm is any weapon that discharges a projectile by use of an explosive charge, or is designed or is readily convertible to such a use. Both the federal and Florida definitions include the frame or receiver of any such weapon, and any firearm muffler or silencer. F.S. 790.001(6). Firearm mufflers and silencers are generally illegal to possess, and will be covered elsewhere in this book.

The federal definition also encompasses any **"destructive devices"** which include all explosives, poison gas, bombs, grenades, rockets with more than 4 ounces of propellant, missiles with an explosive or incendiary charge of over one quarter ounce, mines, and most devices which are not shotguns that have a inside barrel diameter (bore) of one half inch or more, and will fire a projectile. The definition also includes any combination of parts by which such a device can be readily assembled.

The only exception to the definition is when the item is not generally considered to be a "weapon". One such example would be a "potato cannon", which is generally considered to be a recreational device made of PVC irrigation pipe that is used to fire potatoes or golf balls by use of a propellant such as ignited hair spray or MAPP gas. Since its use is really not as a weapon -- it is not considered a "destructive device". However, if you used it as a weapon -- then it should qualify for the definition, and could get you in some very serious problems. Another example would be legal fireworks, and probably illegal fireworks, to the extent they are not being used as a weapon, but are being used merely as fireworks.[11]

ANTIQUE FIREARMS -- AND OTHER EXCEPTIONS:
One of the exceptions to the usual definition of a firearm is the class of weapons known as "antique firearms." An antique firearm is usually, but not always, a black-powder gun of some sort, and is generally classified as a "weapon", rather than as a "firearm". This is a major distinction in definition, because "weapons" that are not legally defined as "firearms" escape a large number of state and federal regulations that otherwise would apply.

In order to be an "antique firearm" under Florida law, the weapon must have been manufactured during or before **1918**, or be a replica of such, and it may not use "fixed ammunition" unless this fixed ammunition is no longer manufactured in the United States, and is not readily available in ordinary commerce. Likewise, Federal law defines an antique firearm as any firearm manufactured before **1898**, or a replica thereof. If it's a replica, it can't use rimfire or conventional fixed ammunition unless that ammunition is no longer manufactured in the U.S., and not readily available for purchase. "Fixed ammunition" is defined as self-contained ammunition consisting of a case, primer, explosive charge, and projectile.

A 1998 amendment to the federal law [18 USC 921(16)(C)] also defines an antique firearm as any muzzle-loading firearm that is designed to use black powder or a black powder substitute, cannot use fixed ammunition, and cannot be converted from a modern firearm, or readily convertible to any firearm that can fire fixed ammunition.[12]

You should be aware that if you use an antique firearm in the commission of a crime -- it becomes a firearm, and loses it's status as an "antique firearm".[13]

Unfortunately, in Bostic v. State, 902 So. 2d 225 (Fla. 5DCA 2005), the Fifth District Court of Appeals, somewhat muggled up the Florida definition, and held that the black powder muzzle loading rifle the defendant used for hunting (Thompson Center Arms Model Black Diamond) was not an "antique firearm", but was instead a "firearm" because it was not a "**reasonably exact reproduction**" of a muzzle loading firearm produced on or before the year of 1918. Thus, since Mr. Bostic was a convicted felon, he was subject to being found guilty of a second degree felony (15 year maximum prison sentence with three year mandatory minimum prison sentence) as a felon in possession of a firearm pursuant to F.S. 790.23. The Opinion of the court was right for all the wrong reasons.

Why?

Well, if you trace the history of the definition of "antique firearms" you find out that prior to 1969 there was no Florida law that defined an "antique firearm". A convicted felon back in those days, according to Florida law, could legally own any firearm other than a pistol, sawed-off rifle, or sawed-off shotgun. Federal law added some other restrictions, but in essence, a convicted felon could own most long-guns. However, with the assassination of Martin Luther King on April 4, 1968, and Robert F. Kennedy on June 5, 1968, Congress passed the Gun Control Act of 1968 which made sweeping changes in gun laws. The federal law also created a class of firearms known as "antique firearms", and left them as an unregulated category of guns by stating any such gun was not to be defined as a "firearm". The theory was that these firearms were not as powerful or capable as modern firearms, and didn't really pose a criminal threat. Thus, an antique firearm could still be purchased and shipped through the mail, and owned and possessed by convicted felons. In a more modern context – an "antique firearm" does not need a NICS check at point of sale, nor any waiting period. Well, at least not until the <u>Bostic</u> case came along.

The problem in the Opinion comes from the lack of clarity in both the federal and Florida statutes as to what is a "replica". According to Florida law as defined in F.S. 790.001(1), an " 'antique firearm' means any firearm manufactured in or before 1918 *(including any matchlock, flintlock, percussion cap, or similar early type of ignition system)* or *replica thereof,* whether actually manufactured before or after the year 1918 . . . ." The 1968 federal statute (18 USC 921 (16)) has many substantial similarities, and defines an antique firearm as:

(A)   any firearm (including any firearm with a matchlock, flintlock, percussion cap, or similar type of ignition system) manufactured in or before 1898; or

(B)   any replica of any firearm described in subparagraph (A)if such replica:

(i) is not designed or redesigned for using rimfire or conventional centerfire fixed ammunition, or

(ii) uses rimfire or conventional centerfire fixed ammunition which is no longer manufactured in the United States and which is not readily available in the ordinary channels of commercial trade;

Common sense tells you that the Florida law was meant to be given similar meaning to the federal definition. Moreover, in the case of <u>Modern Muzzleloading, Inc. V. Magaw</u>, 18 F. Supp. 2d 29 (Dist. Columbia 1998), both the government and the court recognized that the definition of a "replica" included "any matchlock, flintlock, percussion cap, or similar early type of ignition system" so long as it was "not designed or redesigned for using rimfire or conventional centerfire fixed ammunition". This was in accord with a longstanding interpretation by ATF, and confirmed in ATF Industry Circular 98-2. The only controversy was whether a modern muzzleloader that could use a modern primer was still an "antique firearm", and whether muzzle loading firearms that used interchangeable barrels that could also be converted to fire modern ammunition were "antique firearms", or to be more accurate – "replicas". Congress solved the problem, and changed the law to add another subsection, as follows:

> (C) any muzzle loading rifle, muzzle loading shotgun, or muzzle loading pistol, which is designed to use black powder, or a black powder substitute, and which cannot use fixed ammunition. For purposes of this subparagraph, the term "antique firearm" shall not include any weapon which incorporates a firearm frame or receiver, any firearm which is converted into a muzzle loading weapon, or any muzzle loading weapon which can be readily converted to fire fixed ammunition by replacing the barrel, bolt, breechblock, or any combination thereof.

This subsection made it legal to use modern primers on muzzleloaders, and still retain the classification of an "antique firearm" – but denied this status to those muzzleloaders that had the interchangeable barrels. (ATF Firearms Update, November 18, 2004). Florida has made no such change, so assuming you could forget about the Bostic case, and interpret Florida law along federal lines, you'd soon realize that any muzzleloader that can use a shotgun primer, or interchangeable barrel is not an "antique firearm", not a "replica", and therefore is a "firearm" subject to all the restrictions on sale, possession, etc.

So, it looks like the Bostic case was right, after all, but not on the basis of the Opinion.

Why?

Because the Thompson Center Arms Black Diamond can use a shotgun primer! [14] On the other hand, just because I think the reasoning in Bostic is wrong doesn't invalidate the Opinion. Until the Legislature amends the statute we're all stuck with Bostic's reasoning.

Why is this such a big deal?

Well, since an "antique firearm" is not legally defined as a "firearm", unless used in a crime, a convicted felon could legally own one if he or she were not on parole or probation, and did not carry it concealed. Of course, make an error on whether it's "a reasonably exact reproduction", and you have big problems under Florida law as a convicted felon. Also – if it's a "firearm" vs. "antique firearm" – you now need the NICS background check before purchasing from any dealer. Convicted felons beware!

OTHER EXCLUDED DEVICES:
Also excluded from the definition of a "firearm" are starter pistols that are not capable of discharging any projectile, air guns, BB guns, and pyrotechnic devices that are used for signaling, or throwing safety lines. However, case law makes it clear that a starter gun can be classified as a firearm if it is "readily convertible" to the firing of a projectile. On the other hand, air guns and BB guns are not considered to be firearms since they don't expel a projectile by use of an explosive, although they can be defined as a weapon, or even "deadly weapon", depending upon their use, or intended use.[15]

AGE ON PURCHASES FROM A FIREARMS DEALER:
Now that you know what a firearm is, you probably want to know some of the requirements for purchasing one. In Florida, the age of majority (ie: not a "minor") is 18 years unless otherwise specified by the Florida Constitution, or state beverage laws. For our purposes -- that means 18 years of age, or older.

However, in order to purchase a *handgun* from a federal licensee (ie: a licensed firearms dealer) -- you need to be at least 21 years of age. On the other hand, in order to purchase a rifle or shotgun from a federal licensee -- you need to be at least 18 years of age. The same age requirements apply to the purchase of ammunition for these firearms from a federal licensee. In other words, you can't buy .38 caliber ammunition from a federal licensee until you are 21 years of age, because it's not generally used in anything but a handgun. On the other hand, if you were 18 years of age, and wanted to buy .22 caliber ammunition -- if you represented it was for a rifle, it would be legal. If you represented it was for a handgun, it would be illegal. That's because .22 caliber is used in both types of firearms. However, if you misrepresented it's use, and really wanted it for a handgun -- you'd be committing a federal felony.

If you present falsified identification, or lie on an application to obtain a firearm -- you have just committed a federal crime, as well as a third degree felony in Florida.[16] You could actually be prosecuted in both state and federal court, at the same time. If you are lucky enough to have the feds prosecute you, remember that federal prisons have lots of room. You will stay there for a long time.

JUVENILE FELONY OFFENDER:

You should also know that if you had a conviction or even "withheld adjudication" as a juvenile offender on a crime that would otherwise be a felony F.S.790.23(1)(d) makes it a second degree felony for you to own or possess a firearm, electric weapon, or carry any concealed weapon including chemical sprays until you reach the age of 24 years old.[17]

AGE FOR NON-DEALER PURCHASE:

Both Florida and Federal laws are primarily aimed at sales made by licensed firearms dealers (ie: "FFL")[18] to private citizens. This leaves a few loopholes when the sale is strictly between private persons, or if the transfer of a firearm is a gift between private individuals, and no licensed dealer is involved. Under Florida and Federal law, any citizen of the age of 18 years, or more, who is not under some other legal disability, may possess or own a handgun, rifle, or shotgun.

In other words -- even if it would be illegal to purchase a handgun from a licensed firearms dealer because you're not yet 21 -- it may still be legal for you to purchase, or receive it privately -- as long as you're at least 18 years of age, or older, and suffer no other legal disqualification.

PURCHASES UNDER 18 YEARS OLD WITH PERMISSION:

In Florida, it is a first degree misdemeanor to give, lend, or sell a person under the age of 18 years any type of weapon (not just firearms) -- except an ordinary pocketknife, unless they are given permission to do so by one of the minor's parents, or by the minor's guardian.[19] If it's a firearm, then it's a felony. This proscription is primarily directed to private persons, since the penalty is greater for federal licensees, and other dealers.[20]   Moreover, federally licensed firearms dealers cannot sell a "firearm" to anyone unless that person meets the federal age requirements of 18 or 21 years, regardless of whose permission they have.

PURCHASES DISALLOWED, EVEN WITH PERMISSION:

It is also illegal for any person who deals in weapons (any type of weapons -- not just federally licensed firearms dealers) to sell a dirk,[21] Bowie knife, brass knuckles,[22] electric weapon, or slungshot (ie: a flexible handled weapon with a weight on the end used for striking) to anyone UNDER the age of 18 years -- even with their parents permission.   However, it is legal for the parent to purchase such a weapon, and then give it to the child as a gift.

USE DISALLOWED EXCEPT UNDER ADULT SUPERVISION:

Furthermore, it is illegal for any child under the age of _16 years_ of age to use any firearm, BB gun, air rifle, or electric weapon except under the attending supervision of an adult, who is acting with permission of a parent.   If an adult who is then responsible for the child knows that the child is in possession of an air gun, or electric weapon in violation of this section -- then that adult is guilty of a second degree misdemeanor. A firearm is a felony -- and will probably result in civil liability for any damages caused by the minor, as well.[23] F.S. 790.22

In addition, Florida has made it a felony for an adult who is responsible for the child to knowingly and willfully permit a child under the age of 18 years to possess any firearm at any place other than the child's home, unless the following criteria are met:[24]

a.   The child is engaged in lawful hunting, and is at least 16 years of age, or if under the age of 16, is being supervised by an adult while engaged in lawful hunting.

b.   The child is engaged in lawful shooting competition, or practice, or other lawful recreational shooting activity, and is at least 16 years of age, or if under the age of 16, is being supervised by an adult who is acting with the consent of the minor's parent or guardian.

c.   The firearm is unloaded, and is being transported directly to or from the event authorized in either (a) or (b).

Moreover, if the firearm is being kept by the child at home, it must be unloaded.   Under federal law, the child could not keep a handgun in his possession at home, even if unloaded.   He could only have a rifle or shotgun.[25] We'll discuss this in the next section.

YOUTH HANDGUN SAFETY AMENDMENT:
The 1994 Crime Bill passed by the United States Congress, section 110201, now codified in 18 USC 922(x), adds some additional restrictions for minors (ie: under 18 years) in possession of handguns, or handgun ammunition, which somewhat overlap the Florida statute. These additional restrictions require that the minor have the prior written consent of a parent or guardian, that the written consent be kept on the minor's person at all times that he is in possession of a handgun, and that the handgun be transported unloaded and in a locked case directly to and from any lawfully enumerated activity if being transported by the minor.   Remember, the restrictions here apply to handguns -- not shotguns or rifles.

It should be noted that the Florida statute does NOT permit a minor to use or possess a firearm (handgun or long gun) in the course of employment, or during ranching or farming -- whereas the federal statute does.   In case you're curious about the apparent conflict, the Florida statute controls because it's more restrictive.   Whether it's constitutional or not, is another question.

SOME QUESTIONS ABOUT AGE:

QUESTION: I wanted to give my nephew a really great gift on his 16th birthday, so I bought him a bow and arrows. I didn't ask his folks if I could do this because I thought they might be mad. Could I get in trouble?

ANSWER: Sure! If Mom and Dad wanted to make an issue of it, you just committed a first degree misdemeanor[26] -- because you didn't have their permission to give it to the kid. On the other hand, if his Dad said it was OK -- and his Mom didn't -- you'd still be legal, although, you probably wouldn't be invited over for dinner anymore. The same thing would apply to an air gun, most knives, sword, electric weapon, mace, etc. If the kid is under 18 years of age -- you need the permission of a parent, or guardian.

QUESTION: I am a licensed firearms dealer. An 18 year old wanted to buy ammunition for his rifle, which was of a caliber that could also be used in a handgun. Can I legally sell it to him?

ANSWER: Sure. As long as he represents it's for a long gun (rifle or shotgun), and you have no real reason to doubt he's telling the truth -- you can freely do so. Obviously, the type of ammunition must be typical for the weapon he says it's for -- otherwise you're on notice that the sale could be illegal.

QUESTION: I'm only 19 years old, but I really want a handgun. My father said I could get one if I maintained at least a "B" average in school -- and I have. How do I purchase the gun?

ANSWER: As long as you are 18 years of age or older, you may legally purchase a handgun from a private owner. You do not need your parents permission. You may receive it as a gift. There may be a problem with having somebody else buy it for you from a licensed firearms dealer, although you could receive it as a gift.[27] If you pay someone to buy it for you as a "gift" you both have just committed a very serious federal crime.

QUESTION: I am not a licensed firearms dealer, but I have a store, and carry a selection of knives. A juvenile and his uncle came in last week, and the uncle wanted to buy a Bowie knife for his nephew. He gave the nephew the money, who handed it to me. I refused the sale. Was I right?

ANSWER: Absolutely. Otherwise, you would have committed a second degree felony. You could not sell the knife directly to the minor, even if he had been there with a parent, rather than the uncle -- since a direct sale is prohibited. You could have sold it to the uncle, even if you knew he was going to give it to his nephew -- although that might not be wise from a civil liability standpoint if there was any hint that it was without parental approval. And, of course, if the uncle then gave it to his nephew without the actual permission of a parent -- he would have committed a first degree misdemeanor, although you should be legally O.K.

RESIDENCE, LOANS, RENTALS & BEQUESTS:

Federal law strictly prohibits the transfer or receipt of any firearm to a non-resident by a non-licensee, and also restricts many transfers by a licensed firearms dealer to a non-licensee. It is therefore a federal crime for an ordinary citizen to sell, transfer, give, or receive a firearm when the person receiving the handgun is not a genuine resident of the state in which the transfer is made. In such instances, anyone willfully involved would be guilty of a federal felony.[28] There are a few exceptions which we will discuss, shortly.

These restriction also apply to transfers made by a federal licensee to a person who does not reside in the dealers state. However, there are again, some exceptions.

One of the exceptions occurs when the transfer is a temporary one, in the sense of a loan or rental[29] of a firearm. However, the loan is restricted to only those instances which are for a lawful sporting purpose.[30]   This exception applies to both dealers, and private individuals. But, don't try to get cute with the "temporary" nature of the transfer. It's not something to play with.

Another exception is where the transfer is the result of a bequest or devise, due to the death of the owner of the firearm. In this case, a non-resident may receive the firearm bequeathed to him, regardless of his state of residence, although he still may not transport it into his residence state, unless it is legal to have it there.[31]

Rifles and shotguns are treated somewhat differently from handguns, and federal law does not prevent a qualified citizen who resides in another state from purchasing a rifle or shotgun in a face-to-face transaction with a federally licensed firearms dealer outside his state if: the purchase would be legal in both states, and if the regulatory requirements of both states are complied with. 18 USC 922 (b)(3)

OUT-OF-STATE PURCHASE BY NON-FFL:
    Of course, an FFL (federal firearms licensee) can purchase a firearm from anyone in any state, dealer or not.   And, assuming you see a firearm you want to buy from out-of-state, there still is a method of legally purchasing it. It goes like this:

If a person or federal licensee sells a firearm to a non-resident it's legal, so long as the seller has the firearm delivered to a federally licensed firearms dealer in the buyer's state of residence, and the buyer picks the firearm up in his home state at the federal licensee's business location (ie: gun store) after filling out the Form 4473, and getting approved by a NICS computer check. Again, the firearm cannot be given to the purchaser by the seller, as the seller (unless he's an FFL) must have it transported to an FFL in the seller's home state for shipment to the out-of-state FFL. Remember, you can't give it to the buyer to transport unless the buyer is an FFL, because it's a federal felony to do so. 27 CFR 478.147.

The legal theory on how this works is that the sale is not complete until delivery, and since delivery is at an FFL in the residence state of the purchaser, it's legal. This would also apply to a "gift" of any firearm to an out-of-state resident.[32] So, if you want to make such a gift, you'll have to arrange to have it sent to a federal licensee in his home state.[33] And, if you want to obtain firearms from out-of-state, you'd better make sure you buy them from a federally licensed dealer, who ships them to a federally licensed dealer in your home state for your eventual pick-up. Almost all gun shops will assist in this process for a fee.

As a strong word of warning, you should know that it is illegal for a third person to purchase a firearm with the intent of transferring it to a non-resident, or to someone who has a legal disqualification. This is known as a "straw man" purchase, and is a federal felony for anyone involved, as well a felony under F.S. 790.065. Thus, if the dealer has reasonable cause to suspect that this is the intent of the purchaser, he cannot make the sale without committing a federal crime.

For instance. Your nephew from New Jersey comes down to Florida for a visit. He is staying with you, is over 21 years of age, has never been arrested, and is an all-around wonderful person. He knows you have a couple of handguns, and that you even have a Florida Concealed Weapons Permit. You've taken him out shooting with you at the range -- and he's a better shot than you. He's always wanted a handgun, but New Jersey law won't let him get one. He asks you if you can buy him one, and he'll pay you back. You say "sure".

You've heard it's illegal to purchase a handgun for somebody else who lives out of state, and your gun dealer tells you "no way" will he sell you one -- even if you promise to swear that it was only for you. So, you decide to give your old 38 caliber revolver to the nephew as a gift.

"What's the harm?"

The harm is that you just violated the Gun Control Act of 1968, and are subject to five years imprisonment in a federal penitentiary, and a fine of up to $5,000.00. Your nephew is also subject to the same penalty. What a great uncle, you are! Won't the family be pleased?

DUAL RESIDENCE:

It is possible for a person to have a dual residence, and thus be able to purchase a rifle, shotgun, or handgun in more than one state legally. This means that the state you are attempting to purchase the firearm in is not a place that you are merely visiting -- but is one in which you reside at, and maintain as your home. Examples would be a college student living away from home part of the year. Persons who owned permanent homes, or leased apartments in different cities where they regularly lived or worked. And people who kept permanent vacation homes where they resided part of the year. Mere ownership of property does not constitute residence. Of course, to prove residence you are probably going to have to have a driver's license from both states, or at least a state issued photographic identification card. Otherwise, most dealers would be wise not to make the sale to you. Military on active duty have their residence at their permanent duty station, and residence.

PURCHASE BY ALIENS:

According to federal law[34], an alien (ie: citizens from another country -- not from another planet), except those with a non-immigrant visa, may purchase a firearm so long as they are legally in the United States, are a resident of the State in which the firearm is purchased, and have been a resident of that State for an uninterrupted "ninety continuous days" immediately prior to the purchase. [35] This requirement applies to both resident/permanent aliens (ie: green card), and those non-immigrant aliens who are not prohibited, such as those who have a valid hunting license. The old practice of allowing a non-resident alien (ie: non-immigrant alien) the purchase a firearm by virtue of a letter from his consulate or embassy was eliminated in April 1997. The "90 continuous days" requirement means exactly that. Plus, if he or she goes to another country within the 90 days, even for a day, they must start the 90 day period anew when they return to Florida. (ATF Ruling 2004-1).

The dealer who sells a non-prohibited alien a firearm must obtain proof of residency by examination of documents such as a lease, utility bills, or similar types of proof that show at least 90 days have elapsed since the initial date. These can be furnished with different addresses if all are within Florida. The proof must be noted on the Form 4473 by the FFL. Photo identification must also be presented, and documented on the Form 4473. See, 27 CFR 478.124 & 478.125. The alien must also provide the dealer with their INS admission number (ie: the number on the Form I-94 or I-94W). If it appears that the firearm is going to be taken out of the country, the alien must notify the Office of Munitions Control, and obtain a DSP Form 5, in order to export it. A legal resident alien may also purchase ammunition anywhere in the United States as only the firearm prohibitions have the 90 day residency requirement.

Those aliens who are "non-immigrants" here on a "non-immigrant" visa may also purchase/possess ammo and firearms only under specialized conditions set forth in 18 USC 922(y)(2). The 90 day residency requirement applies to firearm purchases from federal firearm licensees (FFL's) in an over-the-counter sale. Since purchase usually requires a current hunting license, expiration of such a license would make possession illegal. If you're wondering how a visiting alien can do a temporary shoot (rental) at a firing range, they can't legally unless they fall within one of the exceptions such as a valid hunting license, although no residency would be required to purchase ammo or rent a firearm at a range if they met the exception.

Another warning here: If your legal status as an alien ever changes or expires so that you're illegally in the U.S.A. – your ownership or possession of a firearm or ammunition will constitute a felony.[36]

LEGAL DISABILITIES PREVENTING PURCHASE:
If you're purchasing from a private individual, you already know that you must be a resident of the same state where the purchase was made (or the transfer was made through an FFL in the purchaser's home state), and the purchaser must be at least 18 years of age. Another requirement of any purchase or receipt of firearms or ammunition – no matter who you get it from – is that you don't have a felony conviction where the "possible" imprisonment (imposed or not) was over one year, or a misdemeanor conviction where the possible imprisonment (imposed or not) was over two years.

A "conviction" means that you were actually convicted of the crime. In Florida this means an "adjudication". Federal law follows the state's interpretation of its own laws. Thus, under Florida law, a "withheld adjudication" does not constitute a "conviction" of a felony for most firearms purposes. However, if you plead "guilty" vs. "no contest" — it might, under current federal interpretations. United States v.Chubbuck, 252 F.3d 1300 (11ᵗʰ Cir. 2001). On the other hand, that interpretation doesn't apply to a "withheld adjudication" in a juvenile court felony due to F.S. 790.23. In that situation, you can't own or possess firearms and certain other weapons in Florida until you reach the age of 24. Violation is a second degree felony.

If you have a federal, or out-of-state conviction, the federal law, or laws of the state of conviction control your legal status to possess a firearm -- not Florida law. On the other hand, if you were "adjudicated" or "convicted" under a Florida felony -- you're obviously going to have to read the upcoming chapter on removal of legal disabilities. Tough luck!

Other disabilities which would make it a crime to sell, transfer, possess[37], or receive, the firearm include:

a.   The purchaser is under Indictment or Information for a felony, or crime punishable by more than a year in jail. However, this would not bar "possession" until adjudication of guilt is imposed.

b.   The purchaser is a fugitive from justice (ie: any person who has deliberately fled another state to avoid prosecution for a crime, or avoid testifying in a criminal proceeding).

c.   The purchaser is an unlawful user, or addicted to illegal drugs (21 USC 802) (Yeah -- if you occasionally smoke marijuana -- you could be determined as "prohibited").

d.   The purchaser has been adjudicated a mental defective, or has been committed to any mental institution, anytime. The term is defined in 27 CFR 478.11, and F.S. 790.065(4). The case law interpreting "commitment" holds that involuntary placement in a mental facility for "observation" is not a commitment unless there is a determination by some board or agency or court of mental illness or mental defect and need for (involuntary) treatment. Voluntary admission to a mental facility is not included. Also included would be a finding of "not guilty by reason of insanity" in a criminal case, and can also include involuntary commitment for drug or alcohol use. [38] Pursuant to the NICS Improvement Amendment Act of 2007 the term also includes an administrative decision by a federal board, agency or commission that you are a danger to yourself or to others or are incompetent to manage your own affaires, but this stigma is extinguished if the federal agency that made the decision later: (1) sets the decision aside or expunges it; (2) the person has been fully released or discharged from all mandatory treatment, supervision or monitoring by the agency; or (3) the person was found by the agency to no longer suffer from the mental health adjudication. However, this exception does not apply to anyone found "not guilty" or acquitted in a criminal case, or military tribunal due to a lack of mental responsibility, insanity, or incompetence.

e.   The purchaser was dishonorably discharged.

f.   The purchaser renounced his/her U.S. citizenship.

g.   The purchaser is subject to a court order restraining the purchaser from harassing, stalking, or threatening an intimate partner[39], or child of such, or engaging in other conduct that would place the intimate partner in reasonable fear of bodily harm to the partner or child -- so long as such order was issued after a hearing of which the purchaser received actual notice, and had an opportunity to participate -- whether or not the purchaser did participate. And, in such restraining order the court must find that the person represented a credible threat to the physical safety of the other, or alternatively, that the court order expressly prohibits the use, threatened or attempted use of physical force.[40]

h.   The person was convicted of a crime of a "misdemeanor crime of domestic violence". 18 USC 922(g)(9). A misdemeanor crime of domestic violence means an offense that has, as an element, the use or attempted use of physical force, or the threatened use of a deadly weapon, committed by a current or former spouse, parent, or guardian of the victim, by a person with whom the victim shares a child in common, by a person who is cohabiting with or has cohabited with the victim as a spouse, parent, or guardian, or by a person similarly situated to a spouse, parent, or guardian of the victim[41] It doesn't apply to casual relationships unless you were living together. Under current federal law it likely includes cases where a *"guilty"* plea was entered vs. *"no contest"* plea, or where there was a trial with a *"guilty"* verdict, even if adjudication was later "withheld". It will always include an "adjudication".[42]

There are some defenses to these federal firearm prohibitions where the domestic violence conviction occurred when the individual was not represented by an attorney, and where he or she did not "knowingly and voluntarily" waive the right to counsel, or when the individual was entitled to a jury trial, and did not "knowingly or intelligently" waive that right. Likewise, an expunction or pardon is a defense to the prohibition.

All of the foregoing disabilities are imposed by federal law, and violations are taken very seriously by your friendly federal government, and ATF agent (Bureau of Alcohol, Tobacco, Firearms, and Explosives). They apply equally to sales by licensed dealers, and private individuals. Florida has similar laws in F.S. 790.065(2)(c)(1); and F.S. 790.233. Moreover, Florida defines "domestic violence" somewhat different than federal law in F.S. 741.28.[43]

FLORIDA DOMESTIC VIOLENCE INJUNCTIONS:
You should also know that Florida has a statute, F.S. 741.31(4)(a), that allows law enforcement seizure of a person's firearms and ammunition if a judge orders their surrender pursuant to the issuance of an injunction for protection against domestic violence. Under these circumstances, it is a first degree misdemeanor to refuse turning the guns and ammo over to the police. Once the injunction ends – you are entitled to get them back. Likewise, it is a first degree misdemeanor under Florida law to continue to possess firearms or ammunition in violation of a final injunction for protection against domestic violence. These prohibitions do not apply to firearms and ammunition of a law enforcement officer for use in his or her official duties, although a misdemeanor domestic violence conviction or withheld adjudication would prohibit even a police officer from

owning or possessing firearms or ammunition.   Of course, if you are in violation of the federal definition, the penalties are more substantial. 18 USC 922(g)(8).

PURCHASE FROM A LICENSED FIREARMS DEALER:

In order to legally sell firearms as a business, a person or corporation must be federally licensed. This requirement does not apply to the sale of ammunition[44], although a federal licensee who also sells ammunition must comply with certain federal laws that a non-licensee who sells ammunition, does not.   Whatever, anybody who sells firearms as a business with the idea of making a profit vs. enhancing his personal collection -- must be licensed by the feds. A failure is a very unpleasant federal prison sentence. This requirement applies to pawnshops, antique dealers, or whoever. Only sales from legitimate private collections are exempt -- and these better be very on the level.

Now, purchasing a firearm from a dealer is a very different animal than buying it privately. There are a lot more regulations that you both have to comply with, certain forms, record checks, and you may find that while you could legally buy the same gun from a private person -- you can't legally purchase it from a dealer. Doesn't make much sense, does it?

QUESTION: What are the differences in a private sale?

ANSWER: No three day waiting period on a handgun. Currently, no FDLE background check, or federal Form 4473 to fill out, no requirement that handgun purchaser be 21 years old. Eighteen years old would be sufficient. Same age of eighteen applies to rifles and shotguns. But you still can't sell to someone from out-of-state, a convicted felon, etc.

I guess you'd really like me to get into the meat and potatoes of this section, so let me get on with it, and fill you in on the regulations, and procedures for an over-the-counter purchase that I haven't already specified.

FLORIDA FIREARMS PURCHASE PROGRAM:
Florida has instituted, amongst other things, a firearms purchase program administered by the Florida Department of Law Enforcement (FDLE). This program requires any firearms dealer to run a criminal history records check of any prospective purchaser over the phone on a special line to FDLE. There is an five dollar service fee[45] which is charged to the potential purchaser, even if the sale cannot be completed. The records check is a mandatory requirement to purchase a firearm from a licensed dealer.

The records check searches the person's record for anything that would prevent the person from purchasing or possessing a firearm under both federal and Florida law. If anything is found, the purchase will be disapproved. It can also make mistakes, and could even miss an old battery or assault conviction that now qualifies as a "misdemeanor crime of domestic violence". If it that happens, and you make the purchase -- you are still illegal, and could face prosecution.

ARREST FOR "DANGEROUS" CRIME:
If you are trying to purchase a firearm from a dealer, and have an arrest for what is considered a "*dangerous crime*" as listed in F.S. 907.041(4)[46], or for certain other specified felonies, you will get a "*conditional denial*" and not be able to purchase the firearm, until there is proof the case was dropped or you were acquitted of the charge. Hopefully, this will show on the NICS check, but if not, it's your responsibility to get the matter corrected. You will also be denied if you have a current domestic violence or repeat violence injunction entered against you, have a conviction for domestic violence, a "*withheld*" for a domestic violence where 3 years hasn't elapsed since the sentence was completed, or where you are formally charged with the commission of any felony. A "formal charge" means an Information or Indictment has been filed against you in a court of law. The list of arrests that bar your approval from purchasing from a licensed firearms dealer[47] are as follows:

34

CHART OF ARRESTS PREVENTING FDLE APPROVAL:
* includes any attempt or conspiracy to commit

arson *	child abuse*	aggravated battery *	sabotage
child abuse *	hijacking *	kidnaping *	homicide *
illegal use of explosive*, & other explosives violations		sexual battery *	robbery*
indecent or lewd assault or act on or in presence of child under 16 *		aggravated assault *	hijacking*
			car jacking*
sexual activity with child 12 -17 by or through person in custodial or familial authority *		criminal anarchy (felony only)	extortion
any controlled substance violation in Chapter 893, Florida Statutes		domestic violence includ. "withhelds"	abuse of elder or disabled*
any weapon or firearms charge in Chapter 790, Florida Statutes		burglary of dwelling*	
explosives violations *		resisting officer with violence	
treason	manslaughter *	assisting suicide	any stalking *

WARNING ABOUT DOMESTIC VIOLENCE CRIMES:

Federal decisional law is in flux as to whether a *"withheld adjudication"* in Florida can be a *"conviction"* for a misdemeanor crime of domestic violence. The 11th Circuit Court of Appeals in Atlanta currently says if you plead guilty, or were found guilty in a trial — a *"withheld adjudication"* is still a *"conviction"* for federal purposes— although they admit they may be mistaken on this interpretation.[48] Thus, only a plea of *"no contest"*, and a *"withheld adjudication"* are currently safe for federal purposes, unless the case was dropped or you won at trial. Moreover, F.S. 790.065(2)(a)(3), states that a *"withheld adjudication"* on any felony, misdemeanor crime of domestic violence, or any misdemeanor crime of violence will result in a non-approval for purchase of a firearm from a federally licensed dealer until 3 years has elapsed after you've "completed" any sentence. Completion would include finishing probation, and paying any fines and court costs.

STATE DISABILITIES RECOGNIZED BY FEDERAL LAW:
      Section 922 (b)(2) of the (federal) Gun Control Act of 1968 [18
USC 922(b)(2)] states that it is illegal for a licensed dealer to transfer
a firearm to any person whose purchase or possession would be in
violation of State law.   Florida law does not seem to permit the
following additional persons to possess firearms, so they should also be
legally excluded from purchasing from a licensed dealer, although this
may constitute a loophole for sale from a private individual. Even if
this loophole exists, it would be risky, and could subject you to some
very costly civil liability if something went amiss.   Anyway, here's
the additional list:

      a.   Person who is a habitual or chronic alcoholic.
      b.   Vagrants
      c.   Person on Florida probation

PERSON ON FLORIDA PROBATION:
      Ah, yes!   The great zinger of Florida law!   Pursuant to F.S.
948.03(1)(l), a person on any type of Florida probation cannot possess,
carry, or even **own** a firearm — unless authorized by the court, and
consented to by the probation officer.[49]   There is also authority,
although mistaken, that this extends to other weapons.[50]

      QUESTION: You mean that if I get a lousy DUI, I've got to
                sell my firearms, when placed on probation?

      ANSWER: Yes, amazing, huh?   Unless the courts correct
                this error in interpretation, it applies equally to
                misdemeanors, felonies, and even criminal traffic
                offenses where probation is imposed — at least,
                unless you can get the judge and probation
                officer to agree otherwise.

      QUESTION: How could I own or possess a firearm on
                felony probation, even with the agreement of the
                judge and probation officer?   Isn't that always
                illegal?[51]

      ANSWER: If you had a *"withheld adjudication"*[52] you
                would not be a "convicted felon", and could

36

technically still own firearms if you could get this permission. I assume it would have to be by a written order of the judge to be valid. Same theory applies on a misdemeanor (adjudicated or withheld) except domestic violence.

QUESTION: So, what happens once I'm off probation?

ANSWER: Unless you were convicted of a felony, the "probation" restriction disappears.

QUESTION: Any way around this?

ANSWER: My only suggestion is to legally transfer ownership of the firearms to a trust, with the trustee directed to return the firearms only upon the expiration of probation. Hire a lawyer to set up the trust, it's actually pretty simple. Don't get cute, and ask someone to "hold them" for you — because if you do, you still have *"constructive possession"* of the firearms, and could face a probation revocation or new prosecution. This can be very serious stuff if the feds decide they want to prosecute you because you're a *"prohibited person"* under federal law.

DENIAL FOR FELONY RECORD:

The criminal history check run by FDLE will also search to see if you have any felony "convictions", or if you received a suspended sentence, or a "withheld adjudication" for any felony. If you were actually "convicted" of the felony -- you will not be eligible to purchase, own, or possess a firearm under any circumstances -- unless the legal disability has been removed. Also, as previously explained, the case of U.S. v. Chubbuck[53] makes it clear that the feds will still prosecute and convict you on a Florida crime if you plead "guilty", or were found guilty after a trial, even if you got a "withheld adjudication", even though they realize they're probably wrong on the law. If you think that's unfair — be warned. The Eleventh Circuit is very conservative, highly pro-government, and technicalities often prevail over justice. In other words – they really don't care.

THREE YEAR WAITING PERIOD:

If you received a suspended sentence, or a "withheld adjudication" on a felony -- then you can't get an FDLE approval to purchase from a licensed dealer until you have expunged your record, or three (3) years has passed from the date that your probation was over, and any of the conditions set by the court have elapsed.[54] Once the 3 years is up, you're eligible to purchase from a dealer again, however, the loophole here is pretty clear -- you can still purchase from a private individual.

One word of caution. Don't get a friend to buy you a firearm from a dealer, or anyone else if you don't qualify under these sections. This is called a "straw man" transaction, and is a state and federal crime. If you do, both you and your friend will be guilty of a felony.[55] Same thing goes for giving false identification.[56]

WAITING PERIOD FOR HANDGUN PURCHASES:

A few years ago Florida passed a constitutional amendment that provided a three (3) business day waiting period (weekends and legal holidays don't count) for the purchase of a handgun unless you have a concealed weapons permit, or it's a trade for another hand gun. (Fla. Const., Art. 1, section 8) In November 1998 another amendment (Fla. Const., Art. 8, section 5) changed this somewhat, and now each county may place a waiting period of up to five (5) days on any firearm — if any part of the transaction takes place on *"property to which the public has the right of access"*. This applies to most gun shows because they are often held in government owned convention centers. It also applies to streets, sidewalks, parks, etc. It should not apply to a private home, business, property, or stores as the public does not have a "right" to access private property. Each county may also require a criminal history records check on private sales conducted on public property. Again, this is a county-to-county thing. However, neither provision applies to sales to a concealed permit holder. It is likely that in order to avoid the Article 8 provision you are stuck with a "straight trade", handgun for handgun without additional money or items allowed, whereas the Article 1 provision should allow any handgun trade regardless of what else is thrown into the pot. Of course, there is no case law on either of these interpretations. By the way, police officers are not exempted from either of these requirements unless they have a concealed permit.

If you think these Constitutional provisions are kind of stupid — you're right. They could have passed either in the legislature by statute, and had it uniform, so we would all know what the law was. To do it by constitutional amendment was absurd. However, almost everybody in Florida voted for it. Score another one for ignorance, and the media. So, here's my quote for the day:

> *"Experience should teach us to be most on our guard to protect liberty when the Government's purposes are beneficial . . . . The greatest dangers to liberty lurk in insidious encroachment by men of zeal, well-meaning, but without understanding." Justice Brandeis in <u>Olmstead v. United States</u>, 277 US 438 (1928).*

QUESTION: So, if I have a concealed permit, I don't have to wait three days to get my handgun?

ANSWER: Correct. However, you will still need to have a NICS background check. Your permit is currently issued by the Department of Agriculture which is not a law enforcement agency, and therefore cannot do the NICS check required by federal law. Only "law enforcement agencies" can access NICS, and therefore the federal exemption that normally applies to concealed weapon permits, does not apply to those issued in Florida.

To make all these disabilities a little easier to remember, I've prepared a chart to help you which you'll find on the next page. Remember, there are some exceptions to the chart as previously discussed.

CHART OF PERMITTED/NON-PERMITTED SALES:

	Handguns		Rifles & Shotguns	
	Private	Dealer sales	Private	Dealer sales
Age	18 years	21 years old	18 years	18 years old
Residence	same state	same state	same state	any state
3 Day Wait	none	yes, except CWP holder	none	none
Felony conviction	not allowed	not allowed	not allowed	not allowed
Felony "withheld"	allowed	after 3 years	allowed	after 3 years
"Dangerous crime" arrest	allowed	not allowed	allowed	not allowed
Indictment or Information for felony	not allowed	not allowed	not allowed	not allowed
fugitive	not allowed	not allowed	not allowed	not allowed
unlawful drug user	not allowed	not allowed	not allowed	not allowed
illegal alien	not allowed	not allowed	not allowed	not allowed
mental defective or was committed	not allowed	not allowed	not allowed	not allowed
dishonorable discharge	not allowed	not allowed	not allowed	not allowed
renounced citizenship	not allowed	not allowed	not allowed	not allowed
conviction of domestic violence, or restraining order	not allowed 18 USC 922(d)(8)	not allowed	not allowed	not allowed
legal aliens if Fla. resident	allowed	allowed	allowed	allowed
on Probation in Florida	not allowed	not allowed 18 USC 922 (b)(2	not allowed	not allowed
chronic or habitual alcoholic	not suggested	not allowed	not sug-gested	not allowed

CHAPTER THREE

WHAT TO DO
AFTER THEY TURN YOU DOWN

Ah, ha! They turned you down. Those lowly pencil-pushing, dirty so-and-so's had the nerve to turn you, the all-knowing, all-seeing, all-perfect one, down! A pox on all of them! What do they know?

Well, that's actually a good question, Oh Knowing One. You've raised an interesting point.

To answer that, let's first see how it actually works in FDLE Land. It may surprise you. And, by the way, these are generally pretty nice people . . . so don't get down too hard on them. If problems arise -- it's usually not their fault.

THE APPROVAL (OR DISAPPROVAL) PROCESS:
In 1989 Florida passed a law requiring licensed firearm dealers to do a telephone records check on non-licensee purchasers with the FDLE prior to completing any sale. The purpose of the law is to do a statewide and national criminal records check before an approval for purchase is given. Philosophically speaking, this is a pretty good idea. A rare thing in government. It was also pretty good anticipation of the Brady Bill. Score one brownie point for Florida!

Anyway, under Florida law, sales of firearms between private individuals from their private collections are normally not covered by these "record checking" regulations, although sales between private individuals are still subject to certain federal and state restrictions, and in certain counties, sales on public property may require a record check, and even up to a five day wait on certain purchases to non-permit holders. Otherwise, there currently is no FDLE check in a private sale. However, since we're now talking about dealer sales, and not staring into a crystal legislative ball -- let's get back to the subject at hand.

41

IDENTIFICATION NEEDED TO PURCHASE:

The procedure when purchasing (or trading) a firearm from a licensed firearms dealer is to have the buyer complete a federal **Form 4473**. This is required by both state and federal law. It is not generally required as to sales between private individuals. The purchaser must also furnish government issued photo identification establishing his or her name, residence address, and date of birth.[57] Photo identification is normally done by a drivers license, or state identification card. Other acceptable photo identification includes a Concealed Weapons Permit, Military identification card, passport, and immigration card. Production of your Social Security card is also recommended to clear-up any potential misidentification when FDLE does the records check. A five dollar processing fee is then collected, and the dealer calls FDLE at a special toll-free number.

THE COMPUTER CHECK BY FDLE:

At this point the FDLE operator conducts a computerized state and national criminal records check. Based on the findings of that check the operator will provide the dealer with an approval, non-approval, conditional approval, or conditional non-approval number. The operator is <u>not</u> allowed to release any criminal history over the phone, and the dealer may not ordinarily reveal the results of the check with anyone except the buyer.[58] Of course, giving false information to the firearms dealer in order to secure a firearm is also a state and federal crime -- a felony.[59]

HOW THE FDLE CALL-IN SYSTEM OPERATES:

When FDLE gets the call, they have a limited amount of time to make a determination of your eligibility, assuming your record is unclear. The <u>maximum</u> delay is 24 working hours. "Working hours" mean Monday to Friday, from 9:00 a.m. to 5:00 p.m., legal holidays excluded. If the record shows no disability -- the approval is immediate.

If FDLE can't make a determination one way or the other within this time frame, the dealer is given a CONDITIONAL APPROVAL NUMBER, and you are allowed to purchase the firearm. However, if FDLE receives information at a later time that you were really ineligible, this conditional approval is revoked, the conditional approval number becomes a "non-approval number", and local law enforcement is alerted. Obviously, you can't keep the firearm, and that brings up some interesting civil questions on whether the dealer would be obligated to take it back, and give a refund.

If you have a pending arrest on any "dangerous crime", domestic violence, or one of the special enumerated felonies I listed in the last chapter -- you get a CONDITIONAL NON-APPROVAL until the case is disposed of, and you inform FDLE that you're now off-the-hook. At that point, if you check-out as OK -- the qualified non-approval number becomes an approval number. If an Indictment or Information is filed against you for any felony (not just an arrest), then the same rule applies, and you receive a conditional non-approval until the case is resolved in your favor. If resolved against you, your conditional non-approval becomes a literal non-approval.

Obviously, if the check comes back that you have a felony conviction, are a deserter, were found mentally incompetent, or had some other legal disability, you will be disapproved. Same thing if it comes back with a withheld adjudication on any felony unless three (3) years have elapsed from the date all probation and any other conditions set by the court, including restitution, have been completed. If the amount of probation is unknown, then FDLE will use the three years, as a rule of thumb, until it can be shown otherwise.

Whatever happens, the dealer writes the approval, non-approval, conditional approval, or conditional non-approval number on the Form 4473. He retains this in his records, and you do not get a copy -- so don't bother trying. The records are confidential. You should get the denial number, or NICS transaction number (ie: NTN).

WHAT HAPPENS IF THE COMPUTERS ARE DOWN:
If computers are down -- FDLE has until end of next business day (5:00 pm) to notify the licensed firearms dealer that the purchase is prohibited. Otherwise, they must issue an approval, or conditional approval number, and you can purchase the gun.

The "next business day" is a Monday thru Friday, holidays excluded. This is true even though FDLE is required to have these phone lines working 7 days a week, 9:00 a.m. to 9:00 p.m. -- except

Christmas and New Year's Day.

If telephone service is not working at the licensee's premises due to the fault of the telephone carrier, or because of any natural disaster, act of God, war, invasion, insurrection, riot, other bona fide emergency, or any reason truly beyond the control of the licensee, then the FDLE phone check and approval is not necessary. In that case, all that's done is fill-in, and sign the federal Form 4473, and if everything else is OK -- you can buy the gun, then and there.

PROBLEMS WITH MIS-IDENTIFICATION:
When you apply for the records check, the computer is trying to match you with millions of disqualified people. If somebody has the same name, sex, date of birth, and skin color -- you've got a problem. Same thing if somebody else has been using your name, or identification illegally. Identity theft is rift in America! Since the law of averages says that this is very possible -- problems can occur. A non-approval usually happens like this:

a.   All identifying data in the inquiry matches.

b.   Where it's for a female, if there's a match on race, date of birth, social security number, and first name.

c.   Regarding possible misspelling matches -- where the first name of the applicant has another common spelling or ending (Bill, Billy, Billie, William, Wil, etc.); or the last name has a common similar spellings or ends in "s" or "z" (Rodrigues, Rodreques, Rodreguez, Rodriguez).

d.   Regarding, possible name matches – where the purchaser gives a full name, and there is a match with a person with the same last name who has a matching initial for the first or middle name.

APPROVAL, OR NON-APPROVAL NUMBERS FROM FDLE:

Once you're approved, the approval number is valid for a total of thirty (30) days from issuance, or until the purchase transaction is completed. It expires upon use. If a non-approval number is assigned, the sale cannot be completed, and the dealer is supposed to advise the purchaser of his right to "appeal" the non-approval. There is a form for doing this which the dealer is supposed to provide, and he also should complete the "dealer" section. Any appeal must be filed within 21 days.

If the "appeal" is successful, FDLE sends the buyer a letter notifying him that the firearm may be purchased. The buyer may bring the letter to any dealer who can then make a sale without any further FDLE check. The letter will have a cut-off date, after which it becomes invalid. The letter is then kept by the licensed firearms dealer, and attached to the federal Form 4473. This "appeal" procedure is explained in the next section.

APPEAL PROCEDURE & CRIMINAL HISTORY REVIEW:

Actually, this "appeal" procedure is not really an appeal, but is a formal "criminal history records check", where you provide FDLE with your fingerprints to assist a more in-depth examination of the (hopeful) mix-up. The procedure is outlined in Section 11C-8.001 of the Florida Administrative Code. There is no charge for the records check by FDLE, but you must obtain a set of your fingerprints from a local law enforcement agency on the appropriate fingerprint card (FBI FD-258), or on the fingerprint portion of the appeal form. The local agency may charge you a fee for doing the fingerprinting, although the Sheriff is supposed to do it for free, upon request. Once you have the fingerprinting done, you send the card and the "Firearm Purchase Non-Approval Appeal Form" to FDLE, on the address listed on the form. Make sure the card is in an appropriate envelope, because a bent fingerprint card is not going to do you much good if somebody is trying to compare prints. The address is:

FDLE
Firearm Purchase Program
Post Office Box 1489
Tallahassee, Florida 32302-1489

If a positive fingerprint identification is made against an existing criminal record, then FDLE will return the fingerprint card, appeal form, and a single copy of the record directly to the applicant, unless you submitted it through a law enforcement agency. If you still think there is a mistake, there are additional procedures you may follow, but they get very complicated, and I suggest you hire an attorney to assist you with them. Again, FDLE must receive your "appeal" within 21 days of the denial.[60] You may also appeal thru the FBI. This is a more complicated procedure which I recommend an attorney for from the beginning. The procedure, in brief, can be found on the FBI website at [http://www.fbi.gov/hq/cjisd/nics].

A QUICK HINT:

If you get turned down, and think it's a mistake -- you may be right. Sometimes the FDLE operator punches in the wrong information (hey, they're human!), and you get a disapproval. If this happens, don't despair. Try again a day or two later, and it will probably be approved. If not -- then, you may have a problem, and will have to get a criminal history records check through the appeal process I've already explained.

THE BRADY ACT & NICS:

The Brady Act's[61] permanent provisions went into effect on November 30, 1998, and did not substantially affect Florida, since many of its provisions were already operational here. There were some temporary problems due to Federal law requiring background checks through the NICS (National Instant Check System) system, as that computer system has a wider data-base than what Florida formerly used. The NICS system check includes injunctions against repeat or domestic violence, misdemeanor crimes of domestic violence, involuntary commitments, etc.

Other than that, Brady, required sales of multiple handguns (ie: more than one handgun in five work days from same dealer) to be reported by dealers on both the ATF[62] form, as well as to State or local government -- so that your local police, etc., will now have a "track" of purchasers buying more than one handgun in a week's time from the same dealer, and raised the application fee for becoming a federally licensed dealer. Under Florida law, when you purchase a firearm with a CWP, and thereby avoid the Florida Constitution's three day waiting period on handgun purchases, a copy of your permit is made and attached to the Form 4473 by the dealer, or your permit number is copied into the form.   If you do not have a concealed permit, you must still wait three days to pick-up the handgun. There is no waiting period on a rifle or shotgun as long as you got the FDLE approval or qualified approval which is being run through the NICS system.

QUESTION: You say that the FDLE check is run through the NICS system, right?   Then, why is there a problem purchasing a firearm with a concealed weapons permit issued after November 30, 1998?

ANSWER: The main problem is that the Dept. of Agriculture handles the concealed permit program — not FDLE. Since the Dept. of Agriculture is not a "law enforcement" agency per federal law, it can't do NICS checks when it issues the concealed permit. Thus, the legislation would have to be changed to allow the Dept. of Agriculture to run the permit applications through FDLE, a law enforcement agency, who can then run it through NICS. Even so, there would still be some problems before the permit would be recognized by the feds as the concealed weapons license could be issued to a federally "prohibited person" such as a person who was committed to a mental institution, but who later had their competency restored under Florida law.   Under current federal law, there is no remedy for this type prohibition to be remedied.

(this page reserved)

CHAPTER FOUR

REMOVAL OF LEGAL DISABILITIES

Sometimes the computers are right -- and there's really no mistake about it. You've got a felony conviction, or other type of legitimate legal disability. Since the rest of us are now somewhat concerned that you may not be the type of person we really want walking around with a firearm -- you may be wondering what your options are. That's what this chapter is all about. Of course, executive clemency includes death penalty matters, and many other things you're not really interested in, and therefore I'm going to keep the chapter geared strictly to persons not in prison who are not seeking a reduction of sentence, but just want their firearms rights restored. Hopefully, it will be of some help in explaining the process.

Now, if you've read any of the previous versions of this book, you'll probably noticed that this chapter undergone a lot of change. That's because the rules relating to executive clemency have changed. Anyway, here's how it works today:

EXECUTIVE CLEMENCY:
The Florida Constitution, Article 4, section 8, grants the governor, with the approval of two (2) members of the Cabinet, the ability to grant full or conditional pardons, as well as the restoration of the civil rights of most individuals. This is also known as the right to "executive clemency". You have no individual right to executive clemency -- it is totally in the discretion of the governor and his cabinet. That means if you're denied -- tough luck! There's no appeal!

Executive Clemency is granted by the Board of Executive Clemency. That literally means the Governor and his Cabinet. Your chance to meet some really important people, who probably will not want to invite you home for dinner. The mechanics of the operation are overseen by the Office of Executive Clemency which makes sure things run the way they're supposed to, and screens applications to make sure the person applying meets the application qualifications. The Board of Executive Clemency meets four times a year to decide on applications. Waivers, which we'll discuss later, are considered at other times.

While there are numerous applications from prisoners for commutation of sentences, the main areas of executive clemency you are likely to be concerned with fall into the following categories:

a.   Full Pardon
b.   Pardon without firearm authority
c.   Pardon for misdemeanor
d.   Specific authority to own, possess, or use firearms
e.   Restoration of Civil Rights in Florida

Now, you should know that any form of executive clemency can be granted as "conditional". That means just what it says — the Executive Clemency Board added some type of condition to the relief granted. If that happens, the Office of Executive Clemency monitors compliance with the conditions set by the Board. If you violate the conditions, the executive clemency will likely be rescinded. You should also know that when applying for executive clemency the information you provide must be accurate or you are committing a felony, and that your application, if it meets the qualifications — will be investigated by the Florida Parole Commission. If you fail to cooperate with the investigation, your application will be denied.

Applications can be obtained online at the website, Office of Executive Clemency: [http://www.state.fl.us/fpc/exclem.html], or you may contact them by mail at: Coordinator, Office of Executive Clemency, 2601 Blairstone Road, Building C, Room 229, Tallahassee, Florida, 32399-2450.

EXPLANATION OF FORMS OF EXECUTIVE CLEMENCY:
O.K., so you know there are several forms of executive clemency, so which is the one for you? Here's the explanation:

A.   <u>Full Pardon</u> — This is an unconditional release from punishment forgives guilt, and restores all rights including firearms

To be eligible you must have completed all sentences imposed, all conditions of supervision must be completed or expired, for no less than **ten (10) years**, and you may not have any outstanding detainers, pending charges, or unpaid restitution, nor outstanding fines from other criminal or traffic cases that total more than $1,000.00. Figure if you have any fines left — you'll likely be denied. However, if the sum is too great to pay, you should know there is a separate mechanism for remission of fines and forfeitures which can be sought through executive clemency. You should also know that the ten year period is not written in stone as it is subject to "waiver". Again, waivers are treated later in this chapter.

B.   <u>Pardon without firearm authority</u> — same as a full pardon, except no firearm rights. Same time limits and conditions. If this happens you are still illegal under state and federal law to own, use, or possess.

C.   <u>Pardon for misdemeanor</u> — This releases a person from punishment and forgives guilt. On the other hand, since a misdemeanor does not curtail most civil rights — you first need to apply for and obtain a "waiver" before this can be granted.

F.   <u>Specific Authority to Own, Possess, or Use Firearms</u> — This restores all your firearms rights <u>only</u> where the conviction was from a Florida State court. If your conviction was from out of state, or in a federal court -- only the other state or feds have jurisdiction! You can apply for the Florida clemency, assuming you qualify, at the same time you are applying for any other form of executive clemency, or you can do it separately if you've already been granted a partial restoration of civil rights, or partial pardon.

51

Like the pardon, to be eligible you must have completed all sentences imposed, and have all conditions of supervision completed or expired for no less than **eight (8) years**, and no outstanding detainers, or restitution, nor fines from other criminal or traffic cases that total more than $1,000.00. Make sure all fines are paid off on any traffic tickets, etc. — or you may wind-up with a denial.

G.   Restoration of Civil Rights in Florida — This restores all rights of citizenship except right to own, possess, or use firearms. However, it does not relieve a person from registration and notification requirements imposed upon a sexual offender. You may apply for restoration of firearms rights at the same time you apply for your restoration if the eight (8) years has passed, otherwise you need a waiver.

To be eligible you must have completed all sentences imposed including all conditions of supervision. If convicted in a court other than a Florida state court, then the person must a legal resident of Florida at the time the application is made, and until it is decided. There are a number of crimes that will disqualify you from applying unless you have secured a waiver. These are a conviction for a capital or life felony; habitual offender; habitual violent offender; three time violent offender; violent career criminal; or prison release reoffender; any statewide prosecution; any RICO conviction; drug trafficking; any "dangerous crime"; accessory after fact to crime of violence; lewd, lascivious, indecent; crime requiring registration under Sexual Predators Act, sexual battery; crimes against law enforcement, DUI related felony; homicide; public corruption; crimes by elected official; shooting into vehicle or dwelling; leaving scene of accident involving death/serious injury; and possession of a firearm by convicted felon.

WAIVER:
There are always reasons why exceptions should be made, and the Rules of Executive Clemency make room for this. Thus, you may apply for a waiver of any provision of the rules upon a showing of good cause. This is done on a separate form provided by the Office

of Executive Clemency (which can be downloaded from their website), and can be granted by the Governor with one other member of his Cabinet, or by any one member of the Board of Executive Clemency in cases of "exceptional merit".

A waiver cannot be applied for until **two (2) years** have elapsed from the date of your conviction. However, the two year period may be waived by the Governor in cases of extraordinary merit that show a compelling need. If the Clemency Board has not acted on the waiver request within ninety (90) days of receipt of the Florida Parole Commission's "Waiver Report" — the waiver is automatically denied, unless the time is extended by the Governor, himself.

REAPPLICATION:
A person who has been granted or denied executive clemency cannot reapply for at least **two (2) years** from the date the denial became final unless a waiver is granted. However, a person may not reapply for a waiver until **three (3) years** have passed since the date of final action on the last waiver application.

CHART ON EXECUTIVE CLEMENCY APPLICATION:

type of relief	general time limit
pardon	10 years
firearm rights	8 years
restoration	1 year

SOME LIMITATIONS ON PARDON POWER:
Although a full pardon would normally be thought to "blot out guilt" — all pardons now granted have a proviso that the pardon "will not erase or expunge the record of conviction, and it will not indicate innocence". If you want an expunction — you'll have to apply for that separately, assuming you qualify.[63]

53

FEDERAL RESTORATION OF CIVIL RIGHTS:

It used to be that a state restoration of civil rights was insufficient to remove legal disabilities for firearms ownership without also going through an additional approval with ATF in Washington, D.C. Due to a change in federal law, so long as the restoration is "full" including firearms rights, and is from the state of conviction, this is no longer true, (unless it was a federal court conviction). To understand the change, you need to understand the following:

The federal definition of a "conviction" is set forth in 18 USC 921 (a)(20)(B), and states:

"What constitutes a conviction of such crime shall be determined in accordance with the law of the jurisdiction in which the proceedings were held. Any conviction which has been expunged, or set aside or for which a person has been pardoned or has had civil rights restored shall not be considered a conviction for purposes of this chapter, unless such pardon, expungement, or restoration of civil rights expressly provides that the person may not ship, transport, possess, or receive firearms."

Do not read this section literally. The restoration must be total. Thus, until your firearms rights are restored, you do not have a "full" restoration, and cannot possess firearms under either Florida or Federal law. As I said before, if you had a federal conviction, you are plum out of luck, as Congress, since 1992, has refused to fund the federal procedure to remove legal disabilities for firearms rights, and the U.S. Supreme Court upheld it in <u>United States v. Bean</u>, 537 US 71 (2002). Thus, the only current method of getting federal rights restored is by a Presidential pardon. Start those presidential contributions rolling! (Just kidding!)

EXPUNCTIONS & SEALINGS IN FLORIDA:

While not really related to restoration of civil rights, those citizens who were arrested for a crime in Florida, and had their case dropped, or dismissed can apply for an "expunction" of a Florida arrest in most instances pursuant to <u>F.S.</u> 943.0585. To a large extent, the granting of an expunction allows the person to lawfully deny the arrest and any prosecution for most purposes – just like it never occurred. It's not a lie when you do this -- it's called a "legal fiction". There's also something called a "sealing" pursuant to <u>F.S.</u>

54

943.059 which is similar to an expunction, can usually be obtained if the person has no prior record, and received nothing worse than a "withheld adjudication" in the current charge, and they had no prior findings of guilt on other charges. However, it is not as far-reaching as an expunction.

To qualify for an expunction, you cannot have had a previous criminal offense in which you entered a plea of *guilty* or *no contest*, or suffered a previous conviction, and you may not have had a previous sealing or expunction of your record. Likewise, and most unfair, if you went to trial, and won – you cannot obtain an expunction due to an amendment to the statute in 2006.

If you're seeking an expunction (or sealing), there are other things you need to do and know, but quite frankly, you really need a lawyer to accomplish these – so let them handle that.

EXCEPTIONS TO EXPUNCTION PRIVACY:
        Even with an expunction, there are still numerous exceptions on your ability to legally deny the arrest or prosecution, even with an expunction. These include working, volunteering, or apply for a job with: (1) a criminal justice agency; (2) you're a defendant in another criminal prosecution; (3) you're applying for a sealing or expunction in another case; (4) you're applying for admission to The Florida Bar; (5) you're applying for a position or license with the Department of Children and Family Services, the Department of Juvenile Justice, or will be employed or used in a position involving direct contact with children, the developmentally disabled, or the elderly; (6) any position in programs providing care to children, the developmentally disabled, or vulnerable adults; (7) positions with the central abuse hotline; (8) all persons working under contract who have access to abuse records; (9) all mental health personnel working in public or private mental health programs and facilities who have direct contact with unmarried patients under the age of 18 years; (10) persons involved in foster care and substance abuse; (11) child care personnel including schools and day care; (12) care giver of any "vulnerable adult"; (13) those working in delinquency services; (14) those working in nursing homes.

FEDERAL & OUT-OF-STATE CONVICTIONS:

You should know that the State of Florida does not have the power to expunge or seal an out-of-state arrest, nor does it have the power to expunge or seal a federal arrest, even if the arrest was in Florida. If you have an out-of-state problem – you'll likely need a lawyer in that jurisdiction to handle it. When an expunction is granted most of your judicial and almost all law enforcement agency records are actually shredded, and removed from all computers including the FBI, except for the file and computer records kept by FDLE.[64] Those records are generally confidential except by court order, and for verification purposes through FDLE when you apply or work in a position previously described.

In federal land, the federal courts rarely permit an expunction, and they have jurisdiction only to expunge judicial records, and not law enforcement records. U.S. v. Flowers, 389 F.3d 737 (7th Cir. 2004). As a practical matter, this is a very uphill battle, would require a showing of actual innocense, and probably not worth the effort.

PROHIBITED EXPUNCTIONS:

Certain crimes cannot be expunged. Here's the list: Violations of F.S. 393.135 & F.S. 394.4593 (sexual misconduct); any predicate offense for a sexual predator as listed in F.S. 775.21; F.S. 787.025 (luring or enticing a child); C. 794 (sexual battery); F.S. 796.03 (procuring minor for prostitution); F.S. 800.04 (lewd or lascivious acts); F.S.810.14 (voyeurism); F.S. 817.034 (communications fraud); F.S. 825.1025 (lewd or lascivious acts in presence of elderly or disabled); F.S. 827.071 (sexual performance by child); C. 839 (offenses by public officials); F.S. 847.0133 (transmit or show minor obscene materials); F.S. 847.0135 (computer pornography); F.S. 847.0145 (offering or allowing minor to be used for sexual conduct or depictions); F.S. 893.135 (drug trafficking); any violation listed in F.S. 907.041 (ie: "dangerous crimes" – ie: most "forcible felonies"); or F.S. 916.1075 (sexual misconduct).

You might also be interested in knowing that a sealed record can normally be expunged after ten years. F.S. 943.0585(2)(h).

CHAPTER FIVE

FLORIDA CONCEALED WEAPONS PERMIT

Having a Concealed Weapons Permit is the smartest thing anyone can do if they own or carry any type of weapon, whatsoever! If you only have a pocket knife -- get it! If you have a firearm -- you're nuts not to have it, even if you never take it out of the house! Why? Because it takes the worry out of 90% of the situations that could happen, and generally gives you the "benefit of the doubt" if law enforcement is involved. From a federal standpoint — it means you are not criminally liable for driving through a school zone with a firearm! Plus, the fact that you have the CWP is now confidential, and no longer can be disclosed as a public record. F.S. 790.0601.

It's also the best thing that ever happened to the honest Florida firearms, or weapons owner because prior to the passage of this State law, every single Florida county had its own individual set of standards and regulations – which drove everyone who was trying to be honest totally nuts – and left your ability to legally carry a firearm at the mercy of each particular Board of County Commissioners. Politics at its very worst! Of course, the criminals could care less, one way or the other -- but that's another story.

Today, if you meet certain specified qualifications -- you can legally carry a concealed firearm, or any other concealed weapon, almost anywhere in Florida -- with certain exceptions which I will outline later in this chapter. Although the specific purpose of this legislation was to authorize the carrying of a firearm "*as a means of lawful self-defense*", you should remember that it's still only a license to "carry" the firearm (or weapon) in a concealed manner -- and does NOT generally include the use or display of such weapons. The "use" aspect of having a firearm, or any other weapon, is still governed by the criminal laws, and the law of justification and self-defense. "Display" is covered by a number of criminal laws.

WEAPONS COVERED BY LICENSE:

Pursuant to F.S. 790.06(1), the license "technically" covers only handguns, electric weapons, tear gas guns, knives, and billies, however, as a practical matter it covers any weapon or firearm other than a machine gun or destructive device inasmuch as F.S. 790.01(3) exempts persons with a valid Concealed Weapons License from any of the prohibitions of carrying concealed weapons/firearms. Of course, there are no cases interpreting this facet of F.S. 790.01, and therefore if you want to be completely safe, stick to the weapons listed. On the other hand, it seems somewhat irrational to say a person can carry a concealed firearm, but can't carry something less lethal, and I can't imagine a contrary interpretation that would pass constitutional muster, or make any sense. Still, it could be a test case.

QUALIFICATIONS FOR THE CONCEALED PERMIT:

Obtaining a Florida Concealed Weapons License (ie: CWP) is a fairly reasonable procedure. It takes about three (3) months or less to get it, from the time you send in the application -- and lasts for seven (7) years before it must be renewed. The basic qualifications for obtaining the Concealed Weapons Permit/License[65] are as follows:

1. You must be 21 years of age, or older, and a legal resident of the United States.

2. You don't suffer from any physical infirmity which prevents the safe handling of a weapon or firearms.

3. You're not a convicted felon, unless your right to own and possess a firearm was restored by executive clemency.

4. You have not been committed for drug abuse within **three (3) years** of the date of your application for the permit, nor have you been found guilty of any drug crime, including misdemeanor possession, within the same time frame. In this sense, "guilty" is the equivalent of either a conviction, or a withheld adjudication.

5.   You are not a chronic and habitual user of alcohol to the extent that your normal faculties are impaired. This situation is presumed to be true if you were committed for alcohol treatment pursuant to <u>Chapter</u> 396 of the Florida Statutes; were convicted of using a firearm while under the influence of alcohol or a controlled substance; were convicted of DUI two or more times within **3 years** of your application; or have been deemed a habitual offender of the disorderly intoxication laws within **3 years** of your application by three convictions within 12 months.

6.   You have not been adjudicated an incapacitated person under <u>F.S.</u> 744.331, or have waited **five (5) years** after such incapacity was removed by court order.

7.   You have not been committed to a mental institution, unless you have a certificate from a psychiatrist licensed in Florida that you have not suffered from any such disability for **five (5) years**. Of course, if you were involuntarily committed, and the disability is later removed — you will still be prohibited under federal law, even with a concealed permit.

8.   You have not had a withheld adjudication or suspended sentence on any felony, or any misdemeanor crime of domestic violence unless **three (3) years** have passed since you completed probation, and any other conditions set by the court; or unless your record was sealed or expunged. Furthermore, be warned — current Federal law does not permit firearms possession if you plead *"guilty"* vs. *"no contest"* to a felony, or to a misdemeanor domestic violence conviction — *"withheld"* or not. <u>United States v. Chubbuck</u>, 252 F.3d 1300 (11th Cir. 2001). This also applies to police officers, even on duty. <u>F.O.P. v. United States</u>, 173 F.3d 898 (DCC 1999).

9.   There is no injunction currently in force that restrains you from committing either repeat or domestic violence.

10.   You are not prohibited from purchase or possession of a firearm by Florida or Federal law. F.S. 790.06(2)(m).

Since F.S. 790.065, and federal law affect this subsection, the following additional prohibitions currently would **stop** you from obtaining a permit:

a.   if you plead "guilty" instead of "no contest" to any felony, or to any misdemeanor crime of domestic violence, or were found guilty of such after a trial — even if adjudication was "withheld" because the 11th Circuit Court of Appeals says it's still a "conviction". They also admit they're probably wrong, but will still uphold any federal conviction![66] Hence, Florida would be wise to refuse the permit at this point.

b.   even if you had a "withheld adjudication" on any felony, or any misdemeanor crime of domestic violence, and even if you plead "no contest" — you must still wait until **three (3) years** have elapsed since all conditions of the sentence were fulfilled, including fines, probation, parole, and restitution. F.S. 790.06(2)(k)

c.   If you have a criminal indictment or information for a felony pending against you — you can't get the permit until the case is resolved, since federal law does not permit you to purchase from a dealer.

d.   If, while your application is pending, you have an **arrest** for any "dangerous crime" listed per F.S. 907.041; any violation of any firearm/weapons violation in Chapter 790 of the Florida statutes; stalking, resisting an officer with violence, drug crimes under Chapter 893; extortion; explosives; assisting suicide; treason;

sabotage; or criminal anarchy — you will be denied until the charge is disposed of, assuming the disposition does not disqualify you from firearms ownership or possession. It is your responsibility to supply proof of a favorable disposition once the charge is disposed of. This is normally done by obtaining a certified copy of the Nolle Prosequi, or No Information filed by the State Attorney in the court clerk's file. <u>F.S.</u> 790.065(2)(c)(1)

11. You are not a resident of the United States, unless you are a consular security official of a friendly foreign government. (Yes -- you can be an out of state resident, and still obtain a permit. But remember, it's only valid in Florida, and those states that have a reciprocity law with Florida.

There are also training requirements "to demonstrate competence with a firearm". These are to assure the State that you have some intelligent idea of what you can legally do with a firearm, and know how to use it. As varied as this qualification may be in application, it seems to be working extremely well. Very few concealed permit holders are getting in trouble with the law since the program started. The training qualifications can be any one of the following:

1. Completion of any hunter education or safety course approved by the Game & Fresh Water Fish Commission, or similar agency of another state.

2. Completion of any NRA firearms safety or training course.

3. Completion of any firearms safety or training course, or class, available to the general public which is staffed by instructors certified by the NRA, Department of State, or Criminal Justice Standards & Training Commission, and offered by: (a) law enforcement; (b) a college or junior college; (c) a private or public institution, or organization; or (d) a firearms training school.

4.   Completion of any law enforcement firearms training or safety course, or class, offered for security guards, investigators, special deputies, or any subdivision of law enforcement or security enforcement.

5.   Presents evidence of equivalent experience with a firearm through military service (copy of Honorable Discharge, or DD214), or through participation in organized shooting competition.

6.   Is licensed, or was licensed to carry a firearm in this state, any county of this state, or any such municipality, unless the license was revoked for cause.

7.   Completion of any firearms training or safety course, or class, conducted by a state certified firearms instructor, or an NRA certified firearms instructor.

If your training is under subsection 2, 3, or 7 of the above — and you took your instruction on or after July 1, 1998 — the instructor must also certify you "safely handled and discharged the firearm", as part of the course. This can technically be a "one shot" requirement. F.S. 790.06(2)(h), although I would certainly hope for more – including loading and unloading. Plus, the NRA requires its certified instructors to have the student use an actual firearm with live ammunition – not air soft, or blanks – which is totally consistent with the language of the statute. Obviously, the more instruction you get — the better off you are from a practical side, even if this is not necessary for the license. There are many excellent instructors in your geographic area, and no matter what your level of expertise, you'll probably learn something.

Once you complete the course, you enclose a photocopy of your completion certificate with the rest of your application form, and you send it to Tallahassee. If you don't have a completion certificate you may substitute an affidavit from the instructor, school, club, group, or organization that conducted or taught the course/or class that attests to your completion -- or participation in firearms competition.

COMPLETING THE APPLICATION PROCESS:

If you are applying for the permit for the first time the fee, at last glance, was a total of $117.00. This represents both the cost of the permit ($75.00), and the balance ($42.00) for processing the fingerprint card. However, I highly recommend "electronic fingerprinting" through your local sheriff's office which will speed your application by about 60 days. If you are only seeking a renewal, the renewal fee is $65.00 for Florida residents, and further fingerprinting is not required. If you use the fingerprint card rather than electronic fingerprinting – the initial application must be filled out in **BLACK** ink. If you use blue ink, or some other color to fill in anything on the fingerprint card -- it becomes trash, and you'll need another one. The fingerprint card, and almost everything else are supplied to you, on request in writing or online, in a packet from the Florida Department of Agriculture. The address is:

> Florida Department of Agriculture
> Division of Licensing — Concealed Weapon Permits
> P.O. Box 6687
> Tallahassee, Florida 32314-6687
> [http://licgweb.doacs.state.fl.us]

Fingerprinting can be done at any law enforcement agency, but the Sheriff is supposed to do it for no more than five dollars, although the electronic version is still $42.00. You will also have to supply a color photograph taken within 30 days of your application which meets a certain required size format. Separate instructions on this come with your application packet, and most passport photos are OK. Although the application is not available for download, you can order it over the web at http://licgweb.doacs.state.fl.us

If you are currently a law enforcement, corrections, or correctional probation officer, or hold active certification from the Criminal Justice Standards & Training Commission as such, you do not need a background check for the permit, nor do you pay a fee for such. However, you are still stuck with the application or renewal fee. Furthermore, if you are applying for the permit for the first time and held any such position -- and you retired within the year immediately preceding the date of your application -- all fees are waived, no fingerprinting, and it's a one-time freebie. As stated, this does not apply to renewals, but only to initial applications. Officers retired more than a year pay a $30.00 license fee, plus the $42.00 fingerprint fee. If you are a judge, you still must establish proof of the training requirements - but that's it, no fees.[67]

RECIPROCITY:
        A great feature of the permit is that Florida has reciprocal agreements with a number of other states that allow you to carry concealed in their state with your Florida permit. A number of these states also require that you <u>not</u> be a resident of their state to do this, and that you are also an actual resident of Florida if you're using a Florida permit. This varies state-to-state, but is something you must know. There are a few other warnings that must be given: if you carry in a reciprocal state you must carry pursuant to <u>their laws</u>, and not those of Florida.   Sometimes, these vary greatly from Florida! Another warning repeats what I've already said — a concealed carry permit covers only concealed carry.   Anything else, including use or display of the firearm is NOT covered.   Last, is that in many of these states the concealed permit covers only **handguns**, nothing else! Thus, although your Florida permit covers knives, tear gas gun, handgun, billie, and electric weapons — carrying anything else but a concealed handgun in another state could result in your being arrested.

        The answer to these questions is to know the law of concealed carry in each state.   To facilitate this, the Florida Department of Agriculture website has links to the laws of each of the reciprocal carry states, and also a summary of reciprocal restrictions. If you haven't linked up to the web by now — here's a heck of a good reason to do so.   The list of reciprocal states as of the date this chapter was written, April 2009, are as follows:

        Alabama, Alaska, Arizona, Arkansas, Colorado, Delaware, Georgia, Idaho, Indiana, Kansas, Kentucky, Louisiana, Michigan, Missouri, Mississippi, Montana, Nevada, New Hampshire, New Mexico, North Carolina, North Dakota, Ohio, Oklahoma, Pennsylvania, South Carolina, South Dakota, Tennessee, Texas, Utah, Vermont, Virginia, West Virginia, Wyoming [total of 33 states besides Florida]

Remember that Florida does not recognize an out-of-state permit that was issued to a non-resident of the licensing state, or anyone under 21 years of age. F.S. 790.015. There is also some current controversy in Wyoming on whether their reciprocal laws should be curtailed to states who allow persons with drug offenses (misdemeanor or "withhelds") to get a CWP.

PROHIBITED PLACES WITH CONCEALED PERMIT:
The issuance of a Concealed Weapons Permit allows you to carry any type of the listed weapons in a concealed manner.   These are handguns, knives, billies, electric weapons that do not shoot a projectile, and tear gas guns. F.S. 790.06(1).   Thus, chemical sprays, long guns, nun-chuks, throwing stars, swords, hatchets, brass knuckles, etc. are not covered by your license, although they should still be legal by virtue of F.S. 790.01(3).   The permit does not apply to any automatic firearm (ie: machine gun).   Likewise, open (unconcealed) carrying of weapons and firearms are not covered by your permit. There are also some limitations on where you can carrying concealed. Some of these make good sense, some do not. Here's the full list of where you can't carry the weapon or firearm under your license:[68]

1.   Any police station or facility (Sheriff, FHP, local police, etc.)

2.   Any jail, prison, or detention facility.

3.   Any courthouse or courtroom, unless you're a judge. Also, a judge may issue an order allowing a person to carry a firearm in his courtroom.

4.   Any government meeting involving the governing body of a school board, county commission, city commission, or special district.

5.   Any meeting of the Legislature, or any of its committees.

6.   Any polling place.

7.   At any elementary school, secondary school, college, or university "facility". The definition of a "facility"[69] normally relates to buildings, and structures -- thus, an entrance road or parking lot should not ordinarily fall within this definition. However, there are no Florida decisions regarding this, and the interpretation, for now, is purely mine.[70] If you want to play it safe, just keep it "securely encased" and out of sight inside your vehicle as allowed by F.S. 790.115(2)(a)(3), and keep it off your person. Please see the section on schools for a more detailed analysis!

Anyway, under this subsection of the statute, F.S. 790.06(12), you are also prohibited from bringing your concealed weapon to any "area vocational-technical center", and any school administration building. A willful violation of any part of this subsection by a permit holder is a second degree misdemeanor. Without a permit — it's a felony.[71]

There is an exception to the prohibition, as applied to colleges and universities only, and only where the permit holder is also a registered student, faculty member, or employee, and the weapon is a stun gun or other non-lethal electric weapon that does not fire a dart or projectile, and is designed solely for defensive purposes. Chemical weapons are not permitted. These persons may carry such electric weapon into buildings and structures on the college and university campus so long as it is concealed. F.S. 790.06(12)

You should also know that F.S. 790.115 has a blanket prohibition on the "possession" of any firearm or weapon on the "property" of a school,[72] school bus or school bus stop, and further prohibits the "display" of a weapon on such areas, as well as within 1000 feet of a school, if the display is done in the presence of others, and in a rude, careless, angry, or threatening manner — and not in lawful self-defense. However, it then exempts CWP holders from the penalties of F.S. 790.115, and refers to their punishment as a second degree misdemeanor under the concealed weapons statute, F.S. 790.06(12). That's confusing – because it leaves four possible interpretations: (1) if you are a permit holder and violate F.S. 790.115, you've committed only a civil infraction unless done "willfully"; or (2) it's a second degree misdemeanor only if done "willfully"; or (3) it's a second degree misdemeanor willfully or not; or (4) assuming that F.S. 790.06(12) allows concealed carry on "grounds" vs. "facilities" with the CWP then it's legal if concealed, and you don't go on or into any structure.

Of course, the last interpretation is legally dangerous, and will probably make you a "test case" because I think you'll be arrested in this situation unless an appellate court first decides my last interpretation is right. Don't chance it!

8.   Any athletic event of a school, or college -- and also for any professional athletic event (Marlins, Dolphins, the Heat, Buccaneers, diving contest, skateboard, etc.) of all types. There is an exception to this prohibition only if the event is one that is related to firearms.

9.   Inside the passenger portion of any airline terminal, and the "sterile area" of any airport (ie: the X-ray machine checkpoint, and beyond). Usually the area reserved for passengers making flight departures, or arrivals.

However, there is an exception for anyone who is a passenger, is in the terminal (but not the sterile area), and is carrying a firearm for shipment as baggage on an airline so long as that firearm is already unloaded, and encased in a locked container. More on that in the next chapter, especially in light of federal regulations.

10.   Any other place a firearm is prohibited by federal law, including any federal office or building.[73] This means, amongst other places -- a post office, IRS, social security. It does not mean a bank. If you go to a bank, and take out lots of money -- you may need a firearm. If you go to an ATM (automatic teller), and it's after hours, statistics show you'd better have one! Likewise, if you go into a store that

sells stamps or has a small post office inside it should be a "contract post office" pursuant to 39 CFR 241.2. Such a site should not be considered a federal office or building as the regulation defines it as being wholly private.[74] Thus, there should be nothing illegal if you have a valid CWP on you.

11.　　In any portion of a restaurant, bar, nightclub, or other establishment licensed to serve alcohol for consumption on the premises (not a liquor store which only sells the packaged stuff vs. serving it) in the portion of the premises that is primarily devoted to that purpose.

In other words, if you go into a restaurant, you can't go in the bar, you can't even walk through the bar -- but you can sit at a dinner table, go to other places within the establishment not within or through the bar area, and even order drinks with your meal, or just order drinks. However, be warned, that in many of the reciprocal states you are prohibited from going in any establishment that serves alcohol, with a concealed weapon or firearm.

A question I'm often asked concerning this subsection is: "What if I work in a bar, or own it?" Well, I think that since you could carry even without a permit pursuant to F.S. 790.25(3)(n), you are legal, and carry would be pursuant to the statute rather than the permit. The subsection in the permit law, F.S 790.06(12), doesn't say it negates legal carry pursuant to F.S. 790.25 – it just says the license doesn't "authorize" carry in certain places. Thus, if you're legal under F.S. 790.25 – you should be legal even with the permit, because you're not carrying "pursuant" to the permit. Again, this is just my opinion since as there's no case law on it, but it's just common sense. On the other hand, if you're a school teacher don't think you can bring it into the school. That would be an entirely different matter, governed by different statutory sections, and illegal. Possession at schools is only allowed to specified persons at specified times.

12.   Last but not least, you can't carry in a house of prostitution, crack house, or place of illegal gambling, as these constitute "public nuisances" under F.S. 823.05.

LICENSE VIOLATIONS:
There are certain problems that can arise when you have the Concealed Weapons Permit. In comparison to what could happen to someone without the permit -- these consequences are really mild. One thing you need to know is that if you are carrying a concealed weapon or firearm, you must also have your actual permit on your person.[75] A failure to do so is a noncriminal violation with a $25.00 fine. Same thing goes if a police officer asks to see your permit and other identification while you're carrying -- and you don't have it, or refuse to show it (that would be really stupid). Of course, you may get arrested for a felony since the officer is probably not going to take your word that you "must of left it at home". But, you'll finally be able to beat that charge, since you do have the permit somewhere. Of course, this will occur long after you are hassled-to-death by the system, as it tries to sort-out your screw-up.

Another problem is if you violate any of the use restrictions I just outlined in the preceding numbered paragraphs, 1 -12. If you do, and that violation was done "willfully" (ie: deliberate violation of the law)[76] -- it's a second degree misdemeanor. Moreover, if you carry into the sterile area of an airport -- it's also a federal felony, unless you can establish the defense that you are a total idiot, and really forgot that you had the .357 Magnum in your pocketbook. You'd be surprised how many people do this every year! You should also know that this type of incident is seriously scrutinized since 9/11.

LOST LICENSES, OR CHANGE OF ADDRESS:
You are also required to notify the Department of Agriculture of any change in your permanent address, or if your permit was lost, stolen, or destroyed -- all within a period of 30 days. A failure is a noncriminal violation, and another big twenty five dollar fine. If you move, the process is real simple. You can mail or fax a letter (fax to: 850-487-7950), or do it over their web site, stating your new address, and asking that your records be changed. [http://licgweb.doacs.state.fl.us/license/changes.html]. Make sure you include your concealed permit number. No charge, unless

you want to receive a replacement license. If you do, it's fifteen bucks, plus you need to send a color passport photo.

If it was lost or stolen, your permit is automatically invalid until you pay the Department of Agriculture a fifteen dollar ($15.00) fee to reinstate it, a photo, and you receive back the replacement license. In order to get this, you also have to send them a notarized statement that the permit was lost, stolen, or destroyed -- along with the fee, and the passport photo. The address for all of this is, including on line web form is:

> Florida Department of Agriculture,   Division of Licensing
> Concealed Weapons Permit Program
> P.O. Box 6687
> Tallahassee, Florida 32314-6687
> http://licgweb.doacs.state.fl.us

QUESTION: Does that mean that if I lost my original, but have a copy -- I don't have the protections of a concealed permit?

ANSWER: Silly, huh? Yeah, that's the way the statute seems to read. From a constitutional standpoint there may be a way around it, but who would want to be in that position? Remember, test cases are only good for lawyers.

SUSPENSION OR REVOCATION OF YOUR PERMIT:
The State is not happy if you suddenly do something you shouldn't have, and still have your permit to carry. Most of the time this makes good sense. However, if you use your gun for self-defense, get arrested because somebody on the government side is too chicken to stand-up against possible adverse publicity, and temporarily/permanently lose your permit -- it (pardon the expression) stinks. However, this is not where I am going to lecture you on my personal philosophy of life, so let's get back to the law.

Most of the things that would disqualify you from getting the permit will also cause you to have it suspended or revoked.   F.S. 790.06(3) & (10). If you plea to, or are found guilty of a felony while you hold the permit, obviously, it's history. Same thing if you get a conviction or "withheld" for any drug crime, even if it's a misdemeanor; or a conviction on a misdemeanor crime of domestic violence. You'll get a suspension if there's an injunction in effect that prevents domestic violence, or repeat violence, or if you're arrested or charged with a crime that could disqualify you from a permit. As to other exciting reasons why your permit will be revoked or suspended, here's the rest of the list:

1.   committed as an alcoholic, or deemed a disorderly intoxication habitual offender.

2.   convicted of a second DUI within 3 years of any prior one.

3.   adjudicated an incapacitated person.

4.   committed to a mental institution.

5.   develops or sustains a physical infirmity which prevents the safe handling of a weapon or firearm.

6.   chronically and habitually uses alcoholic beverages to extent that normal faculties are impaired.[77]

7.   May revoke if licensee is found "guilty" ("adjudication" or "withheld adjudication") of one or more crimes of violence within the preceding three years.[78]

8.   Shall suspend the license upon notification by FDLE, a court, or law enforcement agency of the arrest or formal charge of a drug crime, a felony, a second DUI within three years, pending final disposition of the charge.

If this list isn't real clear to you, I've included a chart on the last page of this chapter to make it easier. Remember, that if you plead "guilty" rather than "no contest", or were found "guilty" after a trial, you will still be considered as "convicted" under the current interpretation of federal law. This is true regardless of whether you were "adjudicated" or received a "withheld adjudication".[79] Florida law would be different, but then, who wants to be prosecuted by the feds for something you're actually innocent of?

HOW YOU CAN CARRY CONCEALED:

Carrying a concealed weapon or firearm under F.S. 790.01 means "on or about your person". "On or about" your person generally means within your reach or immediate control. Thus, with the permit you may legally carry your firearm or weapon in a briefcase, bag, etc. -- as well as on your immediate person, so long as it's concealed. Logically, this means you could have it within reach, under a towel in your car. No, it doesn't have to be in a holster!

DEALING WITH POLICE OFFICERS:

Now, just because this is legal, don't think you can't get arrested. The problem is that many police officers have not been trained very well in this area, and have their own idea of what the law is. I personally handle at least half a dozen cases a year where the police arrest someone for something that is totally legal. Unfortunately -- they just didn't know the law. More unfortunately, some innocent slob got arrested for being legal. That's life in the big city. It happens.[80]

The only thing I can tell you is that once you finish reading this book, keep it in your vehicle. Then if a police officer pulls you over, and suddenly announces you're being arrested for something the law says you can do -- you can politely tell him or her that you're sure he or she knows the law, and you don't want to sound like a "wise guy" -- but you've got this book on firearms in the car that's being used by seven police academies, and over eighty law enforcement agencies -- and it says that it's O.K. Would he/she please "just take a look?"

With a little bit of the Irish luck, he'll realize he may be making a slight error, and with even more luck, he'll say something to the effect of:

"I don't care what the book says, I know the law. But, I'm gonna give you a break. Don't do it again."

At this point, thank him. Then, shut your mouth, and be thankful you didn't have to go to jail to prove your point. Got the point? Of course, if you are arrested, see a good civil lawyer once the case is dropped, as you've got a great false arrest claim. By the way — don't threaten the officer that you'll sue him if he arrests you — that will only get him angry, and is a sure way to complicate whatever situation you're already in. Even in a tough situation try to be respectful. Most of them really deserve your respect.

WHY CONCEALED PERMITS ARE THE BEST:
If you haven't already guessed, I'm the greatest believer in concealed permits there is. Well . . . at least, I'm one of them. I think that it takes the edge off situations where you might otherwise get arrested, and normally puts you in a position where a police officer will give you the benefit of a doubt. It also fills in the gaps where you need to carry concealed, or unintentionally do carry concealed. In other words -- it's there.

More importantly, you join the ranks of over 561,681 (as of 3/31/09) active permit holders. Dems alot of votes, partner! The more permit holders there are, the less likely it will be that politicians are going to try to take any of your rights away. And, if you don't think there are forces out there that would love to see you disarmed, and easy prey for everything and everybody -- you better start getting educated, because the battle is raging around you, every single day.

CONCEALED WEAPONS BADGES:
I keep getting asked by people whether they should buy a concealed weapons badge. My answer is a definite "no". It has no statutory basis, no real useful purpose, is not a substitute for the permit, and is a possible way to get arrested assuming you are taken as pretending to be a law enforcement officer by the way you've used and displayed it. F.S. 843.08 On the other hand, if its just something you want to put on your mantle to impress folks (assuming they're stupid enough to be impressed by something anyone can buy for a few bucks) – it's legal because F.S. 843.085 which made it unlawful to display law enforcement badges by persons who were not law enforcement personnel was declared unconstitutional because the statute did not require an intent to deceive by the possessor.[81]

MOMENTARILY UNCONCEALED – "PRINTING":

I've received quite a few questions on my opinion as to whether momentary or inadvertent disclosure of your legally concealed weapon violates the protections of the permit. I have found no cases on this subject, however, I think common sense, and constitutional Due Process would protect you if a gust of wind or some other inadvertent situation occurred that momentarily disclosed your actual weapon. Even in this circumstance it is still "partially concealed". Moreover, the mere fact that your firearm may occasionally "print" under your clothing doesn't mean it's not legally concealed. However, I would always do my best to make sure any weapon I carried with my permit was not obvious. That's also common sense. Likewise, there are several defenses to an arrest for this including something called "lack of scienter" – which simply means you didn't know the firearm was so exposed at the time the incident occurred. (ie: lack of knowledge)

The next page has a chart on what can get your license suspended or revoked. Hope that helps.

CHART ON LICENSE SUSPENSION/REVOCATION:

Suspension or Revocation of Permit -- 790.06(10) & 790.06(3)
Physical infirmity that renders handling of weapon/firearm unsafe.
Felony conviction.
Found guilty of any drug crime.
Committed as substance abuser.
Three convictions within 12 months for disorderly intoxication.
Two DUI convictions within 3 years.
Adjudicated as an incapacitated person.
Committed to mental institution.
Chronic user of alcohol or other substances.
Convicted of using firearm while under influence. — F.S. 790.151
Withheld adjudication on any felony, or any misdemeanor crime of domestic violence (until 3 years elapsed since completion of sentence & all conditions).
Current injunction against repeat or domestic violence.
Otherwise prohibited from possession/purchase of firearm by Florida or Federal law — F.S. 790.06(2)(m) – which would be: •   felony indictment or information -- pending. •   withheld adjudication on felony, or misdemeanor crime of domestic violence if plead "guilty", or if found "guilty" after trial. •   arrest for any "dangerous crime" per F.S. 907.041 — pending. •   arrest for any violation of C.790 — pending. •   arrest for resisting officer with violence, drug crime, extortion, explosives, assisting suicide, treason, sabotage, criminal anarchy — pending.
Found guilty (or suspended sentence) for any misdemeanor or felony which involves violence (until 3 years elapsed since completion of sentence & all conditions). F.S. 790.06(3)
Upon notification and verification of an arrest, indictment, information, or formal charge for any crime that would disqualify person for license. [same as F.S. 790.06(2)(m)]

(this page reserved)

CHAPTER SIX

TRANSPORTATION AND CARRYING OF WEAPONS, AND FIREARMS

When I do a speaking engagement, the questions I am asked most frequently are those related to the transportation of firearms. In other words: "Where the heck can I keep it, and how?"

Leading the confusion chart are questions relating to transportation of a gun in your own car while you're in Florida. But what about private boats, private aircraft, public aircraft, in a taxi, while you're camping, going to the range, going to a gun show, or traveling state-to-state in your car, etc.?

If you're a Concealed Weapons Permit licensee -- you have a much easier problem to contend with. However, with the number of state and federal laws that govern this area, the legal carrying or transporting of firearms, as well as other weapons, is far from simple -- permit, or not. That's what I'll try to show you in this chapter. And although the statutory law is not perfectly clear on all points, it has been pretty much clarified by the case law. Whatever the circumstances, I'll make it as clear as anybody can. However, before doing that, let's take a look at the most asked question about firearms law:

SUMMARY OF WHERE HANDGUN CAN BE KEPT IN VEHICLE:
Most questions on firearms law concern where a person can legally carry a handgun in a vehicle, with or without a concealed permit, here's the short answer on what's definitely "securely encased":

a.   in a snapped holster — anywhere — loaded or unloaded.
b.   in a closed console — loaded or unloaded.
c.   in a closed glove compartment — loaded or unloaded.
d.   in a zippered gun case — loaded or unloaded.
e.   in any other type of <u>closed</u> container which the gun cannot be fired from until withdrawn — loaded or unloaded.

That's the easy correct answer, and it applies equally to all commercial vehicles.   If you do the above, you're legal in Florida except in certain special situations related to schools.   More on that in another chapter.   On the other hand,   just because you know the law doesn't mean the police know the law.   I handle at least a couple of cases a year where honest citizens are arrested for completely legal carry.   The usual outcome is we get the case dropped, and then sue or settle with the offending government agency that was responsible.   More on that later, but for now, let's get back to the meat of this chapter.

THE LEGAL CARRYING OF FIREARMS -- LISTED:
   Since Florida generally prohibits open carry of firearms[82], and (without a permit) concealed carry of almost everything[83], there is a statute, F.S. 790.25, that gives certain listed exceptions to this — lot's of exceptions!   The statute seems contradictory in parts, but the case interpretations of the statute have been extremely consistent, and clearly indicate that these sections allow both concealed carry on the person without a permit (except in private conveyances), and open carry.[84] However, I advise you to use some discretion.   Like I've said before, many police officers don't know this area of law — others don't care -- and you certainly don't need to be arrested, mistakenly or otherwise.

   Anyway, the chart on the next page gives you the statutory list of exceptions from F.S. 790.25(3), which would allow you to carry without a permit, open or concealed:

CHART OF EXEMPTIONS UNDER F.S. 790.25:

Members of the military or National Guard, while on duty.
Carrying out training for emergency management duties pursuant to C. 252
Law enforcement officers of this state; or those of other states, or the federal government while carrying out official duties in Florida.
Florida or federal officials authorized to carry concealed weapons
Guards or messengers of common carriers, express companies, mail carriers, armored car carriers, banks, and other financial institutions while actually employed in and about the transportation or delivery of any money, treasure, bullion, bonds, or other thing of value within this state.
Regularly enrolled members of any organization or club organized for target, skeet, or trap shooting, while at such practice or event, or going to or from such.
Regularly enrolled members of clubs organized for firearms collecting, while such members are at, or going to/fro any gun show, convention, or exhibit.
A person engaged in fishing, camping, or lawful hunting, or going to or from such an expedition.
Any person/employee of a business engaged in the manufacture, repair, or dealing in firearms while engaged in the lawful course of such business.
Legally firing weapons for testing or target practice, under safe conditions, and at a safe place, not prohibited by law, or while going to or from such place,
A person on a public conveyance transporting a securely encased weapon, which is not in his manual possession.[85]
A person who carries a pistol unloaded, and in a secure wrapper, from the place of purchase to his home or business, or to a place of repair, or back therefrom.
A person at his own home or place of business (but this does not pertain to "common areas" shared with other individuals in an apartment building or condominium, or a shared parking lot).
A person in a private conveyance (vehicle, aircraft, or boat) where the weapon is "securely encased", or not readily accessible for immediate use. However, in this circumstance the law says it CANNOT be carried on your person.
An investigator employed full-time by the Public Defender or Capital Collateral Representative, in the course of their official duties, who meet other requirements of statute.

Now, if this list seems perfectly clear to you -- you should know it's not quite as simple as you may think. Some of these areas are pretty clear-cut, others are confusing as heck, and need explicit explanation. You may also have noticed that in some of these instances I mentioned weapons other than firearms. However, most weapons other than firearms, are not regulated by the Florida state statutes unless they are carried "concealed". With only some exceptions, it is technically legal[86] to carry most weapons, other than firearms, in the open -- just about anywhere other than at schools, school bus stops, school buses, vehicles, and public transportation.   I'll cover that later in a separate chapter, but since you still need some further instruction in the areas I've just covered in the preceding numbered paragraphs -- the next portion of this book contains the explicit explanation sections -- to whatever extent that is really possible.

LEGAL CARRYING IN AUTOMOBILES & PRIVATE VEHICLES:

The most often asked question in the State of Florida related to firearms -- is how can they legally be transported in a private vehicle. By "vehicle" I mean a car, truck, motorcycle, or any other type of private conveyance you can think of that normally drives on the road. By the word "private", I mean any vehicle that is not driven by somebody for hire, but is privately owned and driven. By "conveyance" I mean a trailer, motor vehicle, ship, railway car, or aircraft.[87] A bicycle is <u>not</u> a conveyance.[88]

A vehicle that is driven in a car-pool is private, even if you all chip in on the gas. A non-private vehicle would include a taxi-cab, or rented limo. Any other interpretation of what is or is not private can probably be figured out by common sense. And by the way, these definitions were my interpretations, not the legislature's -- because the legislature didn't bother to give us any definition -- and the courts haven't gotten around to interpreting these definitions, either.

So, now that you know what is probably private, and what is not -- you still need to know the definition of the next two phrases: "<u>securely encased</u>", and "<u>not readily accessible for immediate use</u>". Each of these phrases apply to very different legal ways of transporting a firearm in your private vehicle. Here's how it works.

SECURELY ENCASED:

"Securely encased"[89] means that the weapon or firearm is in some type of holster, bag, enclosure, box, or container that is secured with a clasp, lid, zipper, strap, snap, flap, or other device, so that in order to fire or use the weapon, the device must first be opened, removed, or undone.[90] It does not require a lock. The purpose behind this was to give a person a very brief opportunity to think about it, before actually using it. This includes a closed glove compartment or console; zippered, snapped, or Velcro-closed bag,[91] holster, or case which first must be unclasped in order to fire; any type of box or enclosure with a closed lid; or even a purse -- assuming you can't operate the firing mechanism through the fabric, and there is some physical act required to open the top of the purse and unhook/unclasp/unzip it. A briefcase or suitcase also falls into this category. A cardboard box with the lid closed also complies.[92] A man's plastic purse with a flap over the opening is also included because the flap must be moved in order to withdraw the weapon. Urquiola v. State, 590 So.2d 497 (Fla. 3DCA 1991). Likewise, in Alexander v. State, 477 So.2d 557 (Fla. 1985), the Florida Supreme Court held that a man's zippered leather pouch containing a firearm was "securely encased" even though there were other items in the pouch, and even though the man had opened and zippered the pouch several times in the presence of a police officer.[93]

So, you can see the courts are fairly liberal on what is "securely encased". As long as the statutory purpose is met, a firearm can be kept in just about anything in a vehicle if it has a lid, closure, or something must be opened to get it out.

QUESTION: Can the handgun be loaded if I do this?

ANSWER: Absolutely. It won't do you any good, otherwise.

QUESTION: I heard it must be in a holster if I have it in the glove compartment, and the glove compartment must be locked?

ANSWER: Nope. All you need is to have the glove compartment closed.

81

QUESTION: What if it's in my console, loaded, and ready to go?

ANSWER: Totally legal as long as the lid is closed.[94] If the lid is open wide enough to remove the firearm you are in big trouble.[95]

QUESTION: What if the lid is partially opened?

ANSWER: The courts should focus on whether the weapon can be obtained without removing/opening the lid wider to gain access. If you still have to move the flap – the statutory purpose has been met, and it should be "securely encased". How wide the opening is will be the deciding factor, and is a factual question.

QUESTION: OK, I hear what you're saying, but I really don't understand. How can a firearm be "securely encased" if all I have to do is flip open a lid?

ANSWER: Well, it seems clear that the statutory definition of "securely encased" doesn't really mean that the weapon is "encased securely". It just means that the method of carry meets the statutory definition. If it does, it's "legally" secure, even if it's not factually secure.[96]

QUESTION: I've heard that keeping a firearm in a car is a two step, or three step rule. What does that mean?

ANSWER: It means that the person who gave you that advice couldn't remember what the statute actually said, so they made up their own definition to substitute for it. Forget it. Just remember the statute.

QUESTION: If a police officer stops me, and the gun is legally in my handbag along with my drivers license -- what do I do when he asks me for my license?

ANSWER: Make darn sure you take your drivers license out before you exit the car, and leave your purse inside. You are only legal inside the vehicle, unless you have a Concealed Weapons Permit. If you carry it outside -- it could be a felony -- "carrying a concealed firearm". If it's another weapon other than two ounce chemical spray, a stun gun, or common pocketknife, it's a misdemeanor -- "carrying a concealed weapon".

If you tell him you have a firearm in the purse before you exit, and he thereafter tells you to hand it to him outside the car, you would have a legal defense since he ordered you to do it. Obviously, in this situation, don't hand him the firearm, itself! That would be stupid! He'll be nervous, and he also has a gun. Instead, give him the entire purse, and leave it closed, unless he instructs you otherwise. Or, stand away from the car, and have him take the purse out on his own. You don't want to get shot over a stupid misunderstanding.

QUESTION: If I tell the officer I have a firearm, what can he do?

ANSWER: Usually, he'll ask for its location, ask you to move to an area away from it, take temporary custody of the firearm, empty the cartridges, and when he's done giving you a ticket (unless he's arresting you for something), he should give you back the firearm and cartridges separately, and instruct you not to load it until either you or he leaves. Such a procedure is totally legal, very intelligent, and completely proper.

QUESTION: Can the officer keep the firearm for safety reasons, and refuse to return it to me?

ANSWER: Not legally unless he takes you into custody, or the firearm was reported stolen, or is somehow otherwise illegal such as having the serial number obliterated. Other than that, it should be returned to you at the end of the stop.

QUESTION: I'm a CWP holder. I've been told I cannot carry a firearm concealed on my person while in my vehicle.

ANSWER: Total misconception. Since you have the CWP you have a choice of carrying concealed "on or about" your person with the CWP, or "securely encased" or "not readily accessible" under 790.25. However, I warn you that many police officers don't seem to understand this, and you should therefore be careful.

QUESTION: I live in a condominium. Can I take it from my car to my condo?

ANSWER: Not usually. Although you have the right to have it either in your car, or in your condo -- you cannot carry it across "common" areas -- such as a parking lot, elevators, or hallways -- unless you have the CWP, or fit into one of the exceptions in 790.25. This was a major goof by the legislature.

QUESTION: What if I'm in the car, and I put it in a paper bag, but I twist the top of the bag really well?

ANSWER: Technically, I think you have a problem since the bag is easy to rip, and you may be able to pull the trigger through it. It certainly isn't a zipper, snap, or anything similar. It's also pushing the "flap" example in the Urquiola case.

Although it's an argument – I wouldn't want to try it. Same thing for a cloth "Crown Royal" bag, which I seem to get a case on at least once per year. From a legal standpoint the issue will be whether it can be fired without opening the bag, and what steps need to be taken to get the bag open. Test case time, again.

QUESTION: What if I have it in an unsnapped holster?

ANSWER: If the gun is in a concealed area of the car, it's the third degree felony of carrying a concealed firearm. If the gun is in the open -- it's a second degree misdemeanor of "open carrying of weapons."[97]   If the unsnapped holster is in the glove compartment, closed purse or briefcase, or closed console -- you're OK.[98]

QUESTION: Why?

ANSWER: Because you're still legal under another part of the same section of the statute (ie: in a glove compartment, or other closed container).

QUESTION: What if it becomes unsnapped without my knowledge?

ANSWER: Assuming it unsnaps without your knowledge - you have a defense of "lack of scienter", or "lack of guilty knowledge". The terms are synonymous. Unfortunately, if the officer doesn't believe you it becomes an issue of proof.

QUESTION: What if I have it on my person in a snapped shoulder holster, but the holster can be detached intact from the shoulder harness?

ANSWER: Remember what I said before? It can't be on your person **unless** you have a Concealed Weapons Permit! If it is -- you are not protected by the law, and have committed a crime, whether it's securely encased, or not.

QUESTION: Is there any special place the firearm or weapon must be kept, if I have it in a securely encased bag or holster?

ANSWER: Nope. Anywhere you want except on your person. It can even be under the seat -- as long as it's securely encased in a container or box with a closed lid; or a zippered, snapped, or Velcro-closed pouch, holster, or gun case.[99]

QUESTION: What about weapons other than a handgun?

ANSWER: F.S. 790.25 applies to any legal weapon, including rifles and shotguns. Thus, any weapon that is "securely encased", or "not readily accessible for immediate use" is legal in a private conveyance. However, there is case law and statutory authority that rifles and shotguns may be openly carried in a vehicle if being transported for lawful purposes. Still, my recommendation is that they be transported in a closed case or gun rug – "securely encased".

QUESTION: What about a motorcycle?

ANSWER: What about a motorcycle? It has the same rules as a car. It must be securely encased, and cannot be on your person unless you have a CWP.[100] Otherwise, it must be in a closed container such as a saddlebag actually attached to the bike – not you.

READILY ACCESSIBLE FOR IMMEDIATE USE:

There's another legal way to transport a firearm in a private conveyance (ie: "vehicle") called "not readily accessible for immediate use".[101] Under the law, you can transport a firearm in a vehicle "securely encased", "not readily accessible for immediate use", or both. Any combination is legal. Likewise, if you have a concealed permit, you can have the additional method of carrying concealed on or about your person. Your choice, nobody should really care because legally it doesn't matter – if you're legal, you're legal.

However, while "not readily accessible for immediate use" may sound like "securely encased", and to some extent there may be an overlap, it's a separate concept entirely. Not readily accessible for immediate use means that the firearm or weapon cannot be used without some type of difficulty that significantly hinders it's immediate use. Court cases establish that this should include a loaded firearm with a trigger lock; or an empty firearm without any ammunition in "close proximity", although recent case law has held that if the ammo is "securely encased" separate from the firearm, the firearm is not "readily accessible".[102] Likewise, if the ammo was in the trunk it would be fine. Same thing if the ammo were in a locked box. If you have a weapon in the trunk, and can access the trunk by folding down the rear seat – it should meet the definition of both securely encased and not readily accessible for immediate use. Seems like a no-brainer to me.

Another example of "not readily accessible for immediate use" occurs with a weapon that just can't be used inside the vehicle, as a practical matter. Thus, in the case of Boswink v. State,[103] the appellate court held that a loaded shotgun and rifle in the back of a small pick-up truck was not "readily accessible" because the cab was too small to use the weapons from the inside without difficulty, and the occupant would normally have to exit the truck in order to retrieve, and use them effectively. Thus, they were not subject to retrieval "as easily and quickly as if carried on the person." Again, I wouldn't suggest relying on this case, too much. If you're truck or long gun was a different size — you might wind-up as another test case.

UNCONCEALED SHOTGUNS AND RIFLES:
An interesting point not raised by the Boswink case is whether it's illegal to have an unconcealed, but loaded shotgun, or rifle in a private conveyance, at all. This question arises because F.S. 790.25(5), states that:

> "Nothing herein contained prohibits the carrying of a legal firearm other than a handgun anywhere in a private conveyance when such firearm is being carried for a lawful use."

Thus, if "legal firearm" means any legally possessed long gun not being carried for the commission of a crime -- it"s legal. This seems clear because the statutory language would otherwise be meaningless. Moreover, in <u>Mitchell v. State</u>, 494 So.2d 498 (Fla. 2DCA 1986), the appellate court found that a rifle on the back seat of a vehicle did not furnish probable cause for an arrest. Likewise, a <u>Dept. of Hwy Safety Legal Bulletin</u> 88-02, reviewed the 1982 enactment of this section and confirms my definition. This makes even more sense when you remember that our border states, Alabama and Georgia generally require <u>open carry</u> of rifles and shotguns in vehicles. Since a lot of north Florida residents hunt in these border states, I can almost guarantee that the language was included for that reason. On the other hand, I don't know anyone who has ever raised this question in court before, so it could wind-up as a "test case" in some of our more populated areas. Get rural -- it would be an entirely different story. Under any circumstance, you could legally have a loaded rifle or shotgun in a locked gun rack, as it would not be "readily accessible for immediate use". Still, I have personal problems with a shotgun or rifle on the back seat in an urban setting. I just think too many police officers would make the wrong legal decision in this situation. I'm not saying it's illegal – because in my view the law is clear on this – I'm just saying it's probably smarter keeping your rifle or shotgun in a case.

THE WAY IT USED TO BE:

I thought I'd get off the track here for a moment, and give you a little historical insight from our not too distant past. I get a perverse kick out of how some liberal legislators, and other "anti-gunners" think that permitting a firearm in a car is a recent, and overly generous gift to the citizens of Florida. If you look back into Florida's history, not all that far -- you'll find it wasn't originally thought of as a gift -- but was thought to be pretty much a <u>basic right</u> -- part of the right of an individual to self preservation. So, just in case you'd like to see how it used to be viewed by the majority, let me give you a quote from the 1941 Florida Supreme Court case of <u>Watson v. Stone</u>: [104]

"The business men, tourists, commercial travelers, professional man on night calls, unprotected women and children in cars on the highways day and night, State and County officials, and all law-abiding citizens fully appreciate the sense of security afforded by the knowledge of the existence of a pistol in the pocket of an automobile in which they are traveling. It cannot be said that it is placed in the car or automobile for unlawful purposes, but on the other hand it was placed therein exclusively for defensive or protective purposes. These people, in the opinion of this writer, should not be branded criminals in their effort of self preservation and protection, but should be recognized and accorded the full rights of free and independent American citizens."

INTER-STATE TRANSPORTATION OF FIREARMS:

If you are traveling from state to state in a vehicle, the transportation of firearms and other weapons is governed by each state's law that you pass through. In Florida -- you know how you can transport it. But what happens when you get to the Georgia border, or beyond?

Federal law says that if you are traveling state to state, you can legally carry a firearm if such is for a lawful purpose, and it would be legal for you to possess and carry it in your final destination state. However, to qualify for this -- the firearm must be unloaded, and neither the firearm or ammunition can be readily or directly accessible from the passenger compartment of the transporting vehicle -- which means it should be locked in the trunk, unloaded. If your vehicle has no separate compartment from the drivers compartment, then the firearm or ammunition must be kept in a locked container that is neither the glove compartment or the console. This section usually applies to trucks. 18 USC 926A.

If you follow federal law, you may legally transport your firearms state to state, even if some of the intervening states would not otherwise permit it. Of course, don't take the gun out of this protected area until you arrive at your destination, unless you know that such would be lawful in whatever other state you are traveling in.

Federal law also states that if there's a more liberal way of transporting the firearm in the state you're traveling in -- you can do it that way while you're in that particular state -- without losing your federal state to state protection during the rest of your trip. There's a book called "Traveler's Guide to the Firearms Laws of the Fifty States" written by attorney J. Scott Kappas in Covington, Kentucky, that gives a short summary of each state's carry law for travelers. You can purchase it on the web, and I believe the NRA also carries it.

The NRA also publishes pamphlet summaries of the laws of each state. Give them a call at 1-800-392-8683, and if you're a member they'll send it to you free, or you can download it from their website at http://www.nraila.org/library.asp.

PRIVATE BOATS:
Private boats that qualify as a "conveyance" are just like motor vehicles,[105] and the same state and federal laws apply with slight variation. The variation is that once you're outside the three mile limit on the east coast, or the nine mile limit (three leagues) on the Gulf Coast, you're in international waters -- and you can do most anything you want short of piracy, shooting at other people, boats, protected marine life, or carrying automatic weapons. Of course, once you come back into the jurisdictional limit -- make sure you're "Florida legal".

THE BAHAMAS & FOREIGN PORTS:

If you are thinking of traveling to the Bahamas -- I contacted their Customs agency and was advised that any firearms other than fully automatic weapons are permitted to be kept on board. Under any circumstance, you will have to declare your firearms and ammunition with Customs when you come into port, or are checked by any Customs vessel, and must leave them on board in some type of secure enclosure. Bahama firearm laws on the internet state that possession of firearms on a non-Bahamian vessel by persons who are not Bahamian residents is legal so long as the firearms and ammunition do not leave the ship, are not used in Bahamian waters, and are declared to Bahamian Customs within 48 hours of arrival. However, keep them under lock and key, as well. U.S. Customs also advises you must list all firearms being taken out of the United States on a Form 4457, and keep a copy with you at all times. I have also heard that a failure to have this form on international trips by sea or air can result in serious problems with certain foreign governments - especially Mexico. Please note that Mexico is experiencing serious crime problems with guns, and you should make specific inquiry as to their laws before having firearms in their territorial waters, or airspace.

If you are within the territorial waters of any other nation, or use their airspace you must normally comply with that nations laws. What that may be is outside the scope of this book, however, I understand that our jails are pleasure palaces next to those of nations south of the border.

WEAPONS, AIRPORTS, AND COMMERCIAL AIRCRAFT:
Since 9/11 things have changed somewhat, and the Transportation Security Administration is now in charge of airport security instead of the F.A.A. Things are also beginning to be taken more seriously, and as a passenger you need to know what you can and can't do. Even if not prosecuted criminally — the TSA is beginning to levy civil fines up to $10,000.00 for baggage and carry-on violations involving weapons pursuant to 49 USC 46303. Even if not prosecuted, you will be paying the TSA some money.

Both Florida and Federal law permit you, assuming you are at an airport as a passenger on a commercial aircraft, to take an unloaded firearm with you if it is checked-in as baggage, and declared with the carrier at the ticket counter. You must have any firearm placed unloaded, in a locked, hard-sided container, in which you are the only person on the aircraft with the key or combination. 49 CFR 1540.111. Moreover, any ammunition must now securely packed in a fiber, wood, or metal package/box specifically designed to carry ammunition. 49 CFR 175.10. I would declare this, as well. Call the airline ahead of time to find out exactly what their policy is, and make damn sure your possession will be legal in your destination airport. Last, but not least — do not mark the outside of any container to show it contains any weapons or ammunition.

As a passenger, you may also transport one self-defense chemical spray not exceeding 4 ounces, so long as the spray has "a positive means to prevent accidental discharge". This can only be in checked on baggage. Carry on is a serious violation! Again, make sure it's legal at your destination airport, and declare it at the main concourse ticket counter before you try checking any baggage.! I would also call the airline ahead of time to make sure there are no potential problems, and you know their procedures. Likewise, you can check in with baggage other weapons that are not firearms. This includes knives, box cutters, etc. Again, this is check-in baggage only, and I once again warn you to declare it, and call the airline ahead of time.

The law considers most anything that resembles a weapon, or can be used as a weapon as prohibited — at least for carry on. Many of these are termed "dual-use items" as they have a practical function, but could also be used as a weapon. This includes a hammer, crowbar, screwdriver, drill, ax, box-cutter, baseball bat, hockey stick, billie club, etc. Same thing for most pointed scissors[106], although rounded edge scissors are permitted for carry-on . No explosives anywhere — so fireworks are out completely. Same thing for micro-torches, and the like. Anything that can explode is usually completely illegal to transport.

Another thing they only permit in checked baggage is a "realistic replica" of a firearm. So, if your toy gun looks real — it needs to be in your checked in baggage. The screeners have full discretion on any item. If you don't like their decision — try walking to Vermont. Generally, if your mistake was innocent, and doesn't involve a firearm, or obvious weapon — you'll have the choice of putting the rejected item in checked in baggage, or returning it to your vehicle. If that's not an option, your only other option is to "abandon" the property to the screener, and if so, the property is automatically transferred to the federal government. If you need more information, check the web site of the Transportation Security Administration (TSA) at www.tsa.gov. They have a list of what you can't have, and lots of other useful information.

Please don't bitch and moan if a screener tells you an item is not OK for carry on, because it will rarely accomplish anything other than result in your missing your flight — or worse. To a large extent, you leave the Constitution back at your car once you enter the "sterile area". One last word of warning. Make sure that any weapons being transported are legal at your final airport destination. I'd hate to try transporting a handgun to JFK in New York, because if anyone got wind of what you were doing once you landed — you'd have all hell to pay.

Anyway, the real bad news is that intentionally attempting to carry a dangerous weapon on a commercial aircraft is punishable by up to ten years in a federal prison. 49 USC 46505   Same thing for placing a loaded firearm in checked-in baggage, or not declaring it. If you forgot you had such a weapon with you, then the federal standard of knowledge is "should have known". This is a fairly easy standard to prove, and prosecution will likely depend on the discretion of the Transportation Security Administration. If you were prosecuted under state law, it would be a slightly more liberal defense on the level of knowledge required, but just as an unpleasant experience. Conversations with the TSA indicate that they will generally not prosecute federally if they really believe you carried the weapon on by pure accident. In these instances, it is probably not a great idea to claim your Fifth Amendment "right to silence", and I would be as frank, humble, and horrified as possible. Don't take it casually, as people who seem to take it casually are usually the ones they prosecute. Moreover, this is one of the few instances in which I would definitely not insist on speaking to an attorney before speaking to them. Failure to make instantly clear that this was one big, stupid mistake for which you are **terribly embarrassed** can often lead to prosecution. Be humble! Be apologetic! Make sure they understand it was a mistake, and you forgot – or didn't realize it was there!

Furthermore, don't wait and try to declare any of these items at the gate, because once you enter the "sterile area" you probably have committed a federal crime. If you don't remember what the sterile areas is, it's the area from the X-ray machine or security checkpoint, on. It's the portion of the passenger terminal usually reserved for the arrival and departure of passengers on scheduled flights. This rule applies equally to persons holding a Concealed Weapons Permit. Current penalties are pursuant to 49 USC 46505, which are up to ten years for a dangerous weapon, explosive, or incendiary device, or if done "willfully" and with reckless disregard to human life — up to twenty years, or if a death occurs, up to life. Moreover, you can receive a civil fine up to $10,000.00, even if they don't decide to prosecute you. [49 USC 46303].

Please remember that if you are in a hurry, and usually carry a gun in a bag, briefcase, or on your person (especially a derringer or small pistol) — you are likely to forget it's still there as you rush from your car to the gate! When that happens — you are going to have a rude interruption of your travel plans! Make a pre-departure checklist to put the gun somewhere else! There are numerous examples of this happening in a federal criminal prosecution, and so far the federal courts have varied between a standard of "actual knowledge" or "should have known".[107] Most of these people wind-up being convicted if the government decides to prosecute!

Since post-9/11 airport security falls primarily under the jurisdiction of the Transportation Security Administration [www.tsa.gov] I highly recommend that you take a look at their website under the 'Travelers & Consumers" link. That section lists all prohibited items for passengers. Many of the items that can't be taken in carry-on, can be taken in checked baggage. Again, no weapons are allowed for carry-on, including pepper spray, and if you mistakenly put a <u>loaded</u> firearm in check-in, or have your ammo rolling around -- you can be prosecuted for a felony, or hit with a hefty civil fine.

Last, but not least, your CWP does not permit you to carry anywhere inside the terminal – including the baggage area unless it is a completely separate building from the terminal. You can carry in most airport parking garages since they're separate from the terminal building.

PRIVATE AIRCRAFT:
When it comes to a private aircraft not being used for commercial purposes, in which you are not a paid passenger, you may carry firearms and ammunition according to State law, so long as it's done with the permission of the pilot. Ammunition should be limited to amounts that do not exceed a reasonable amount for personal use. The F.A.A. strongly recommends that ammunition be boxed in suitable containers. You may not carry any mace, or other chemical sprays, even if legal in your state as these are considered "<u>hazardous materials</u>". Of course, if you land at an airport, you are still subject to the rule about not having any ammunition, firearms, or weapons in the passenger "sterile area", and not having any firearm in the passenger terminal unless it is unloaded, and in a secured container as a passenger due to transport.

TRAINS, BUSES, AND OTHER PUBLIC TRANSPORTATION:

If you are traveling interstate -- federal law controls, and you should deliver the firearm unloaded, in a locked container to the carrier for transportation, after declaring it as such. I suggest you follow the same guidelines as commercial aircraft passengers, and I suggest calling the carrier before so you know their regulations. There is also a question whether this applies if the bus or train you are on is traveling on an interstate run. If it is, I think the better advise is to follow federal law on this issue, as similar questions have come up on commuter aircraft flights, and it was determined against the passenger.

If you are traveling by public transportation that operates solely within Florida -- F.S. 790.25(3)(L) says the firearm or weapon must be "securely encased", and not in your manual possession.[108] Since "manual possession" normally means that the weapon is actually in your hand[109] -- my best guess is that this subsection means something a bit more secure than the normal definition in a private conveyance.

Obviously, if you were holding a holster, it's probably in your manual possession, although "securely encased". If it were in a zippered gun case, I am again unsure, as "not in your manual possession" might be interpreted as requiring more than being in just a gun case. From a conservative standpoint I would want to have any firearm or weapon "securely encased" inside a locked bag or locked briefcase, or in a holster or gun rug inside my luggage, bag, or briefcase. If I wanted to be extra careful — it would be unloaded, and checked as baggage.

Naturally, there is no case law interpreting this section, and there are just too many stories of law enforcement officials going on buses, and pressuring people into random searches -- and then seizing their firearms, whether they're legal or not. I wouldn't want you to be the test case if you were pushing this interpretation to the limit, so my advise is that it's better to be safe -- than sorry. Or — just get a Concealed Permit.

CARRYING IN YOUR HOME OR BUSINESS:

Now that we've beaten-to-death the subject of how you can carry a firearm (and any other weapon) in any type of vehicle or other transportation -- the next most important area is your home, or business.   The good news is that you can carry or possess a firearm, or any other legal weapon, anywhere in your home or business, concealed or in the open -- your choice.   No Concealed Weapons Permit necessary!   This area of the law is very well settled.

Why?

Well, F.S. 790.25(3)(n) makes it lawful for persons to possess a firearm or other weapon on their home or place of business, either concealed or in the open.   Despite several challenges in the courts, this law stands stronger than ever.   From the standpoint of your home – we're talking about an apartment, house, or condo.   If you're inside the unit, you're totally legal.   Once you step outside – it changes a bit.   If it's a single family type dwelling – all the surrounding property that is actually deeded to the home is exempt.   That's what the Florida Supreme Court pretty much held in Peoples v. State, 287 So. 2d 63 (Fla. 1973).   This was expanded on in several other appellate court cases that followed the Peoples decision.   For instance:

> "It is not unlawful for a person to possess firearms at his home or place of business, including surrounding property, as well as buildings and structures situated thereon." State v. Anton, 700 So. 2d 743 (Fla. 2DCA 1997).

> "(The) home exemption applied to the defendant's driveway and yard." Sherrod v. State, 484 So. 2d 1279 (Fla. 4DCA 1986)

On the other hand,   if you live in a condo or apartment building – the Sherrod case held that the exemption afforded by F.S. 790.25(3)(n) would not apply to "common areas" used by all residents such as the parking lot, pool area, garage, and walkways.   Whether the walkway area immediately in front of your apartment is considered "part of your home" is unresolved – but there is a fair likelihood that it isn't, so I wouldn't take the chance.

Like the home exemption – you also have an exemption for your "place of business".   Similar to the home exemption the Anton case held that   "place of business" includes surrounding property owned by the business, and buildings situated thereon.   It likely includes an adjacent sidewalk, according to the case of Collins v. State, 475 So.2d 968 (Fla. 4DCA 1985).   The safe way of interpreting this is that the property must be the portion where your duties actually take you, or usually take you.   And, similarly to the home exemption

– areas common to other businesses such as common parking lots, walkways, etc. – are likely not protected by this exemption.

However, on the good side of the business exemption, the cases interpreting this section have made it very clear that you don't need your employer's permission to carry.[110] State v. Commons, 592 So. 2d 317 (Fla. 3DCA 1991). On the other hand – if you disobey a company directive and get caught – you can usually get fired for it, although there is a limited exception that we will discuss later for employee parking lots when the employee also has a CWP.

So, for those of you who are standing guard over your homestead or business premises without the permit – it's legal to carry there concealed, or carry open.   However, without the permit, make sure you're on your own property or business premises! On the other hand, for those of you who "open carry" –   you'll be legal, but I almost guarantee that some liberal neighbor will call the cops, and cause you more grief than it's worth.   In those situations, open carry in the presence of others should not be done in a "rude, angry, careless, or threatening manner" to avoid possible problems with F.S. 790.10.

Like I already hinted at, the problems arise with getting the firearm to, or fro. This is where the Legislature goofed-up real good -- and was probably due more to oversight than anything else. So, what are the problems?

PROBLEMS WITH CONDO'S & APARTMENTS:
Problem number one is when you live in a condominium or apartment. When this happens, you must park in a common parking lot,[111] go through common hallways, use common elevators, and have access to common facilities. By "common" -- I mean that almost everybody in the complex has a right to use it. Unfortunately, unless you have a Concealed Weapons Permit, or you're coming back from a hunting, fishing, or camping trip -- or one of the other interesting exceptions I mentioned before in F.S. 790.25 -- you can't legally carry while you're on or in any of these "common" areas, concealed or otherwise.

QUESTION: So how the heck am I supposed to get my firearm from my car to my apartment?

ANSWER: You're not! Go get a permit, or tell your state legislator that the law is stupid as written, and you want it changed. Heck, it certainly is.

QUESTION: What if it's my own home, a duplex, and I'm renting the other half?

ANSWER: No problem for you, and no problem for your renter as long as you don't share any common areas. Technically, since you're the sole owner, and the other guy is only a renter -- he can't use the common areas for carrying a firearm, but you can.

QUESTION: What if I hear a noise on the stairway outside my apartment, and I think it's a burglar?

ANSWER: Another interesting test case. Technically, you have no right to go out with a firearm on a common area. However, since you do have a constitutional, and statutory right to self-defense, and defense of property -- you may have an exception to the general rule. Get a good lawyer.

As you can see from these questions and answers -- there are certain restrictions on carrying if you don't live in a private residence. If you do live in a private residence, even if you rent it -- you have a right to carry and possess firearms anywhere on the property, not just inside the dwelling.[112]   Same thing if you're renting a room in a motel, as far as the room itself goes. During the rental period it's considered as your "dwelling", although only temporary.[113]   Since your property includes the driveway -- no problem getting the gun from the car to the house. This applies to every member of your family.

QUESTION: I'm a construction worker, and I'll be working on a project at one location for the next six months. Does that qualify as "business premises"?

ANSWER: I seriously doubt it. However, the construction trailer of the company you work for should. Test case time.

QUESTION: I heard that you couldn't shoot anyone except if you were in your house. So, how can I legally carry a gun outside my home, even if it's on my property?

ANSWER: You are confusing two different areas of the law. You're thinking about the old "retreat rule" or "castle doctrine" which really concerned the **use** of a firearm, rather than when and where you can carry it. **"Carrying"** a weapon or firearm is an entirely separate matter. The law says you can carry a firearm, concealed or in the open, anywhere on your property. In the house, in your business, or on the premises, outside. It doesn't matter. On the other hand, **how** you use it, point it, or handle it does!

QUESTION: You say I can get fired if I carry a gun against my employers directions. Isn't Florida a "preemption" state?

ANSWER: The preemption law only covers government — not private entities or persons. The parking lot law modifies this somewhat.

WHEN YOU STILL CAN'T HAVE IT:
There are always exceptions to the exceptions of legal possession and carrying. One big exception is when you're about to commit, or are committing a crime. Another concerns people in national parks. Another concerns schools. They uniformly apply to all persons, whether you have a permit or not. There are still other instances which could penalize otherwise legal possession, but let's just cover the areas I've mentioned, for now:

SCHOOLS, COLLEGES, UNIVERSITIES:
Rather than go over the rules that pertain to schools, and colleges -- let me tell you that this is gone over extensively in the chapter about children -- Chapter Eight. It's a real important area, and I highly suggest that you read it. Whether you have kids, or not, you'll find that it applies to you in some way.

NATIONAL FORESTS:
Unlike National Parks, National Forests follow state law. Under current Florida law [Rule 62d-2.014] a CWP holder can carry concealed on their person in a National Forest. Without the permit, you can carry only if you are engaged in lawful fishing, hunting, or camping, and the weapon or firearm must be concealed. However, you can also keep a weapon or firearm in a vehicle or tent if it is "secured from minors". This goes for CWP holders, as well, if not on your person. That means in a locked container of some sort.

NATIONAL PARKS & WILDLIFE REFUGES:
Recent changes in federal regulations would have permitted <u>concealed</u> carry in National Parks [36 CFR 2.4], and in National Wildlife Refuges [50 CFR 27.42] as allowed per state law, except inside any building on such premises normally used by federal employees. Unfortunately, an injunction was issued in March 2009 by a federal district court to prevent the National Park and National Wildlife regulations from being enforced, and as of April 2009, the injunction stands. However, an almost identical regulation was not challenged that covers federal reclamation lands and water bodies. 43 CFR 423.30 . Assuming the injunction is defeated or lifted – weapons and firearms may still not be taken inside any building in these areas that are regularly used by

federal employees, as doing so would be a violation of 18 USC 930. Of course, open carry of firearms in permitted areas for hunting, during season, with the proper firearm and a valid hunting license are unaffected.

STATE FORESTS AND PARKS:

In 2006 the Legislature did away with firearms restrictions in national forests and state parks by repealing Florida Statutes 790.11; 790.12; and 790.14 [HB 1029]. Since National Forests follow state legislative restrictions on weapons (don't confuse this with "National Parks"), that basically put legal carry in National Forests and state parks in Florida under Florida Statute 790.25. The Legislature then left it to the Florida Department of Environmental Protection to pass a rule implementing this. That rule, 62D-2.014 states:

"weapons shall at all times be in the possession of a responsible party or properly secured within or to a vehicle or temporary housing . . . while in state parks. "Properly secured" means the weapon shall be locked away and not accessible to minors , and if in a tent, the weapon shall be secured in a locked container. No person shall use or openly display in any state park weapons . . . Except when such are used for resource management purposes as authorized in this subsection."

Obviously, the Rule doesn't follow all that 790.25, and other Florida Statutes allow. How that will work out in the future will probably fall on those "test cases" where the courts will hopefully uphold what the Legislature directed, rather than the more restrictive version of what the Florida DEP enacted. Although I've already covered it in the previous section on National Forests, the safe side of what the rule means is that anyone with a CWP can carry weapons and firearms concealed, upon their person (including any bag or knapsack you personally carry), in a state park or national forest in Florida. It also means that if you don't have the CWP – and so long as you are engaged in "lawful" fishing, hunting, or camping, a weapon or firearm can be carried on your person, so long as it is carried concealed. "Lawful" generally means with a valid hunting or fishing license, in season if hunting, and for hunting or fishing, in a place where being there is not otherwise unlawful. However, any individual (CWP or not) may keep a weapon or firearm in their tent or vehicle if it is in a locked container. Under a literal reading of the Rule, a minor could not carry any type of weapon, nor could an adult carry a partially or fully exposed weapon on a belt, or for that matter, any electronic or chemical weapon that wasn't fully concealed. A holster or sheath that fully covers the entire weapon, including the handle, should be considered "concealed" even though the content is obvious. However, if any part of the weapon is visible - it is likely not "concealed" under the law.

MAILING & SENDING FIREARMS:

As a general rule, it is illegal to send any handgun or ammunition through the mail. [18 USC 1715 & 1716] You can send a rifle or shotgun if you declare it as such -- but not a handgun. Send the handgun by a carrier such as UPS, but you must declare any firearm to the carrier in writing, and it must be unloaded and securely encased. Remember, you may only send a firearm out of state if it's for repair or return to a federal licensee (ie: firearms manufacturer, dealer, importer, or gunsmith), otherwise it is a federal crime, or you are a federal firearms licensee.

QUESTION: What if I need to get a firearm repaired, and the factory is out of state?

ANSWER: You can mail it if it's a long gun, or UPS it if it's a handgun. However, the preferred method is never to send a firearm by the mail. By the way, Federal Express, or any other common carrier or trucker, can qualify for your shipment. I just know that UPS does a lot of these. However, remember to declare it to the carrier or it's a felony. Also, don't mark the package showing that the contents are a firearm. That's also a "no no", even if it's otherwise obvious.

QUESTION: What about mailing a hand gun to a relative within Florida?

ANSWER: Buy a toothbrush, and meet your new cellmate, Guido. This is a violation of federal statutes. However, you may legally UPS it (not the U.S.

Mail) so long as it's within the same state you sent it from, and the person receiving it is not legally disqualified.

QUESTION: So, how the heck does my firearms dealer get his stuff, with all these regulations?

ANSWER: Try to remember that he's a federal licensee, and can receive or ship to or from any other federal licensee. The rules are different because of his qualifications.

If you need to ship a firearm to somebody in another state, and that person can legally possess it there, you might consider having a federally licensed gun dealer in your home state do it for you, or you could make arrangements to send it direct to an FFL in the state you are sending it to. He'd charge you a fee, and send it to a dealer in the other state. The person you're sending it to would be able to pick it up from the dealer in the other state after complying with the law there — which is usually a short waiting period plus the NICS check.

QUESTION: Didn't you say earlier that I could ship to an out of state dealer (FFL) if I had made a sale to an out of state resident?

ANSWER: Yes, according to ATF this is perfectly legal so long as the delivery to the out-of-state resident is thru an FFL in your home state who does the actual shipping to another FFL in the buyer's home state. The legal theory on this is that the sale or transfer is not complete until "delivery", and the "delivery" is being made by the out-of-state FFL, who is also doing the transfer paperwork. [NICS check and 4473].

QUESTION: How about a bequest or inheritance?

ANSWER: Yup, an exception to the usual rule, and does not
           require an FFL intermediary. This is per 27 CFR
           478.30, although I would advise that only the
           executor or administrator of the estate send it
           (UPS), and he or she make darn sure the person
           receiving it is legal in the state of receipt.
           However, if it's an NFA weapon (machine guns,
           etc.) the executor can only transfer it to a
           beneficiary after approval by ATF on a Form 5.
           Also, if the machine gun was a "dealer sample"
           (ie: manufacture/import after May 19, 1986) it
           can only be transferred to an FFL Class III dealer
           via an approved Form 4.

           An interesting aside on machine guns — if you
           transfer it contrary to law – it becomes
           "contraband", and is illegal to possess. The
           recipient can't legally send it back to you to
           "undo" the mistake, because once screwed-up it
           becomes "contraband" forever, and cannot be
           made legal. Thus, it's a very serious federal
           crime to keep it in your possession.

INDIAN RESERVATIONS:
        Indian land is protected under 18 USC 1165. It is a crime for
anyone to go on Indian lands to hunt or fish without the permission of
the tribal authorities. Quechan Tribe v. Rowe, 531 F.2d 408 (9th Cir.
1976). Likewise, it is a felony to have any type switchblade knife on
Indian land. [15 USC 1241-1245] Otherwise, everyday Florida law
and statutes control what you can or can't do. F.S. 285.16. Thus, it
is not "technically" illegal to have a firearm in a casino with a CWP
– although it is highly likely that such is not permitted by the casino,
and thus could result in a trespass warning, and maybe even an arrest.

SEAPORT RESTRICTED ZONES:

<u>F.S.</u> 311.12(7), enacted in 2006 states it's a first degree misdemeanor to have a "concealed" weapon inside any designated "restricted" area in a seaport, even if securely encased in a vehicle. While seaports are generally open to the public, the legislation makes clear that any unauthorized person in a marked (ie: posted) "restricted area" or "restricted zone" is subject to trespass. I assume that means that if the area or entrance to the area is conspicuously posted – you could get arrested. Likewise, I assume the defense to any such arrest would be you didn't see the signs because they were not conspicuously located, or the signs weren't posted where you entered the restricted area. It would be likely up to you to prove this defense.

The loophole in this statute is the word "concealed" because only "concealed" weapons get you in trouble under this section of the law. On the other hand, I would think that the trespass statutes (likely with the same defenses) are still going to apply even if the weapon is not concealed. Unfortunately, if the weapon is on your person – it might be prosecuted as an "armed trespass", which is a felony. Not a fun charge to face, or defend.

If you want to get around the statute legally – you can. However, you need the written permission from the seaport director to possess. Still, law enforcement officers are permitted to have them, although there is no requirement in the statute that they need be on duty. Security guards working in these areas should obtain written permission, or a blanket written OK for the entire security service would probably be fine, as well.

HOSPITALS & MENTAL FACITILIES:

<u>F.S.</u> 394.458 states that "except as authorized by law" it is a third degree felony for any person to bring, carry, possess, or transport a "firearm or other dangerous weapon" (or alcoholic beverage) upon the grounds of any "hospital (or mental health facility) providing mental health services". As a practical matter, almost every hospital and hospital emergency room provides mental health services – so, from a technical standpoint, the statute seems to prohibit firearms or weapons anywhere on its grounds, with some important exceptions.

What are the exceptions?   Well, the answer lies in the phrase "except as authorized by law".   F.S.790.25 authorizes "securely encased" weapons in vehicles.   Hence, a securely encased weapon or firearm in a vehicle should be considered   "authorized by law". Likewise, for all you CWP holders, F.S. 790.06(12) lists all the places you can't go with a CWP – and "hospitals or mental health facilities" are not on the list. Thus, logic holds that carrying in those situations are also "authorized by law".   Of course, there are no court decisions on this area for now, so I urge caution.

PARKING LOT LAW:
    F.S. 790.251, also known as the "parking lot" law, passed in 2008 allegedly made it illegal for a business or employer to prohibit the use of parking areas to customers or employees who keep a lawful firearm and/or ammo in their locked vehicle, forbade retaliation against the employee or customer for doing so, forbade questioning of the employee or customer to determine if he or she had such a stored firearm,   and   forbade   searches   of   vehicles   to   determine   such. Unfortunately,   the bill suffered from severe drafting problems, and terrible shortsightedness.   At this time a federal district court [Florida Retail Assoc v. Attorney General, 576 F.Supp.2d 1281 (N.D. Fla. 2008)]has held the statute only protects employees who have a concealed weapons permit, and correctly held that the provisions applying to customers and other invitees were unconstitutional because of substantial drafting issues in the legislation.

    Likewise, the statute granted several overbroad exceptions so that it doesn't apply to company vehicles, any property involving school grounds, correctional institutions, property used for national defense, aerospace,   domestic   security,   manufacture/storage/or   transport   of combustible or explosive materials, or any other property prohibited by state or federal law.   That phrasing arguably eliminated most theme parks that use fireworks, service stations, etc.   Plus, as a practical matter, the enforcement provisions of the statute for private individuals are worse than dismal,   and the Attorney General seemed more interested in politics than trying to enforce it.   Should the Legislature ever get around to re-writing it properly – it would easily pass constitutional muster as it did in another federal appeal,   Ramsey Winch, Inc. v. Henry, 2009 WL 388050 (10th Cir. 2009).

CHAPTER SEVEN

COMMON WEAPONS VIOLATIONS AND RELATED CRIMES

The only people who don't have to worry about weapons violations are criminals, and juveniles who are becoming criminals. They don't care -- so whatever regulatory laws we pass aren't going to stop them. The only thing that will stop them is a jail sentence, and except for juveniles, we already have more than enough laws to accomplish that, if anybody would bother to enforce them. The rest of us who are just trying to defend ourselves, and stay out of trouble -- have all the problems obeying this stuff. Since you are hopefully in this later category of the population, God bless you, you need all the help you can get.

CARRYING CONCEALED WEAPONS AND FIREARMS:
By this time you should all know, with certain limited exceptions, you can't carry a concealed weapon or firearm without a permit unless you're at home, or your business premises. If you don't understand that by now -- you need a remedial reading course.

Carrying a concealed firearm without a Concealed Weapons Permit is a third degree felony. Carrying a concealed weapon, which is not a firearm, is a first degree misdemeanor, unless you have a permit. F.S. 790.01. Of course, there are the exceptions that we've already discussed in a previous chapter, and a few more I'm going to update you on in a moment.

If you're an off-duty law enforcement or corrections officer, you can carry a concealed weapon or firearm only if you have a Concealed Weapons Permit, or if you have the permission of your superior to do so while off duty, for professional purposes. If your department has a written policy that you're always "on duty", even when not in uniform -- you're legal.[114]   Otherwise, you're just like the rest of us.

Sometimes, people forget they are carrying a concealed weapon. This normally happens when they're in a rush, are preoccupied, and are legally transporting the weapon in a bag, or briefcase with other things -- and then forget it's there. If you wander into a courthouse or airport, even if you have a concealed permit -- you're gonna be in big trouble when the metal detector suddenly goes off![115] And, if you're thinking that this could never happen -- I can assure you that it happens all the time. Remember -- we're all just human!

"So", you ask. "Are there any defenses?"

Well, now that you've mentioned it, the answer is "yes". Under Florida law there is a defense which I like to term: "complete and utter stupidity". The court definition is a bit more legally precise, and is blandly referred to as a lack of knowledge, mistake of fact, or lack of scienter.[116] Since you were caught voluntarily placing a heavy metal object directly into a metal detector -- most people will probably come to realize that you did it innocently, and by mistake, rather than with a criminal intent. In other words, if you honestly forgot it was there, and can convince your friendly local prosecutor, or jury of that -- you will get out of it. Of course, you'll go through hell getting to that point. And, of course, this is normally subject to the assumption that you have no real criminal record, and aren't carrying drugs, other weapons, or a large amount of cash at the same time. Any of those additional factors would not be very helpful. Likewise, in federal land, the defense also exists, but in a more restricted sense. There, the federal courts have a "should have known" standard, and it is much easier to prove the case against you.[117] Likewise, if it's at an airport — there are some stiff civil monetary penalties you could face regardless of mistake.

PEPPER SPRAY, TEAR-GAS, AND POCKET KNIVES:
While carrying concealed is generally illegal without a concealed permit, there are some exceptions to the general rules which were expanded by the legislature. The exceptions allow you to carry a "common pocket knife", "self-defense chemical spray", "nonlethal stun gun", or other "nonlethal electric weapon or device". F.S. 790.01(4). I'll explain the specifics for each one of these, shortly. Prior to this law, unless you had a concealed permit, you could only carry a "common pocketknife", or a "chemical defensive spray"

containing no more than one half ounce of chemical.[118]   This has changed.

COMMON POCKETKNIVES:

A common pocketknife, according to Florida law, is not a "weapon", unless it is used as a "deadly weapon". Thus, anyone may carry a concealed "common pocketknife" without a permit so long as it is not on school grounds, a school bus, or school bus stop. Until recently, this was a very confused area. The cases that interpreted the statute couldn't decide what the word "common" meant — and you took your chances whenever you had something even slightly unusual.[119]   Federal law has been fairly clearcut,[120] and does not consider a "pocketknife" with a blade less than 2 ½ inches to be a "dangerous weapon".[121]   However, under federal law you still can't take these into any "sterile area" at an airport. In 1997 the confusion in Florida law was changed by an opinion by the Florida Supreme Court in L.B. v. State, 700 So.2d 370 (Fla. 1997).

Adopting a close version of the Attorney General's definition, and somewhat expanding on it, the Florida Supreme Court has held that a common pocketknife is not a "weapon" when it is a folding knife with a blade four inches or less. In fact, the Court noted there might be some instances where a pocketknife might still qualify as a "common" pocketknife if it had a blade length over four inches. In making the decision the Court stated:

> "Webster's defines "pocketknife" as "a knife with a blade folding into the handle to fit it for being carried in the pocket." From these definitions, we can infer that the legislature's intended definition of "common pocketknife" was: "A type of knife occurring frequently in the community which has a blade that folds into the handle and that can be carried in one's pocket." We believe that in the vast majority of cases, it will be evident to citizens and fact-finders whether one's pocketknife is a "common" pocketknife under any intended definition of that term. We need not be concerned with odd scenarios construing smaller but more expensive knives as "uncommon".

This definition should still exclude butterfly knives, automatic knives, or knives that do not fold in the traditional manner. A recent case held a 3 ½ inch bladed folding knife with a large finger guard, and notched combat-style grip still qualified as a weapon. J.D.L.R. v. State, 701 So.2d 626 (Fla. 3DCA 1997). Thus, if it has significant features normally reserved to a combat type fighting knife — it may be considered a "weapon". My personal interpretation of that decision is that a finger guard is not a typical feature of a "common" pocketknife, and smacks more of a hunting knife, or combat style. Also, it's not illegal to possess a common pocketknife at a school, school grounds, school bus stop, or school bus. F.S.790.115, although rude, angry, careless, or threatening display is still illegal. Still, a student in possession could get expelled for doing so if against school regulations.

ELECTRIC , TASER & CHEMICAL WEAPONS:

Most pepper sprays have a maximum effective range of about ten feet. If the wind is blowing — make the proper adjustments, and make sure you aren't firing into a strong wind, or it may blow back on you. Make sure you buy something with at least 1.5 million SHU heat units — or it may be ineffective. Forget about percentages — it's the SHU's that count!

In 1997 and 2006 the legislature amended some of the carrying restrictions concerning chemical and electronic weapons -- in favor of the ordinary citizen. You may now carry, for lawful self defense purposes, concealed or in the open, any "self-defense chemical spray". A "self-defense chemical spray" is a device carried solely for lawful self-defense, that is compact in size, is designed to be carried on or about a person, and contains no more than two (2) ounces of chemical.[122] "Chemical" does not refer to the propellant portion.

You may also carry openly or concealed, for lawful self-defense, any "nonlethal electric weapon or device", including a stun gun, and Taser type weapons (ie: "dart firing stun guns"). The necessity for having a Concealed Weapons Permit to carry a Taser ended in June 2006. (C. 2006-298). F.S. 790.001(15); 790.01; 790.053

Of course, you still can't have these weapons at schools, school buses, and school bus stops. I'll discuss these restrictions in Chapter Eight. It is also a felony to take them into any state prison, county jail, or juvenile detention facility. F.S. 944.47; F.S. 951.22; F.S. 985.4046.[123]1 Technically, there doesn't appear to be any current criminal prohibition against taking either a nonlethal stun gun or self defense chemical spray into a city jail facility or state courthouse (except maybe if you have a concealed permit, are carrying a nonlethal stun gun, and you do so "willfully").[124]   On the other hand I would strongly recommend you don't try it as there's no way you're getting in if they find out, it will likely get you arrested, and they'll probably close this loophole at some point, anyway.

QUESTION: Do you mean I can take a stun gun or pepper spray into a bar, concealed or in the open?

ANSWER: Yes, unless maybe if you have a CWP, as permit holders are not permitted to take a concealed weapon in any area prohibited by F.S. 790.06(12)[125]. Still, even if you don't have the permit I wouldn't recommend you "open carry" as it will probably upset the world. Moreover, the establishment can request that you get rid of it, and if you chose to ignore this request you have probably committed a misdemeanor trespass,[126] and if it's another weapon that qualifies as a "dangerous weapon" or firearm, it becomes a felony. F.S. 810.08(2)(c).

One warning about these exciting exceptions to concealed and open carry laws — knowing and willful use of such weapons against a law enforcement officer engaged in the performance of his/her duties is a third degree felony. Moreover, unless the weapon is initially being carried for purposes of lawful self-defense — it's not covered under the statutory exception. Last, but not least, if you misuse the weapon for something other than lawful self-defense, you may still be prosecuted.

Before we get into the next section, let me add one point for general reference. Pepper spray, mace, tear gas, similar sprays, and most nonlethal electric weapons are not generally considered "dangerous" weapons.[127]   This is because they are designed to temporarily incapacitate an opponent, rather than cause any permanent harm. If they do, it would normally be unintended. Thus, the use of mace, tear gas, pepper spray, stun gun, etc., should not constitute the use of "deadly force", although it would certainly constitute the use of "non-deadly force".[128]   This will suddenly become enlightening when you get to Chapter Eleven, which concerns your right to self-defense.

OPEN CARRYING OF WEAPONS OTHER THAN FIREARMS:

Florida does not generally prohibit the open carrying of weapons (other than firearms, and lethal or non-defensive electric weapons) except on a school bus, at a school bus stop, or within 1000 feet of the real property that comprises a public or private elementary, middle, or secondary school.[129]   More on this in Chapter Eight.   The crime of "open carrying of weapons" is covered in F.S. 790.053, and that section applies only to firearms, and certain electric weapons.   Moreover, that section also specifies it is legal for a person to "openly carry" (for lawful self-defense) any self-defense chemical spray, and any nonlethal stun gun or electric weapon, including Taser type weapons.   (ie: "dart firing stun gun")

By "openly carry" I mean that the weapon is not concealed from ordinary view, and that anyone with moderate intelligence can see you have a weapon, if they bothered to take a look.[130]

Technically, this means you could carry a knife, machete, bow, cross-bow, sword, spear, nun-chuks, and almost anything else with you -- almost anywhere -- totally legal -- so long as they are not concealed. Amazing, huh?

QUESTION: You mean I can walk down the streets armed with a crossbow, or spear?

ANSWER: Yes, unless prohibited by local ordinance.[131] Although I don't suggest you try it with the more obvious of these weapons.   Somehow, I don't think most people or police officers would appreciate you doing your personal impression of William Tell, or Attila the Hun   -- no matter what the law says.

QUESTION: How about a Taser type weapon, or stun gun?

ANSWER: Sure, as long as it's designed to be nonlethal, and is for defensive purposes -- even a Taser type weapon now complies due to a change in the law in 2006. However, it's a felony to use them against law enforcement officers in the performance of their duties.

QUESTION: Any place I couldn't open carry a weapon, other than a firearm, for sure?

ANSWER: Yes, schools, school buses, school bus stops. Read Chapter Eight for the low-down. Also, you're not getting in the courthouse with one, open or concealed. The same applies to police stations, jails, and prisons.

IMPROPER EXHIBITION OF FIREARMS & WEAPONS:

The crime of improper exhibition of a firearm or other weapon [F.S. 790.10] is a first degree misdemeanor in Florida. It occurs when any person carrying a knife, sword cane, firearm, electric weapon, or any other weapon exhibits it to others in a rude, careless, angry, or threatening manner -- unless in necessary self-defense.[132] This does not mean that all you're doing is carrying it. Self-defense is a very involved topic, and is covered in detail in its own chapter. Therefore, I suggest you try not to figure it out until you get there. However, the normal framework of this particular crime is that you can't go threatening, frightening, or endangering people with the display of a weapon. If you do -- you've got problems, and will probably need my services. If you want to try a more detailed analysis of the statute, let's give it a go, because it really is terribly drafted, and my personal opinion is that it is unconstitutionally vague. F.S. 790.10 states:

"If any person having or carrying any dirk, sword, sword cane, firearm, electric weapon or device, or other weapon, shall, in the presence of one or more persons, exhibit the same in a rude, careless, angry, or threatening manner, not in necessary self defense" the person shall be guilty of a misdemeanor of the first degree.

From reading this statute, which is not a model of clarity, we find that the elements of the crime are as follows:

1.   The offender must have or carry a weapon,
2.   The weapon is being exhibited,
3.   The exhibition is being done in a rude, careless, angry or threatening manner,
4.   The exhibition is not in necessary self defense
5.   The exhibition is in the presence of one or more other persons

The big problems with the statute are:

A.   What is meant by "exhibited"?   Does that mean that an unintentional display, or displayed where the exhibitor was unaware others were watching?   A very good question — without any current answer. I'll guess on the side of caution, and so should you.

B.   What constitutes "rude, careless, angry or threatening manner"?   Is that from the standpoint of any onlooker, no matter how unreasonable, or is it judged from what a "reasonable person" would judge?   The only likely response to this issue is that the "reasonable person" standard must be used.

C.   The next issue is what if the person with the weapon is angry or rude — but doesn't use the weapon to further his or her anger/rudeness/threat?   The statute says the "weapon", not the person, must be exhibited in such a manner.   That means some purposeful or careless use of the weapon should be a required element.   Just being angry and having a weapon on you shouldn't be a violation.   Otherwise, just going to the range to blow off a little steam, against someone you're angry at would be a violation.   Obviously, not an interpretation any court would likely allow.

D.   Last issue — what the heck is "in the presence" of others?   Is that ten feet, twenty feet, a hundred feet away?   What if you don't even realize somebody else is watching you?   Again, a real problem with clarity.   My personal guess is that "in the presence" means the other person or persons are in close enough proximity that you should reasonably know they are there, and are close enough that if your exhibition somehow went amiss — there would be a reasonable possibility they could be injured. Is this the law? Darn if I know! The statute is so poorly written that nobody really knows. The only appellate case that ever discussed it was <u>M.C.M. v. State</u>, 754 So.2d 844 (Fla. 2DCA 2000), where the appellate court held that the careful transfer of a rifle from one car to another was not a violation of the statute, could not be considered "careless" even where certain onlookers were concerned it might cause an accident.   Other than this single case,   almost all other appellate decisions involve aggravated assaults, where the issue was whether reckless display was a lesser possible charge.

So, now that you realize the problems with the statute,   you should also know that since the statute concerns a misdemeanor you can only be "legally" arrested if the police officer observes all the elements of the alleged violation occur in his presence. He can't arrest you on what somebody else said you did unless he has an arrest warrant.   I say "legally",   because a number of police officers lack the training to realize the limits of their authority.   Thus, you can get "falsely arrested" for almost anything.   The remedy for this is a good lawyer.

In summary — you do have the right to openly display a firearm or other weapon on your own property or place of business, and if done in a careful (ie: not careless), or non-threatening manner — it is perfectly legal.   If done in necessary self defense — it can be rude, angry, or whatever — but that is a separate self defense question. Unless the police see it — they can't "legally" arrest you for it without a warrant, although they can investigate it.

In 1994 the Legislature made improper exhibition a third degree felony when done on any school bus, school bus stop, or within 1000 feet of the real property on which any school (excluded are nursery schools, colleges, and vocational schools) is located.[133] [<u>F.S.</u> 790.115] The law does not apply to <u>private</u> property within 1000 feet of a school, when the offender is there with permission.

There are also some other tricky quirks to this statute that are covered in Chapter Eight. I suggest you read that chapter so you fully understand it.

Last, but not least, there is no case law on whether the mere display of a firearm in some type of aggressive or defensive position (not pointed at anyone) is an aggravated assault or a possible "improper exhibition".[134]   As a general rule it will be a jury question as to what your intent was, whether a reasonable person would have been in fear of imminent harm, whether it was meant as a threat, a conditional threat, or just "being ready" in case things got worse, and last but not least – whether it was in lawful self defense. Since the difference between aggravated assault and improper display is a felony with a mandatory minimum prison sentence versus a misdemeanor charge[135] – this becomes a real critical issue, and is why I advise never to display a firearm in a road rage situation ("But officer, it was only pointed at the ceiling!") unless it gets extremely serious. More on that in the self defense chapter.

DISCHARGING FIREARMS IN PUBLIC:
It is a first degree misdemeanor to discharge a firearm in any public place, from the right-of-way on any paved public road, or know-ingly across any road or occupied premises. However, this would not apply if you were acting in lawful defense of self or property, if you were performing official duties requiring the discharge of a firearm, or if the public place or road was expressly approved for hunting by the State.

However, if you fire from a vehicle, and you know there's a person within 1000 feet of you -- hunting or not -- it's a second degree felony. Moreover, if you're the owner or driver of a vehicle, and you direct somebody else to fire from the vehicle -- it's a third degree felony.[136]

If you're wondering what all this means -- it means you can't fire a gun from inside, or on a vehicle unless in necessary self-defense.

DISCHARGING MACHINE GUNS:
First of all -- you can't have one without a special federal approval. Otherwise, you're looking at a possible ten years federal prison sentence, and a very hefty fine. But assuming you're otherwise

legal -- I don't suggest you fire any automatic weapon[137] unless it's at a range. Firing it almost anywhere else with the intent to injure persons or property is a first degree felony punishable by life imprisonment -- whether you hit anything or not.[138]

On the other hand, if you have the right to use deadly force -- your use of a machine gun is, with certain reservations, legal.[139] Again, it's not advised, especially as use of a firearm in the commission of certain felonies, where the firearm is capable of automatic or semi-automatic fire, and has a magazine capable of holding twenty or more center fire rounds requires very strict sentencing pursuant to F.S. 775.087. This requires a mandatory minimum sentence of fifteen years if unfired, and 20 years if discharged. More on this in the self-defense chapter.

MACHINE GUNS, UNDERSIZED FIREARMS, AND OTHER NFA WEAPONS:

Federal law prohibits the ownership or possession of certain weapons pursuant to the National Firearms Act, hence the term "NFA" weapons. These include destructive devices, firearms capable of firing more than one shot with a single pull of the trigger (automatic firearms), shotguns and rifles that have been altered in certain ways usually to make them shorter than legal, anything that qualifies as a silencer or any of its parts, and certain exotic weapons. That's not a complete list, but it gives you a good idea.

Possession of any automatic firearm (machine gun); or a rifle with a barrel length of less than 16 inches (short-barreled rifle), or shotgun with a barrel length of less than 18 inches (short-barreled shotgun) is illegal under both State and Federal law, unless you have first obtained the tax stamp and transfer necessary under federal law. [140] Moreover, both rifles and shotguns must have an overall length of at least 26 inches, or the firearm is classified as "any other weapon" under the NFA. If you have a folding stock, length is measured from the tip of the barrel to the very end of the folding stock in its extended position, even if it can be fired without extension.[141] It is a second degree felony, as well as a federal crime to have such a firearm unless you are a federally licensed dealer with a Class III approval, or a private citizen or corporation which has been pre-approved by ATF, and has already received the special NFA tax stamp on an approved

Form 4, or if by bequest, via a Form 5.[142]   When I talk about "NFA" weapons, I am speaking of those weapons regulated by the National Firearms Act, which falls under Internal Revenue Code jurisdiction, and can be found beginning at 26 USC 5801.

The most basic definition of a machine gun is under Florida law. In that sense, a machine gun is any firearm that shoots, or is designed to shoot more than one shot, automatically, by a single pull of the trigger.[143]   If you're wondering why a "Hell Fire" equipped weapon is OK -- the "Hell Fire" causes multiple pulls of the trigger in extremely rapid succession -- thus although it mimics an automatic, it is "semi-automatic" because the trigger is being moved to accomplish the firing of each round. Not so for the Akins Accelerator due to a change in ATF rulings.

Federal law is a lot tougher on what constitutes a machine gun because the federal definition includes the frames or receivers of machine guns, any parts designed to convert a weapon into machine gun (usually the auto sear), and any combination of parts from which a machine gun can be assembled. Federal law also controls a number of other weapons and accessories under the National Firearms Act. If you're thinking about buying an auto sear – remember – it's considered a machine gun by itself! If it wasn't registered prior to 1986 – it's already contraband. There's a supposed exception as to AR-15 drop-in auto sears manufactured prior to November 1, 1981, per ATF Ruling 81-4.   Assuming you have such an auto sear, and can prove it was manufactured prior to the 1981 date, the ruling says you may possess it without registering it, although you would still be subject to pre-registration and the tax stamp if you have the AR-15 firearm, or even the parts for the AR-15, together with the auto sear – otherwise you have committed a federal felony.   On the other hand, some federal courts have made it clear that any transfer of an AR-15 auto sear still needs to be pre-registered and approved, although there would be no transfer tax collected by ATF. United States v. Cash, 149 F.3d 706 (7th Cir. 1998).[144] Therefore, I would strongly suggest that before you obtain a pre-1981 AR-15 auto sear, you get the transfer pre-approved by ATF.

Some of the weapons and accessories that are a federal crime to possess under the NFA (unless you are a dealer in this type weapon or have obtained a tax stamp and approval after completing the Form

4 application for transfer) include: silencers and parts intended to fabricate a silencer, undersized firearms, destructive devices, cane guns, pen guns, wallet guns, and any pistol that is fitted for or with a shoulder stock -- unless the barrel length is over 16 inches, or the weapon with stock has been placed on the "curio and relic" list by the Secretary of Treasury.[145]   Also made illegal are certain revolving cylinder shotguns that were ruled as "non-sporting" by the Secretary of Treasury. which will be covered later in this book under "destructive devices".

If you want to know how to measure the length of your barrel to see if it's legal -- place a metal rod in the gun with the action closed, and mark where the rod exits the barrel. Measure that distance, and you have the official barrel length. 27 CFR 479.11

"ANY OTHER WEAPON":

There are some areas of the law that are difficult to understand. One of these is the area under the National Firearms Act (ie: NFA) concerning firearms defined as "any other weapon". Under federal law, any such firearm must be registered prior to taking possession, or you have committed a felony.

"Any other weapon" means any weapon or device capable of being concealed on the person from which a shot can be discharged through the energy of an explosive . . . . Such term shall not include a pistol or revolver having a rifled bore. . . ." 26 USC 5845 (e)

Pistol: A weapon having "(b) a short stock designed to be gripped by one hand and at an angle to and extending below the line of the bore(s)." 27 CFR 478.11

PEN GUNS & PISTOLS:

If you read these two sections together you see that any weapon capable of being concealed is an "NFA" "any other weapon", unless **excepted** from the definition. One of the exceptions is if the weapon constitutes a "pistol" with a rifled bore. A pistol, to be a "pistol" under federal law, must also have a handle ("short stock") set at an angle to the barrel, and below the barrel. Therefore, the law currently does not define a pen gun as an NFA weapon because the gun is hinged, and the hinged portion is designed to be bent away from the barrel before it can fire.   Thus, the hinged portion becomes the "handle" which is set below, and at an angle to the barrel.

Of possible interest for all you owners of legal pen guns, and wallet guns[146] – in April 2005 ATF applied to change the definition of "pistol" to eliminate pen guns, wallet guns, belt buckle guns, and pager guns (not Pager Pal) (ATF Notice of Proposed Rule Making 7P, April 2005) The change would affect 27 CFR 479.11, but to date – nothing's happened. In case it does, here's how it would work by redefining the word "pistol":

(a) A weapon originally designed, made, and intended to fire a projectile (bullet) from one or more barrels when held in one hand, and having--

(1) A chamber(s) as an integral part(s) of, or permanently aligned with, the bore(s); and

(2) A short fixed stock designed to be gripped by one hand and at an angle to and extending below the line of the bore(s).

(b) The term shall not include any weapon disguised to look like an item other than a firearm, such as a pengun, wallet gun, belt buckle gun, pager gun or gadget device, or any gun that fires more than one shot, without manual reloading, by a single function of the trigger.

Assuming your once legal firearm suddenly becomes an NFA weapon, you will have a grace period to register it as "any other weapon". For now, you're OK.

Sorry, if I confused you on this "any other weapon" stuff. This area is complicated. To make it simpler, if you have any weapon that discharges a shell by use of an explosive, the weapon can be concealed on your person, and that weapon does not have the normal configuration of a pistol or revolver -- it probably is "any other weapon" under federal law.

WALLET GUN:
Similarly, a derringer that can be fired from within a concealing holster becomes "any other weapon" when placed in such a holster, because the angled grip extending from the barrel is no longer visible.

Same thing with a gun rigged to be discharged from inside a briefcase. Also, there's a single shot pistol built into the handle of a knife which I've seen at some gun shows — which is currently legal because the handle is set at an angle slightly below the barrel. Even that slight angled grip to the barrel brought it within the definition of a pistol, according an ATF ruling. However, if the definition ever changes – it's "any other weapon".

QUESTION: You mean if I have a derringer with a special wallet holster, I am illegal?

ANSWER: Sort of! Once you put the two together ATF says you consider them as a "unit". The unit has now lost the "angled grip" it should have to be a pistol. You have a potential ten year federal felony! 26 USC 5871

QUESTION: Isn't this a "combination of parts" like a machine gun?

ANSWER: No – "any other weapon" does not use the "combination of parts" language used for machine guns and silencers.

QUESTION: Can I fit a shoulder-stock to a regular pistol?

ANSWER: Absolutely not! It is no longer a "regular pistol" once you do. It falls under another NFA definition, a "short barreled rifle", as now it's a pistol designed to be fired from the shoulder, rather than by one hand. Another ten year federal "NFA" felony, unless it's exempted on the curio and relic list by the Secretary.

QUESTION: What if I cut-down my shotgun, and I'm a sixteenth of an inch too short?

ANSWER: Federal crime, and possible jail sentence. Mistakes are just your tough luck, and a possible reason to ask the judge for a more lenient sentence. On the other hand, you may have a shot at a defense that it was not "knowingly" or "willfully" done. Get a good lawyer – you'll need one! My number's in the back of the book.

QUESTION: Can I transport my legal machine gun just like any other firearm.

ANSWER: Within Florida, yes -- so long as you're federally legal. However, you are not covered under your Concealed Weapons Permit.

QUESTION: What else do I watch out for?

ANSWER: Well, anything unusual should be questioned, and anything too exotic looking might be something to stay away from unless you're really knowledgeable.

QUESTION: I've heard it's legal to manufacture a machine gun. What are the procedures I must follow?

ANSWER: For a start, pack your bags, and kiss your family goodbye for ten years while you're in federal prison. It is totally illegal to manufacture a machine gun unless you are a licensed Class III manufacturer making an approved firearm for the military or law enforcement. Only machine guns legally registered prior to **May 19, 1986**, may be possessed by ordinary citizens, and that's only after receiving formal ATF pre-approval. [147] The case law that said otherwise was vacated in United States v. Stewart, 125 S.Ct. 2899. Because of this, on June 30, 2006, the 9th Circuit reversed its decision in the Stewart case, and held that a private citizen who manufactures an NFA firearm without prior ATF approval commits a felony. Since ATF will never allow this, the question is closed forever! [148]

SILENCERS:

Silencers are regulated by the NFA, require a tax stamp and pre-approval, and include the tubes and the wipes. You can't have any of the parts before you have the approval from ATF. If you get the tube ahead of time it becomes contraband (assuming it isn't already), and you've committed a felony even if you get the approval later on. Once contraband – always contraband. Good show! Same thing with the baffles (ie: "wipes). You can't have them, even for repairs, because only an NFA approved manufacturer can legally have them separate from the entire silencer.

If you see any of these great deals on the internet where you can import tubes or wipes from Germany or Sweden for a great price – don't! First of all, you'd need the ATF pre-approval before you could even ship the stuff. Second of all, it's illegal to import them. Third of all, there are numerous regulations to comply with before you can import any military type item, so you've probably added another felony by importing without the proper documents, and approvals.

CHART ON LEGAL GUN & BARREL LENGTH:

Legal rifle length		Legal shotgun length	
barrel	overall	barrel	overall
16"	26"	18"	26"

USING A FIREARM WHILE UNDER THE INFLUENCE:

If you're under the influence of alcohol, or any other harmful or illegal chemical substance, to the extent your normal faculties are impaired, it is unlawful to have a <u>loaded</u> firearm in hand, or to fire it. If you do, it's a second degree misdemeanor, unless you're acting in lawful self-defense, or defense of your property. F.S. 790.151. It will also cause the loss of your Concealed Weapons Permit, if you have one. Of course, if the firearm doesn't have ammunition in it — you're still legal — but definitely stupid.

"Normal faculties" doesn't mean you're "drunk". Normal faculties is a lesser standard normally associated with DUI, and means that your coordination, ability to see, speak, judge distances, perform ordinary tasks, or make decisions is affected to an extent that these functions are noticeably interfered with. If you have a "buzz", you are certainly under the influence, and maybe drunk, as well. If you need to try harder to concentrate -- same thing. If you've just had a couple, and it has relaxed you, but nothing more -- you're likely not under the influence in the legal sense, because although all alcohol has had some effect -- it hasn't yet affected your "normal faculties".

If a law enforcement officer has probable cause to believe you were using a firearm while under the influence, he can require you to take a breath test for alcohol, and a urine test for drugs. If you caused death or serious injury to anyone -- he may take blood, and take it by force if you refuse.

A blood alcohol reading of .10 percent or greater is evidence of being under the influence of alcohol to the extent your normal faculties are impaired. Less than .05 percent means you're presumed to be fine. Anywhere in between means "it depends". Although the DUI standard has changed to .08 percent as the presumed level of intoxication since January 1, 1994 -- a .10 will still apply for this firearms offense.[149]

Personally, I don't think you should be walking around with a loaded firearm if you are anything other than stone cold sober, unless somebody or something is coming at you. Otherwise, it's too damn risky.[150] On the other hand, the statute is more than fair, and does not penalize carry — only actual use, or in hand possession.

SHOOTING AT VEHICLES, VESSELS & STRUCTURES:
The deliberate or reckless shooting, or throwing of any projectile or other hard object which could produce great bodily harm, at or into any building, whether **occupied or not**, or at any boat, train, aircraft, bus, or any other vehicle which is occupied or being used by any person -- is a second degree felony. F.S. 790.19. This is the statute that juveniles are usually charged with when they throw rocks from bridges, and overpasses -- and miss. If they hit anybody, add aggravated battery and possibly homicide to the list. Anything that can produce serious injury qualifies. A rock, piece of debris, shooting with

a firearm or bow, etc. Very dangerous stuff -- especially if the vehicle is moving, as it adds velocity to the impact.

In Juarez v. State, 892 So.2d 1158 (Fla. 5DCA 2005), a woman threw a concrete irrigation donut into an unoccupied garage which she knew was unoccupied. In what can only be described as a terrible decision, the appellate court affirmed her conviction because the house to which the garage was attached was occupied. How this "could produce great bodily harm" under the facts is a complete mystery to all, but she was still convicted of a very serious felony charge. Be warned!

SELF-PROPELLED KNIVES:

It is a first degree misdemeanor to manufacture, sell, or possess any "spring knife", "ballistic knife" or "self-propelled" knife -- which are three names for the same thing: a device that propels a knifelike blade, generally by use of a coiled spring, compressed gas, or elastic. F.S. 790.225. Bows, cross-bows, and spearguns are excluded from this definition if they discharge a bolt, dart, or arrow. Federal law defines these knives as a "ballistic knife", and it is a ten year felony to knowingly possess, manufacture, sell, or import such a knife. [15 USC 1245]

POSSESSION BY CONVICTED FELON:

Under Florida law any person convicted of a felony in this, or any other state, or of a crime that would be considered a felony in Florida[151], or a federal felony, is considered a "convicted felon", and such a person cannot possess, own, or have in his/her care or custody any firearm, ammunition, or electric weapon, without first having his right to own and possess such being restored by executive clemency. A convicted felon is also forbidden from carrying concealed, any "weapon", including chemical sprays. Violation is a second degree felony, with a mandatory 3 year prison sentence[152], unless you qualify as a "violent career criminal". If you do, it's a first degree felony with a mandatory minimum 15 year sentence. F.S. 790.23 & F.S. 790.235. Even juveniles may qualify as violent career criminals, and are subject to the mandatory sentence if prosecuted in adult court.

Juveniles who do not qualify as "violent career criminals" under F.S. 790.235, get a break when they become an adult. Any "convicted felon" status disability expires, unless the prior conviction was in adult court vs. juvenile court.[153] However, their prior juvenile adjudications can still be counted to later qualify them for "violent career criminal" status if they don't clean-up their act. Moreover, any juvenile conviction or "withheld adjudication" on a felony charge prohibits that person from owning, possessing, or carrying these items in exactly the same way as it prohibits a convicted felon – until the juvenile offender reaches the age of 24 years. At that time, if they have no other legal disability, the prohibition on firearms and weapons disappears. F.S. 790.23(1)(d).

PROHIBITION AS TO AMMUNITION:

Federal law on convicted felons is somewhat different because it also forbids a convicted felon from possession or ownership of ammunition. Since ammunition includes any component (ie: a single dummy shell would do, or even an empty casing) — it can be a real trap for the unwary. Moreover, the feds are very pro-active on prosecuting felons in possession.

QUESTION: My boyfriend, and I live together. He is a convicted felon, and wants a gun in the house. Can I buy it for him, if I keep it.

ANSWER: No. If you're buying it "for him", it's a second degree felony for him to have it, and you're violating State and Federal law by making a "straw" purchase. Very serious stuff.

QUESTION: How about if I really just want it for me, and not for him.

ANSWER: First, he should not have access to the firearm. You should keep it on your person, and when not on your person, it should be kept locked in a safe or strong box that he does not have either the key, or combination to. This is technically legal, but very risky as the feds really like to prosecute this type of case. Remember, even if it's yours -- your convicted felon live-in could still be charged with "constructive possession". That means that he has knowledge of where the firearm is located, and has the ability to control it, as well. This is a factual issue for the jury, and in my opinion is not worth the risk. Also, don't leave any ammunition lying around -- as this is just as serious for a felon to possess as a firearm, and the feds will prosecute it if given the chance. Ammunition includes any part of a cartridge, even if empty, and even if it's on one of those cool key chains!

QUESTION: How about an antique firearm?

ANSWER: An "antique firearm" is not considered a firearm by either Florida or the feds unless used in the commission of a crime, therefore it is legal for a convicted felon to have such a weapon (when not on probation/parole) so long as it is not concealed. F.S. 790.001(6). However, recent Florida case law has held that to be an antique, the firearm must be "a reasonably exact reproduction." Bostic v. State, 902 So. 2d 225 (Fla.   5DCA 2005).   Federal law is very different, but since we're talking about Florida – Florida law controls.   Thus, modern muzzleloaders are out, and even if you have plastic grips, or a modern sight added to a fairly accurate replica – this case has so screwed-up the definition that nobody knows what the heck "a reasonably exact replica" is.   Hopefully, the Legislature will cure this serious problem, and redefine antique firearms to conform to the federal definition, which was the intent of the original Florida statute, anyway.

QUESTION: What if I received a felony conviction in another country?

ANSWER: Both Florida and Federal law require the
conviction within the United States or its
possessions. Small v. United States, 125 S.Ct.
1752 (2005).

FIREARMS INVOLVED IN THE COMMISSION OF A FELONY:

The mere carrying of a firearm during the commission of a felony, is a separate felony of the third degree under Florida law. That means that nobody even needs to see it -- only that you have it. If you display it, use it, or threaten its use -- it's a second degree felony. F.S. 790.07 Moreover, whatever felony you were involved with is generally increased one degree, and certain felonies, including most defined as a "forcible felony" receive at least a "mandatory minimum" sentence of three (3) years -- which means that the judge must impose that sentence, as the absolute minimum of prison time, even if he doesn't want to. F.S. 775.087 You will see how this has a very "chilling" effect on your right to self-defense later when we discuss aggravated assault. And, if you committed the crime while being armed with a semi-automatic with a high capacity clip, which is a box magazine capable of holding more than 20 centerfire cartridges, or if you were armed with a machine gun -- make it an fifteen (15) year mandatory minimum.[154]

USE OF BULLETPROOF VESTS:

Any person who, while possessing a firearm, commits or attempts to commit a murder, sexual battery, robbery, burglary, kidnaping, arson, aggravated battery, aggravated assault, escape, or aircraft piracy -- and has the nerve to wear a bulletproof vest in furtherance of the crime -- is guilty of a third degree felony. F.S. 775.0846. It is also a federal felony for any convicted felon to purchase or possess body armor. 18 USC 931. The federal statute has a limited exception when such is certified by an employer as being necessary for work purposes, and it is only used for work purposes.

ARMOR PIERCING OR SPECIALITY AMMUNITION:

F.S. 790.31 governs the "Florida version" of what is, and what is not allowed in most ammunition for firearms. Under the Florida statute an "armor-piercing bullet" is one with an inner core of steel or other metal of equivalent hardness (not lead), and a truncated cone (ie: a cut-off tip) which is designed for use in a handgun as an armor or metal piercing bullet. If it isn't designed for a handgun — it doesn't meet the definition.

Other Florida "no-no's" under F.S. 790.31 include the following list of exotics:

a.   "Exploding bullet" — is one that is designed to detonate by use of an explosive or deflagrant (ie: burning agent) contained or attached to the bullet, and can be fired from any firearm.

b.   "Dragon's breath shotgun shell" which is one that is solely designed to spew a flame or fireball (not a tracer — but simulates a flamethrower), and contains exothermic pyrophoric misch metal as the projectile.

c.   "Bolo shell" which is any shell that expels two or more metal balls connected by a solid metal wire, and can be fired in a firearm.

d.   "Flechette shell" means any shell with two or more pieces of fin-stabilized metal wires or solid dart-type projectiles, that can be fired in a firearm.

Under the Florida statute it is a third degree felony to sell, offer for sale, or deliver any of these five types of ammunition. Also, if you merely   possess armor piercing ammo when it is loaded into a handgun, you are also guilty of a third degree felony. Same thing for the other four types of exotics — except they can't be loaded into any type firearm, not just a handgun. If you possess any with the intent to use it in the commission of a crime, loaded or not, it's a second degree felony — 15 years! Of course, the statute excepts law enforcement use, and sale to law enforcement agencies.

Federal law is a bit different because it   only covers armor piercing ammo, and in that instance, doesn't cover purchase, possession, use, or sale by private individuals — unless used in the commission of a crime.[155] In that situation, it's a five year mandatory prison sentence on top of the crime committed. On the other hand, federal licensees (legal gun dealers or "FFL") are strictly controlled on what they can sell, and cannot sell armor piercing ammo to civilians. To find out how the definitions work in federal land — here we go:

a.   "Armor piercing" is any projectile or its core which may be used in a handgun which is made entirely of steel, iron, brass, bronze, beryllium, copper, depleted uranium, or a combination of tungsten alloys, or

A full jacketed projectile larger than .22 caliber which is designed and intended for use in a handgun, and whose jacket weighs more than 25% of the total weight of the projectile.

Excluded from the definition of armor piercing are shotgun shot required by game regulations for hunting, frangible projectiles designed for target shooting (ie: breaks up on way to target), and projectiles which are determined by BATF to be used for sporting purposes, or industrial purposes.

If you noticed, lead is not one of the prohibited metals under Florida or Federal law. Also, you need not worry about federal law unless you are an FFL, or intend to use the ammunition in the commission of a felony.

QUESTION: I have some old 7:62 x 39 steel core ammo for my SKS. I heard it was illegal to shoot it?

ANSWER: Nope. It's fine unless loaded into a handgun. However, a dealer couldn't sell it to you.

QUESTION: I've got some handgun ammo that is supposed to "explode" like a shotgun shell when it hits someone. Isn't that an illegal exploding bullet?

ANSWER: Nope. An "exploding" bullet must actually have some chemical or such to make it explode or incinerate upon contact. The type of round your talking about is quite common, and works purely from the force of impact. Normally, you're talking about something like "safety shot" which contains a number of small pellets that disburse upon impact. Other bullets may be designed to fragment upon impact, with the idea of creating a greater wound channel — thus stopping the assailant before he stops you.

QUESTION: Why call it "safety shot"?

ANSWER: Since these rounds fragment, or disburse -- they lose momentum quicker, and therefore won't generally penetrate walls if you miss. Thus, you don't hit something or someone you didn't intend to. Lots of pros and cons — buy a book on ammunition.

ALTERED OR REMOVED SERIAL NUMBERS:

It is a state and federal felony to knowingly remove or alter a serial number on any firearm, or otherwise attempt to disguise it's identification. F.S. 790.27 & 18 USC 922(k). It is also a felony to knowingly possess, sell, or deliver such a firearm, and if you find a firearm with the serial numbers missing, or partially or completely filed, you should call your local police department, and turn it in. First, because it's a crime to have it, and it's considered "contraband". Second, because you are on notice that the gun is probably stolen -- and it's also a state and federal felony to possess or sell a stolen firearm. F.S. 790.27

DESTRUCTIVE DEVICES:

A "destructive device" under Florida law encompasses both the state and federal definitions.[156] These are many. In its most basic definition it is any bomb, grenade, mine, rocket, missile, or similar device that contains an explosive, incendiary, or poison gas which is designed or constructed to explode, and is capable of causing bodily harm or property damage. It also includes any breakable container filled with an explosive, incendiary, explosive or expanding gas designed or constructed to explode due to its content, and capable of causing bodily harm or property damage. This is usually a "Molotov cocktail".

It also includes any weapon with a barrel diameter over one half inch capable of expelling a projectile by means of an explosive -- other than a legal sized shotgun[157], line-throwing device (rescue), or signaling device. Ammunition for destructive devices are included in the definition of a "destructive device". A 1994 treasury ruling outlawed three shotguns, the Striker, USAS-12, and Streetsweeper -- unless they are registered under the National Firearms Act, just like a machine gun. The reason is that the federal definition of destructive device includes any "weapon" that expels a projectile by means of an explosive having a barrel bore of more than one half inch, except a shotgun or shotgun shell the Secretary of Treasury finds is generally recognized as particularly suitable for sporting purposes. The Secretary found that these particular guns had no legitimate sporting purpose, and were really riot and combat weapons.

I also note that the federal statute makes the definition of destructive device a bit clearer than the Florida statute. That's because of the following language concerning the required status as a "weapon" before it becomes a destructive device:

> "The term 'destructive device' shall not include any device which is neither designed or redesigned for use as a weapon; any device, although originally designed for use as a weapon, which is redesigned for use as a signaling, pyrotechnic, line throwing, safety, or similar device . . . or any other device which the Secretary finds is not likely to be used as a weapon, or is an antique . . . ."

Thus, you now can understand why a potato cannon is not normally a destructive device. Why? Because it is not something "designed" as a "weapon". Of course, under the Florida definition — if you use it as a weapon — it becomes a destructive device under Florida law.

Whatever!

SWITCHBLADE KNIFE:

It is not illegal to possess a switchblade or "automatic" knife in Florida. It was for a couple of years when one of our appellate courts royally screwed up the definition by confusing it with a "spring knife" (ie: "ballistic knife")[158], however, the Legislature corrected this mistake in 2003 in H.B. 1227, a bill sponsored by the Guild of Knifemakers, that passed the Legislature without opposition, and is now F.S. 790.225(2)(a). The bill amended the statute by clarifying what had been obvious to anyone familiar with knives or the federal statute, but obviously not to the appellate court or the attorneys who handled that case -- that a spring knife did not include "any device from which a knifelike blade opens, where such blade remains physically integrated with the device when open". Of course, you would need a CWP to carry any of these knives concealed, as they are certainly not a "common pocketknife", and are therefore going to be classified as a "weapon".

You should know that it is a federal felony for anyone to sell, transport, or distribute these knives, unless they were manufactured in the state of sale, or were manufactured and possessed for the U.S. Armed Forces under contract. Furthermore, it is a federal felony for an individual to transport them into another state, possess them in any state other than where manufactured, possess them on any federal waters outside of a state's jurisdiction, or on Indian land. The only exceptions to these prohibitions are if the person in possession has only one arm, and the blade is three inches or less, or the person is a member of the armed forces in the performance of duty. So, keep them off your person if you go gambling on the Seminole reservation, on an ocean voyage, or if you travel state-to-state. Otherwise, it's a five year federal felony! 15 USC 1241-1245. Likewise, try to remember you need a CWP to carry these anywhere off your property or business. They are not a "common pocket knife".

Just as an aside, you might like to know that switchblades were extensively used as a utility knife by women in the 1800's, and early 1900's -- because their long fingernails would break when opening ordinary pocket knives. They also served as a "safety" knife, as they could be opened with one hand. Thus, if one hand was trapped, or pinned -- the knife could still be opened to help cut you loose. Even today, automatic knifes are in extensive use with EMS personnel and police due to this important ability.

ASSAULT WEAPONS:

After a bitter fight, Congress incorporated the Assault Weapons Ban into the 1994 Crime Bill. 18 USC 922(v) & (w). This totally unnecessary piece of legislation finally ended on September 13, 2004.

Firearms and magazines that were manufactured or imported during the ban that have the stamp "RESTRICTED LAW ENFORCEMENT/GOVERNMENT USE ONLY"; or "FOR EXPORT ONLY" are now legal to purchase, as are any other firearms that the ban previously labeled as an "assault weapon" or "large capacity magazine"

Why did we need the ban?

No reason whatsoever – it was just "pure politics". The firearms were randomly selected based on cosmetic features – and even the FBI admitted they didn't pose a problem based on statistical crime records.

So, you ask: "Why would anybody need such a firearm?"

Aside from looking really cool, being the primary firearm the Second Amendment would recognize over others, and being just about the most fun firearm around to shoot – I don't know. Why do some people have cars with big engines? Why do people buy new clothes when the old ones are still good? Why own a big screen TV? Get the idea?

USE OF BANGSTICKS:

The use of a bangstick or powerhead for self-protection in the salt water areas within State jurisdiction is generally permitted, although the taking of any marine life thereby is strictly prohibited.[159] In other words, unless one of our finny friends has definite plans on having you for dinner, don't use it.

Moreover, you should make sure that the powerhead is permanently attached to a shaft with an overall length of not less than four feet, so you don't fall within the definition of "any other weapon" under federal law -- which, as we just discussed a few sections ago, is very illegal.[160]

Use of powerheads within National and State Parks is another matter, and will not generally be permitted.

QUESTION: How could a bangstick become "any other weapon" under the NFA?

ANSWER: Well, it's only real purpose is a "weapon" — against sharks. If it can be concealed on the person it then qualifies as "any other weapon" since it's not otherwise excepted. The Revenue Ruling in the last endnote said if it's four foot long with a permanent shaft — it's fine because it really can't be concealed at that length. So, if you want to play it safe — do it the way they tell you.

ARMED TRESPASS:

Trespassing on the property of another while in possession of a firearm, loaded or not --is a third degree felony under F.S. 810.09. Basically, a trespass occurs if you go uninvited onto enclosed or posted lands; if you enter or remain in a structure or conveyance without having any express or implied invitation to do so; or if having been warned to leave, you refuse to do so.[161]

While I have found no Florida cases on the subject, there are many instances in which you go into a store, or shopping center -- and they have a sign posted saying "no firearms permitted".   The next question you must face is whether you commit a trespass by going in the store. If so, then you've also committed an "armed trespass", which is a third degree felony.

My personal opinion is that your going into such a store or shopping mall is not a trespass just because they post a sign saying "no firearms" because you are still an "invitee", and they still want your business -- just without the weapon. Again, that's a personal interpretation. A court could call me wrong, and if you want to play it safe — obey the sign.

On the other hand, if you do follow my interpretation, and they asked you to leave, and you refused, or started to argue with them -- that would be another story, and you'd be in serious trouble because they've now made it clear they want you off the property, and the law says you have only a reasonable time to leave -- not to argue or have a debate with them.   Likewise, if they had a guard posted at the mall entrance, and asked you if you were armed -- and you lied -- again, I think you have a problem.   But, in essence, they really are only posting these things to protect themselves from a liability standpoint in case something happens.   That way, you get sued -- they don't!

Since the offense of trespass by an invitee would require a warning, and a refusal to depart my opinion is that you can't legally "refuse" until someone asks you to leave.   Then, it's time to swallow your pride, and exit very quickly, and very politely.   If the wife, and kids are somewhere else in the mall -- ask security if you can locate them before you leave, or, if not -- ask if they'll make an announcement.   Don't push your luck if they're reluctant or refuse.   Just get the hell out of there, pronto!   If the wife or kids will be confused -- try bribing some honest-looking passerby outside the mall to notify them.   All this is a lot better than an arrest, and a third degree felony on your record!

LICENSED PRIVATE SECURITY GUARDS:

Chapter 493, Florida Statutes, governs the use of firearms by private investigative, security, and repossession services.   The regulations pertaining to this Chapter would take a separate book, so I'll be brief.   First, you cannot carry a firearm or weapon as part of your duties without a "G" license.   If you do, and get caught -- you'll probably lose your license for at least five years.   You'll also be committing a first degree misdemeanor.[162]

Security personnel with a Concealed Weapons Permit may be able to legally carry a firearm without committing a crime in their private lives, but professionally, unless they have also have a "G" license, are required to carry a firearm as part of their duties, and are doing so in connection with their duties -- they will be in serious trouble with the Licensing Division of the Department of State, will be committing a misdemeanor, and will be a walking civil liability case, if anything happens.   This is because there are very stringent training requirements to obtain and maintain a "G" license, and those who don't meet these requirements are deemed to be "unqualified" to carry a weapon while on duty.

PERMITTED FIREARMS FOR G LICENSEE:

The type of firearm which can be carried when required for, and in connection with your duties is set forth in F.S. 493.6115(6), and includes .38 and .357 caliber revolvers, and 9mm and .380 caliber semi-autos. You must be pre-qualified for the firearms carried. Do not load .357 ammo! Use factory ammo only. A waiver may be obtained from the Department for non-listed firearms.

Holstered and non-concealed carry is required except for Class "C"; "CC" and "D", who may carry concealed if they are at least 21 years of age, and hold the "G" license, although the "D" licensee must also be on temporary special assignment where the client requires this type of service. F.S. 493.6305

PROHIBITED AMMO FOR SECURITY GUARDS:

a. Glasser, Mag-Safe, etc. pre-fragmented type bullets
b. exploding bullets
c. full metal jacket
d. teflon coated (KTW) or other armor-piercing
e. full wadcutters & reloads (except for range use)
f. .357 — (use .38 instead)

DECLARED EMERGENCIES:

There are two entirely separate sections in the statutes concerning firearms possession during hurricanes and other emergencies. The first covers the power of the Governor, and is found in F.S. 14.021 and F.S. 252.36. In these situations the Governor issues a "proclamation" as to what the emergency is, and what measures he's authorized to deal with it. Each proclamation is individual in its scope, and must be read to determine what is prohibited or restricted. The statute limits his power in that firearms that are lawfully possessed may not be seized unless the person is engaged in the commission of a crime.   Similar in operation are"declared emergencies" by local authorities under F.S. 870.044.   That statute is directed more to situations involving public rioting, or such when there is:

> *"reason to believe that there exists a clear and present danger of a riot or other general public disorder, widespread disobedience of the law, and substantial injury to persons or to property."*

In those instances the sheriff, chief of police, or mayor of the local community may declare a "state of emergency", and take such measures as are necessary to protect the public welfare. When such is declared the statute automatically prohibits the sale or offer to sell any firearms or ammunition; the intentional display of firearms or ammunition at any store; or the intentional possession of a firearm in any public place. Thus, it appears the statute forbids carrying a firearm for protection in your vehicle when on public roads, and carry in any public area. However, the statute clearly prevents the government from seizing lawfully possessed firearms from private citizens so long as the citizen is not engaged in the commission of a crime.

Federal law is similar to its Florida counterparts, and is found at 42 USC 5207. The federal law does not permit the seizure of firearms by federal authorities unless the possession is contrary to state law. Under the federal statute, the government may require temporary surrender of a firearm only as a condition for voluntary rescue or evacuation being provided for by the government, with the firearm being returned after the transportation is completed. A violation allows the person to seek redress in federal court for injunctive relief and attorney fees to obtain return of the firearm.

CHAPTER EIGHT

LAWS CONCERNING CHILDREN

Whenever I mention children, the first thing I think of is air guns, fireworks, and where the heck should I put my gun to make sure they don't get hold of it. Children, the younger the more common, have a bad habit of playing with things they shouldn't. If they get hold of a loaded firearm -- the results can be devastating. More importantly, when it happens, it happens so quickly that there are only seconds to counter the potential disaster. School shootings don't help much, either. To counter this tragic situation, the Florida legislature has gone a bit too far -- and the federal government, as usual -- has gone off the wall. Whatever the merits or demerits of these laws -- the first part of this chapter should educate you on what to be aware of in this area.

LAWFUL AGE TO POSSESS FIREARMS OR AMMUNITION:
The passage of the Youth Handgun Safety Amendment to the 1994 federal Crime Bill[163] made it a federal crime for anyone to sell, deliver, or otherwise transfer to a juvenile (ie: person under 18 years of age) a handgun, or ammunition suitable only for use in a handgun. This means loaded, or unloaded. This means a gift, a sale, just loaning the darn thing, or temporarily handing it over for a "look-see". This applies to parents, uncles, aunts, friends, relatives, scout masters, and any almost every other form of life on the planet, except for firearms dealers. For firearms dealers -- it's still 21 years of age. The exceptions under the statute are a "temporary transfer" for use during:

a.   In the course of ranching, or farming at the residence of the juvenile, or

b.   In the course of ranching, or farming at a location where the juvenile has the permission of the property owner or lessee, or

c.   during target practice, hunting, or a course of instruction on the safe and lawful use of firearms, or

d.   in the course of employment.

On top of these restrictions, there are additional requirements. The additional requirements that must be met while the permitted activities are being performed. These additional restrictions are as follows:

a.   The juvenile must have the prior written consent of a parent or guardian. The written consent must be kept on the juveniles person at all times he is in possession of the handgun or ammunition (during the permitted activity), and the parent or guardian who gave permission, must not have a legal disability that would make it illegal for that parent or guardian to possess a firearm.

b.   The handgun must be transported unloaded, in a locked container, directly to and from the permitted activity. It must thereafter be returned to an adult.

c.   If the activity is ranching or farming, then such must be done at the direction of an adult who does not have a legal disability that would make it illegal for that person to possess a firearm.

Now, if you thought that wasn't enough, here's another doozie. Subsection (D) only allows a juvenile to use a handgun in defense of the juvenile, or another person, if it's against an "intruder" inside the residence of the juvenile, or a residence in which the juvenile is a guest!

Do you know what that supposedly means? It means that if Dad suddenly goes nuts, and begins killing the family, and the kid grabs a handgun to try to stop it -- he's committed a crime! If mom is bloody on the floor, and gives it to the kid because she couldn't use it herself -- she's facing a year in federal prison -- assuming she survives. Why? Because Daddy is not an "intruder". He lives there! Moreover, if it's at the office, in the car, etc. -- same stupid result.

Anyway, since we're all sick of federal law by now, let's get into Florida law. Don't get too excited -- we've still got some more federal law to go over later in this chapter. It never ends.

FLORIDA LAWS PERTAINING TO MINORS:

In Florida, it is unlawful for anyone to sell, lend, or give a person under the age of 18 years any weapon, whatsoever, except an ordinary pocketknife -- unless a parent (guardian) gives permission. A violation is a first degree misdemeanor for weapons, and a third degree felony for firearms. F.S. 790.17. A "dealer in arms" cannot sell to a person under 18 years of age -- even with permission, although he can legally sell to an adult, who may then transfer it to the child, with permission from a parent. F.S. 790.18

A 1996 amendment to F.S. 790.22 makes it illegal for a minor under 16 years to possess a BB gun, air or gas operated gun, or electric weapon unless such is in the presence of, and under the supervision of an adult who acts with consent of one of the minor's parents. It is a second degree misdemeanor for the adult to knowingly and willfully permit such possession. Since a BB technically meets the definition of Airsoft – it includes these totally non-weapons, as well! Just plain stupid! Change the statute to exclude Airsoft! At worst, they sting, and leave a little red mark (unless you shoot someone in the eye).

If it's a firearm, then it's illegal for a minor under 18 years to possess it unless:

a.   Engaged in lawful hunting, and is
      1.   At least 16 years old, or
      2.   Under 16, and is supervised by adult

b.   Engaged in lawful recreational shooting or marksmanship, and is
      1.   At least 16 years, or
      2.   Under 16 and supervised by adult acting with consent of minor's parent or guardian.

c.   Firearm is unloaded, and being transported by minor directly to or from an event authorized by this statute.

d.   Firearm is unloaded, and possessed at child's home.

CHART OF PENALTIES FOR CHILD VIOLATIONS:

Any parent, guardian, or other adult who is responsible for the minor who knowingly and willfully permits the minor to have a firearm in violation of this section — commits a third degree felony! The other possible penalty for minors and parents are in the following chart:

WITH FIREARM	Type offense	Sentence to jail	community service	weapon	driver license
first offense	misd.	up to 3 days	minimum 100 hours	forfeit	up to 1 year loss
second offense	3d felony	up to 15 days	100 -250 hours	forfeit	up to 2 year loss
1st offense & a crime	1st misd.	15 days minimum	minimum 100 hours	forfeit	up to 1 year loss
2d offense & a crime	3d felony	21 days minimum	100 - 250 hours	forfeit	up to 2 year loss
adult in charge	knowingly and willfully permits child to possess firearm in violation of law is third degree felony.				
parent or guardian	same as above, except may also be required to attend parenting classes, and do community service with child.				
VIOLATIONS WHERE AIRGUN OR ELECTRIC WEAPON ONLY					
child	possible delinquency proceeding under F.S. 985				
adult in charge	second degree misdemeanor				

OTHER PENALTIES:

Other recent additions to the statute (F.S. 790.22) permit a child who is taken into custody for possession of a firearm on school property to be detained for up to 21 days for psychological, drug, and medical examination in the discretion of the court. A further addition is that when the violation involves underage possession of a firearm, and a separate violation of another criminal statute — community control can be imposed, and the court may also order the parents or guardians of the child to pay restitution for any damage caused, unless the parents/guardians can show they made a diligent and good faith effort to prevent such conduct.

In closing, what this law doesn't say, is it's obvious that a number of weapons can be possessed by a child under sixteen (16) without supervision -- if they have permission to have the weapon in the first place. Those would include everything but firearms, BB & air guns, and electric weapons. Thus, knives, hatchets, machetes, bows, etc. -- are otherwise legal if not concealed, are obtained with permission of the parent, and are not possessed by the child at a school, school grounds, school bus, school bus stops, or otherwise in violation of any of the laws pertaining to schools, school sponsored events, school bus stops, and school buses.

QUESTION: So, can I buy my kid an air rifle if he is 12 years old?

ANSWER: Sure. But if you let him use it or possess it when you or another adult is not around (until the age of 16 years) -- you're guilty of a misdemeanor.

QUESTION: What if he's 16 years old.

ANSWER: That changes things a little. Now he can possess and use the airgun without supervision.

QUESTION: What about a real rifle -- a 22 caliber?

ANSWER: Well, from 16 until 18 years — he can have it unloaded at home. If he's taking it anywhere, it must be kept unloaded, and be in transport directly to or from lawful recreational shooting, or lawful hunting. Nowhere else! If you let him do otherwise — you've committed a felony!

143

QUESTION: What if my wife and I disagree? She says "no" -- I say "yes".

ANSWER: Your kid can have the weapon or firearm, but your wife will make both your lives miserable.

QUESTION: So, if I can buy it -- can he keep it in his room?

ANSWER: Yes, if it is unloaded, and is not a handgun.

QUESTION: What about a hunting knife, or bow and arrows?

ANSWER: If a parent, or guardian allows the child to have it -- the child may have it at any age: 3, 5, 10, 14 years old -- whatever age they allow. Once the child reaches 18 years of age -- the "child" can purchase any type of weapon, on his own, including handguns -- but cannot purchase the handgun from a federally licensed dealer until 21.

QUESTION: What if the kid wants a weapon, and the wife and I refuse to give permission.

ANSWER: If a parent or guardian doesn't give permission, then the child cannot legally obtain any weapon, other than a common pocketknife, until he reaches 18 years of age.

QUESTION: What happens at 18 years of age?

ANSWER: The "child" becomes an "adult", for most purposes, and may legally buy any weapon, including a handgun, although he cannot buy a handgun from a federally licensed dealer.

QUESTION: What if his grandfather bequeathed him an antique handgun?

ANSWER: Interesting question. It appears that this was an inadvertent loophole left by both Florida and Federal legislators. An "antique firearm" is not a "firearm" unless being used in the commission of a crime. Even the definition of a "handgun" under federal law must still be a "firearm", thus excluding antique firearms. It's obviously not a BB gun or air gun. It's not a "firearm". I guess it's OK for the kid to have it until somebody gets around to changing the law, so long as it's given to the child with the permission of a parent. Still, you could become a "test case" on this one.

STORAGE OF LOADED FIREARMS:

In this day and age, it should be easy to keep firearms away from children -- but anyone who has been around kids can testify that they can get into anything -- sometimes so fast, it's scary. In order to cut your losses, the Legislature has enacted laws making it a crime to leave a <u>loaded</u> gun accessible to children under the age of <u>16 years</u> except under certain circumstances. F.S. 790.174(3). If it's unloaded -- you don't have to worry about these statutes.[164]   Thus, the storing of a <u>loaded</u> firearm within the reach or easy access of a minor child under the age of sixteen, where the person knows, or should know, the minor is <u>likely</u> to gain access to it without lawful permission or supervision is a felony of the third degree if the minor obtains the loaded firearm and uses it to inflict injury or death upon himself or any other person.[165] If no injury occurs, but the minor still gains access to the loaded firearm -- it's a second degree misdemeanor -- only if the minor unlawfully possesses it in a public place, or displays it anywhere, in a "rude, careless, angry, or threatening manner". Of course, if the child was in presence and under the supervision of an adult, at the time (and it's one of our wonderful federally permitted activities), it's also fine, unless the adult was otherwise culpably negligent under F.S. 784.05

You should know that this law would not impose criminal liability when the firearm was stored in a securely locked box/container, or in a location which a <u>reasonable person</u> would believe to be secure, or if the firearm had a trigger lock, or mounted firearm combination lock.   It also would not apply if the person who left the firearm should not have <u>reasonably known</u> that a minor was likely to gain access to the firearm without the permission or supervision of a parent or person having charge of the minor, or if it resulted from an unlawful entry by any person. And, if the firearm is being carried by an adult on his body, or within such proximity to his person that he could retrieve, and use it as easily and quickly as if he carried it on his body ("readily accessible for immediate use") -- it's also legal. Of course, the big loophole here (probably done intentionally) is: if the child doesn't take possession of the firearm – it's not a crime, at all.

QUESTION: What if my sister's kids come over, and I'm a bachelor. I always keep my gun in a bureau by my bed?

ANSWER: Assuming they don't sneak in the back door, and you have time to take some security precautions, it may be reasonable to contemplate that the kids may go searching around. Thus, unloading the weapon, putting on a trigger lock, or locking it in a container -- instantly take you off the hook. If you want to be a bit riskier it becomes a jury question of whether you acted reasonably, or not. Obviously, if they get hold of the gun -- you have a potential legal problem.

QUESTION: What if I'm driving my kids in the car, and I've got my loaded gun in a closed console next to me.

ANSWER: In my opinion, you're legal as long as you're in the vehicle, you're in the driver's seat, and the console is closed.   That's because the statute exempts situations where you are carrying the firearm on your body, "or within such close proximity thereto that he can retrieve and use it as easily and quickly as if he carried it on his body." <u>F.S.</u> 790.174(1).

CIVIL LIABILITY IF THE KIDS GET TO IT:

If a child under the age of 18 years willfully or recklessly destroys or injures the property of another -- the parent or parents he lives with are legally responsible for the actual amount of damages the child causes. This is pursuant to F.S. 741.24. If you were also found negligent in leaving the firearm in a place where a child could reasonably have been anticipated to get hold of it -- you are probably going to be held civilly liable for any damages caused by that child's use of the firearm -- including the death or injury of somebody else. Conceivably, you might even be subject to a manslaughter or culpable negligence prosecution.

Obviously, the way to get around this is to buy one of the many devices available to keep a loaded gun ready for use -- but safe. There are a number of small gun boxes or safes that have a keypad lock that opens electronically by pushing a combination of push buttons. Since it can be opened by "feeling" the buttons -- it can be accessed in total darkness, right next to your bed. If you have kids -- this is really what you need. I've seen these for thirty five to ninety bucks in catalogs, on the internet at Harbor Freight Tools, at gun stores, and even some office supply stores. I own them, and think they're great.

If you want a full size gun locker -- they're available at almost any sporting goods store, gun shops, gun shows, locksmiths, and even at Wal-Mart. Prices range from really cheap -- to really expensive, and fit all purposes and pocketbooks. Not a bad idea since the majority of illegal guns are stolen by teenagers during burglaries from honest owners just like you. Then the guns are used against the rest of us. Be responsible -- make sure your guns are safe from kids -- and safe from theft.

As far as trigger locks go — I am not a great believer in them, as I think a lock box, or gun safe is far superior. To me, a trigger lock is solely a "storage solution", and not a very good one. A stored gun doesn't have to be loaded — and shouldn't be. Moreover, if you have a trigger lock on a self-defense gun — you are going to be dead before you get it unlocked. There are some recent improvements on "electronically keyed", and other push-button mechanisms installed directly on the gun such a "Safe-T-Lock" mechanism — but if that's your answer to keeping the gun where it can be found — I think you need a better solution.

GUN FREE SCHOOL ZONES ACT -- PART TWO:
Well, just as I promised, we're back in federal land. Congress has a bad habit of passing laws that should really be reserved for the decision of the individual states. I already described in the first chapter how the United States Supreme Court decided that this law was unconstitutional, but Congress didn't really care about such minor problems, and reenacted it, again. The reenacted law, 18 USC 922(q), has been upheld by at least two federal appellate courts. Pierson, 139 F.3d 501 (5th Cir. 1998); Danks, 221 F.3d 1037 (8th Cir. 1999). A later Supreme Court case seems to reassert the invalidity of the law, but the federal appeal courts seem to be ignoring it. Morrison, 146 L.ed.2d 658 (2000).[166] Anyway, here's how this law works:

In brief, the law [18 USC 922(q)] makes it a federal crime punishable by up to five years imprisonment to knowingly possess a firearm in a "school zone" unless you meet certain exceptions. A "school zone" is defined as the grounds of any public, private, or parochial elementary or secondary school — or within 1000 feet of such. The exceptions are any of the following:

1.   You've got a concealed permit
2.   The gun is not loaded, and is in a locked container , or locked firearm rack in a motor vehicle
3.   You're on private property, not part of the school
4.   It's for use in a program approved by a school in the school zone (not necessarily at the school)
5.   You're a security guard under contract with a school in the school zone
6.   You're a law enforcement officer acting as such
7.   The gun is unloaded, and you're traversing school grounds for the purpose of legal access to hunting land, if the school authority has authorized such.

Great reason to have a CWP, isn't it?

FLORIDA SCHOOL ZONE LAWS:
In 1997 the legislature passed another law[167] affecting school type situations which amended F.S. 790.115. It sounds something like the federal law we just discussed, but has very few similarities when

you fully examine it. You should be aware that it has two key sections that are very dissimilar -- one devoted to unlawful "display" of firearms and other weapons, and another devoted to mere "possession". A violation of either is a third degree felony unless you are a concealed permit holder. There is a third section that deals with unlawful discharge of weapons which is a second degree felony. Anyway — here's how it works:

The first subsection (1) deals with <u>unlawful exhibition</u> of weapons and firearms, and <u>does not</u> pertain to mere possession. It makes it illegal to <u>display</u> any sword, sword cane, firearm, electric weapon, destructive device, or other weapon including a razor blade, box cutter, or any knife, including "common pocketknife" in a "rude, careless, angry, or threatening manner, not in lawful self-defense, and in the presence of one or more persons:

1.   On the grounds or facilities of any school
2.   On any school bus stop
3.   On any school bus
4.   At any school sponsored event (even off school property)
5.   Or, within <u>1000 feet</u> of the grounds of any elementary, middle, or secondary school

where such occurs: (a) during school hours, or (b) during the time a school sanctioned school activity takes place. This section does not apply to exhibition of a firearm or weapon <u>on private property</u> within 1000 feet of school grounds if such is done by the owner, or by a person who has been authorized, licensed, or invited by the owner to his property.

Subsection (2) of this statute deals with mere possession, and forbids a person from "willfully and knowingly" possessing any firearm, electric weapon, destructive device, or other weapon, including a razor blade, box cutter, or knife (excluding common pocketknives), except as authorized in support of school sanctioned activities, <u>on the property</u> of any school, school bus stop, school sponsored event, or school bus. The definition of a school is expanded to include preschool, elementary, middle, junior high, secondary, post secondary, and vocational schools -- public or private -- which means everything! There is also no restriction as to time of day. In other words, it doesn't matter whether the school is in session, or not. Fortunately, this subsection does not include the "1000 foot" prohibition. Therefore, so long as you're at least one inch off the school grounds, and you've merely got a weapon on you -- this section of the statute does not apply.

A problem with this subsection is when you have a preschool in a church or temple, or other building. Obviously, when the preschool is in session — you can't possess a weapon in the preschool area — but what about areas of the building not used for preschool activity? What about when the preschool isn't in session? What about an adult education course at a church, temple, business, or other community center?

My best guess on an interpretation (since there currently is none) is that if the area used for preschool is regularly and equally used for other unrelated purposes — it would lose its character as a preschool when the preschool activities were completed for the day. Moreover, those areas of the premises that were not used for preschool activity would not be covered by this law. My best guess on any adult education would be that unless the area is used primarily for regular instruction, it would not qualify as a "school", but would merely be an "area" where instruction takes place. Again, these are my interpretations based purely on common sense, and could be interpreted differently by the courts. Test case time!

As to the exceptions to subsection (2) which would still permit lawful possession of a firearm or a weapon (not unlawfully display), here they are:

1.   To a firearms program, class, or function that has been approved in advance by the principal or chief administrative officer of the school

2.   To a vocational school having a firearms training range

3.   In a vehicle pursuant to F.S. 790.25(5) — ie: securely encased or not readily accessible. However, you should know that the legislature made a very bad mistake here, and receded somewhat from our "preemption" law[168] by

permitting a school district to adopt written and published policies that waive this exemption for purposes of student and campus parking privileges. In State v. Ragland, 789 So.2d 530 (5DCA 2001), the Fifth District Court of Appeal held that any waiver must be very specific to be effective, and that a college or vocation school might not be able to legally enforce a waiver as they are not technically part of any "school district". Under any circumstance, a waiver would not affect a vehicle that was merely dropping off a person vs. actually "parking", and there is an unresolved legal question whether temporary parking by persons other than students, faculty, and campus employees legally falls within the ambit of such a waiver. Test case time!

4.   The penalties of this subsection do not apply to concealed permit holders (although the prohibitions do). Instead, permit holders are punished as provided in F.S. 790.06(12), which makes a violation of that particular subsection of 790.06 a second degree misdemeanor -- except that a license holder who unlawfully discharges a weapon or firearm on school property as prohibited by this subsection commits a second degree felony. As I stated in the chapter on concealed permits — a possible but not suggested interpretation would allow concealed carry by a permit holder on school "grounds" but not school buildings or structures inasmuch as "facility" is normally defined as a building or structure.[169] Still, this definition is probably pushing the legal envelope, and I think a court could interpret this differently. I therefore strongly advise against using this interpretation, as it isn't worth being a "test case".

The third section of this statute deals with the discharge of a weapon or firearm while in violation of the possession prohibitions of this section, unless discharged in lawful self defense, or for other lawful purpose. As previously stated, such is a second degree felony.

A fourth section of the statute deals with safe storage of firearms, and really is a duplication of F.S. 790.174 with some gloss. We already covered it when we discussed that statute.

A subsection of F.S. 790.22 also provides that a child who possesses a firearm on school property may be held for up to 21 days for observation and treatment

QUESTION: OK, I'm a law-abiding citizen walking down the street with my self-defense chemical spray legally clipped to the outside of my purse. I suddenly see a school, 999 feet away. I had no idea it was there before this. Am I now guilty of a felony?

ANSWER: No. Only if the display is rude, careless, angry, or threatening — and done in the presence of another person. Still, you can now see why this is such a bad law. If you were adjusting the spray bottle, and someone saw you -- and told a police officer -- would he think this was "careless"? If he did, you could be arrested for a felony! You'd probably win your case -- but who would want to be in that kind of predicament? This is a really dangerous law, and I suggest you write your state legislators to remove it.

QUESTION: I am a teacher. I have always kept my firearm locked in my car so I have it available when I leave. I drive through some dangerous areas. Can this now be forbidden?

ANSWER: Yes. If the school district (not the principal) actually passes, adopts, and publishes a written policy forbidding you to park on school property — you commit a felony by doing so, so long as you did so "knowingly and willfully".

QUESTION: What if my wife drops me off in the school parking lot, and such a published policy exists? Can we still have a firearm or weapon in the car securely encased or not readily accessible?

ANSWER: Only securely encased. Otherwise, the school district may not restrict anything but actual parking privileges in the sense of leaving a vehicle unattended.

QUESTION: What about the federal restrictions? Doesn't this forbid mere possession within 1000 feet of any school zone?

ANSWER: Very perceptive question. The answer, assuming the law is constitutional, is "yes". Only a concealed permit holder, school security guard, or police officer is going to be able to get within 1000 feet of an elementary or secondary school. However, since only a federal officer is going to make an arrest for this — I wouldn't worry too much   unless you are dealing drugs, robbing a bank, or blowing something up. Better yet, get a concealed permit as it exempts you from the federal law.

QUESTION: I take my child to his bus stop. This is not a great section of town. I carry pepper spray for protection. What can I do to protect myself?

ANSWER: Stay at least "one foot" away from the school bus stop — assuming you can figure out the boundaries of it. Also, write your legislator to revise the statute so that it only pertains to persons under 18 years of age, and those who are actually students using that bus stop. That would also take care of the problem the Legislature was trying to cure.

TRAINING CHILDREN TO BE SAFE:
Most accidents happen due to either ignorance, carelessness, or a combination of both factors. The way to counter these dangers is to train children what to do when they see a firearm. The approved method by the NRA is to teach a child who sees a firearm to do the following:

a.   Don't touch the firearm.
b.   Leave the area.
c.   Immediately tell an adult

This is a great rule, and should also apply to ammunition, and to any toy guns that look real. I don't like the idea of a toy gun that looks real being anywhere near my house -- because the guns I own are real -- and some of the smaller calibers, especially a derringer, <u>look</u> like a toy! I don't want my kid to think it's O.K. to play with something that might be a gun, or could be confused with a toy. Guns are for adults who have been trained in their handling, and for responsible "young adults" who have adult supervision, and training. Guns are dangerous. Only training prevents accidents. Think about it. Maybe you'll stop a disaster!

By the way, the next page has a chart related to possession and display near schools, school bus stops, school sponsored events, and on school buses. It's not as detailed as the chapter, but it's a great shorthand tool to use.

CHART RELATED TO POSSESSION NEAR SCHOOL:

POSSESSION IN SCHOOL AREA UNDER FLORIDA LAW — F.S. 790.115			
when prohibited	where prohibited	weapons prohibited	conduct prohibited
school hours or during school sanctioned activity	school grounds/building school sponsored event school bus school bus stop 1000 feet of grounds	any weapon/gun any knife any razor blade any box cutter	rude, angry, careless, or threatening display within presence of at least one person
	school grounds school bus school bus stop school sponsored event		possession
exceptions:			
lawful self defense	private property if owner or invitee	mere possession with principal's pre-approval to class where firearms allowed, or vocational school with gun range	securely encased or not readily accessible in vehicle
SAFE SCHOOL ZONE ACT — 18 USC 922 (q)			
any time	1000 feet of school grounds	any firearm	knowing possession
exceptions:			
concealed permit	on private property not part of school grounds	firearm unloaded in locked container or locked firearms rack in vehicle	law enforcement in official capacity
unloaded & OK'd to cross grounds to get access to hunting area open to public	for use in program pre-approved by the school.	security guard or other person acting pursuant to contract with school	

(this page reserved)

CHAPTER NINE

DEALERS, FFL's & INSTRUCTORS

I'm sure there are lots of things that licensed firearms dealers, and other weapons dealers should know. I'm also sure they probably know most of them by heart. On the other hand, since I defend these citizens in state and federal prosecutions, and in ATF licensing revocations, I know they can obviously make mistakes, too. Since that's happened more than once, I think it might be a good idea to cover some of the issues and questions that seem to come up, over and over again. As a general rule this chapter is devoted primarily to licensed firearms dealers, rather than collectors, manufacturers, and importers -- but I'll make some exceptions from time to time. Plus, I guarantee that some of the answers will prove very interesting to everyone.

Before getting into details, if you are an FFL (Federal Firearms Licensee) or are thinking about it — you really should have computer access to the web, and regularly visit the ATF website. It now has comic-book style instructional courses on typical over-the-counter transactions, and a host of other features. [http://www.atf.gov] Moreover, anyone who works in the firearms trade needs to download or order the Federal Firearms Regulations Reference Guide. This is the "bible" of firearms dealers and their employees. It should be read and outlined at least twice a year by every FFL, and their employees. If you don't — you'll likely be needing my legal services, sooner or later. Anyway, back to the book:

WHO MUST SECURE A FEDERAL LICENSE:
Any person or business entity (corporation or partnership) that has as its principal objective, from the sale or transfer of firearms, the goal of livelihood and profit -- needs to be federally licensed. The main question in defining this profit motive is predominantly one of obtaining pecuniary gain and livelihood, as opposed to other interests such as improving or liquidating a personal collection. If all you're

doing is making an occasional sale to thin your collection, or make room for some other purchases, or even to liquidate your entire collection, you don't need a federal license. If it's as a business -- you better have an FFL, or you are in deep buffalo chips.

The main problem area here is not dealers, it's when people set-up tables at gun shows who are not licensed dealers. I've also seen it where dealer's are dealing out of their "private collections". If this becomes a "business" – be forewarned – ATF is watching!

WHAT DOES THE LICENSE COVER:
Well, in a nutshell, it allows you to purchase and ship firearms/ammunition to and fro to any other FFL, no matter where they are located -- and otherwise engage in the business of buying and selling firearms, as a business. It also allows you to rent or loan firearms for temporary lawful sporting purposes.   It does not allow you to sell/transfer out-of-state to a non-licensee, unless the firearm is delivered from your actual business location to another FFL in the receiving state, or the sale is a rifle or shotgun sold in a face-to-face transaction where the sale is legal in both states.   If you are at a gun show, I've covered that in the upcoming "question and answer" section, since it's somewhat complicated.   Anyway, since it's easier explaining most of this in a question-and-answer format, here goes:

QUESTION: As an FFL, can I purchase from a non-licensee in another state when I'm not at a gun show?

ANSWER: Yes, so long as the purchase is transported back to your business premises in your home state, and logged into your records.[170]

QUESTION: What about a sale to a non-resident from my business premises?

ANSWER: You may sell any non-NFA firearm to a non-resident so long as the firearm is shipped from your licensed premises to another FFL in the purchaser's home state, where the purchaser will take delivery.   If it's a rifle or shotgun in a face-to-face sale made in your state either at your licensed premises or a gun show — then you may also sell and deliver the firearm in your home state so long as the sale complies with the law of both your state, and the purchaser's state, and federal law.

QUESTION: What about at a gun show?

ANSWER: If you're selling at a show <u>outside of your state of licensure</u> to a non-resident, even if an FFL, you can only take orders and money, but then you must ship from your licensed premises to an FFL in the purchaser's state, assuming it's legal in the purchaser's state. You cannot transfer the firearm at the gun show, even to an FFL. The one exception is that you may sell and deliver a curio or relic to any FFL, anywhere. 27 CFR 178.50. You may purchase from anyone.

If the gun show is <u>in your state</u>, then you may sell and deliver to any FFL, even if the FFL is from out-of-state. You may obviously sell to any resident who is not a prohibited person. You may sell and deliver a shotgun or rifle to any out-of- state resident where the sale is legal in both states (plus any applicable waiting period). You may take orders and money from any out-of-state resident on a handgun, but may only deliver it to an FFL in the purchaser's state. You may purchase from anyone.

QUESTION: Can I carry a firearm pursuant to my FFL?

ANSWER: This is not covered by federal law, and is completely a state law issue. In Florida, this is covered by <u>F.S.</u> 790.25(3)(i), which permits a dealer, or employee, to carry while engaged in the "lawful course of such business." This would not permit an employee under the age of

18 years to carry or even possess firearms in such a business pursuit due to the prohibitions in F.S. 790.22.

CONFUSION WITH CORPORATE OWNERSHIP:

If you have taken your FFL as a corporation — the "corporation" is the FFL — not you. You are simply an employee, officer, or whatever. If this is the situation, you cannot treat the inventory as your personal property, because it's not — it's the corporation's. Thus, any firearm obtained must be logged into the acquisition portion of the bound book, and if taken home by you, it better be logged out to you on the disposition portion of the bound book, with a 4473 — or you have violated federal criminal and administrative law.

If you have personal firearms on display at the store, they must be tagged "not for sale", should probably also be tagged as your personal property, and be segregated from the rest of the corporate inventory so there is no confusion. They actually have to be logged into the bound book because they considered are a "loan" of the firearm to the FFL, and when you take them back — must be logged out, with a 4473. A multiple disposition form is unnecessary as it is not a sale, but merely return of property — somewhat similar to a gun at a pawn shop.

Remember, that if you take a gun out of inventory, and you are not the actual FFL because the corporation is the FFL, you are a mere private citizen in the eye's of the law as far as transfer and purchase of firearms goes. I strongly recommend that both you, and any employee be required to obtain and read the "Federal Firearms Reference Guide" which is available free from BATF in book form, or can be downloaded from their website at www.atf.gov. This publication is a review of the statutes, regulations, and questions most asked by dealers about the business. Moreover, the website now has some on-line training on typical firearm transactions in comic book form. Each segment takes about ten minutes or less to go through. Anyone who works at an FFL should be required to review these before participating in any transactions!

LICENSED COLLECTORS:

The only reason anyone would want to be a licensed collector is if you want to buy, sell, and transport curios and relics, out of your residence state. Other than as to curios and relics -- you are treated exactly as a non-licensee.

A relic is a firearm manufactured at least 50 years previous, and it cannot be a replica, but must be the real thing. A curio must be certified by BATF as curio due to it being novel, rare, bizarre, or connected to a historical event. Before it becomes a "curio", a specified procedure must be followed.

OBTAINING THE FFL:

If you want to become a dealer, assuming you are 21 years of age, and otherwise qualify, you can get the application from your local office of the Bureau of Alcohol, Tobacco, Firearms, and Explosives -- usually referred to as "ATF", or download it from their website at www.atf.gov/firearms. Before your application will be accepted you should have a "place of business" to operate as an FFL (ie: Federal Firearms Licensee). The location must be a permitted use under state and local law -- which means that if you're zoned only for residential -- you better find another location if you want a license. Since your home is probably not zoned for firearms sale or storage -- it is doubtful it would qualify unless you are applying as a gunsmith. Moreover, unless you are a gunsmith, the portion of the premises used for your business must be "open to the public" -- and I doubt you want people walking in and out of your home during regular business hours, or have ATF agents nosing around while administrative and records searches are conducted there. Last, do not use a "cover" address for your license, and then work from your home, as your license wouldn't cover the transaction. U.S. v. Bailey, 123 F.3d 1381 (11th Cir. 1997). Thus, in the Bailey case, the 11th Circuit held that where the sale was made from the FFL's home, rather than the actual business address listed on the FFL, he committed the crime of "dealing without a license" as the FFL only covered the business address, not the home.

DENIAL OF APPLICATION:

Once you apply, your application will be approved or denied within sixty (60) days of submission, unless the application was deficient. If so, you'll be given thirty (30) days to correct it, and send it back. On those rare occasions where no approval or denial is obtained within the 60 day review period -- there is a way to force a decision under federal statute 28 USC 1361. This procedure will not be discussed in this book. Assuming your application is denied, the ATF Regional Director will issue you a Form 4498 denial, and you will then have fifteen (15) days to request a hearing to review the denial. If you don't request the hearing your application is disapproved, so marked, and returned to you. All notices are sent certified mail, return receipt requested -- and you should do likewise, although you are not under that same obligation.

The Regional Director must then give you at least ten (10) days written notice of the hearing date, and it must be held at a location convenient to you -- generally at the nearest regional office vs. Washington, D.C. If the denial stands -- a certified copy of the findings and conclusions are furnished to you on a Form 4501, which is marked as "disapproved".

If you're not real pleased with the result, you can still go another step. You then have sixty (60) days to file a petition for review with the United States District Court in your area, pursuant to the federal statute, 18 USC 923(f)(3), for a de novo judicial review of the denial.

PROCEDURE ON REVOCATION OF FFL:

If the Regional Director has reason to believe that you, or an employee, have willfully violated the requirements of the Gun Control Act of 1968, and any of the regulations you must operate by, he or she may revoke your license by mailing the licensee, by certified mail return receipt requested, a notice of revocation on a Form 4500. This factually states the violations.

At that point, you have fifteen (15) days to request (in writing) a hearing to review the revocation, otherwise the Regional Director will issue a final notice on Form 4501. If you do request a hearing, the

Regional Director, in the interest of justice, may postpone the effective date of revocation, or authorize continued operations pending judicial review. The administrative hearing procedure, and judicial review are the same as followed when an application for the FFL is denied. I suggest you get an attorney experienced in dealing with ATF if you get the letter, ASAP. You can and should request the hearing be held in your local.

If you are unlucky enough to be indicted for a felony, or crime punishable by more than two years imprisonment, or have had a criminal information filed against you for such, you may continue to operate until any conviction becomes final. Even then, you may apply to the Secretary of the Treasury for relief from disabilities if it's established that you are not likely to act in manner dangerous to public safety, and that such relief would not be contrary to the public interest.

If you are convicted of the felony, you may still file for removal of disability to operate as an FFL due to said conviction. If so, you are allowed to operate for thirty (30) days after the date of which conviction becomes final. If you don't file for this relief you must stop operating once the thirty (30) days after the date of the conviction runs.

If you were acquitted of the felony charges, or they are otherwise terminated by dismissal, ATF may not try to revoke your FFL for same reasons.

ADMINISTRATIVE REVIEW OF RECORDS AND INVENTORY:
Any licensee is subject to administrative audit of your books, records, and inventory. Unless it is pursuant to a search warrant, it will be done during normal business hours. You have no right to interfere, and should keep out of the agents way. If you think something is improper, mentally note it for review with your attorney at a later date. Do not play "big shot". It will only cause you trouble. Here is the way it works:

ATF may have a judicial magistrate issue a warrant upon "reasonable cause" to believe violation of the firearms law has occurred, and that evidence of such may be on business premises or other storage area. The warrant allows inspection of all records required to be kept, and all firearms & ammo kept on premises.

ATF agents may also inspect <u>without</u> reasonable cause, and <u>without</u> a warrant where:

1.   Such is done in the course of reasonable inquiry during a criminal investigation of someone other than the FFL.

2.   To ensure compliance with record   keeping requirements, but not more than once in any 12 month period. However, the licensee may elect to conduct this inquiry at the local ATF office, rather than on the business premises.

3.   To determine the disposition of one or more particular firearms in course of bona fide criminal investigation.

If any records are seized, the BATF officer may seize only those records that constitute evidence of a violation, and copies must be provided within a reasonable time to licensee.

<u>SALE OF FIREARMS/AMMUNITION TO LEGAL ALIENS:</u>
Although somewhat confusing, it is legal for a firearms dealer to sell firearms or ammunition to a <u>resident</u> alien. The alien must have been a legal resident in the state of purchase for a "continuous" ninety (90) days prior to the sale for firearms, and not otherwise be a "prohibited person" under federal law. Ammo may be purchased anywhere if the resident alien has 90 days continuous residence anywhere in the United States. While visiting or traveling within the U.S.A. does not break actual residency – any travel outside the U.S. "breaks" the residency period, and it must start anew, as the FBI and ATF check immigration records for firearm sales. Under any circumstance, the "90 day" proof will still be required for purchase.

<u>NON-IMMIGRANT ALIENS:</u>
Non-immigrant aliens are treated differently under the statutes and rules as they are generally a "prohibited person" unless they fall under an exception. They are non-citizens who are normally merely

visiting the United States, or are going to school here. These individuals are generally prohibited from purchasing or possessing firearms or ammunition in the United States due to the passage of the Omnibus Appropriations Act of 1999.[171] (See, 18 USC 922(g) & (y)) This excludes from purchase/possession students, and most temporary visitors except some narrow exemptions. The prohibition even prevents temporary use at a range unless they have a valid hunting license or qualify under another exception. Like a resident alien, a non-immigrant alien's "90 continuous days" is the period "immediately prior" to the purchase. [ATF Ruling 2004-1] However, if the non-immigrant alien leaves the country for even a day, start the 90 day period anew.

There is a rather complicated waiver procedure which exists, which is beyond this book. There are also exceptions for aliens specifically admitted into in the country for hunting or sporting purposes, those here for competitive target shooting competitions, those here to display firearms at a trade show sponsored by a firearms organization, foreign law enforcement officers here on official business, and official representatives of friendly foreign governments. I would check with ATF before doing a sale to one of these exempted non-immigrant aliens because official proof of this status would have to be attached to the Form 4473. The web site has a fairly detailed explanation.

Assuming the non-immigrant alien fits any of these exemptions, such as having a current hunting license (which can be from any state — not just Florida) he or she can obtain a temporary rental of a firearm from an FFL, but may not purchase a firearm unless he or she has been a resident of the state of purchase for at least 90 continuous days immediately prior to the sale, and they have an INS alien number or admission number. An exception would be a purchase for export where the firearm would be exported directly from the premises of the FFL after obtaining an export license from the feds. By the way — a Concealed Weapons Permit does not permit possession or purchase by a non-immigrant alien.

PROOF OF RESIDENCY:
Assuming the person is a resident alien, or otherwise qualifies under the exemptions for non-immigrant aliens — then such person to purchase a firearm must generally furnish copies of certain types of

proof which should be noted on the Form 4473. This includes rent receipts, utility bills, or similar to show the 90 day residence in the state of purchase, government issued photo identification, and must furnish their INS issued alien number, or alien admission number [INS Form I-94 or INS Form I-94W].

Any alien may purchase a firearm if he is not taking possession of the weapon in the United States. Thus, sale for export is allowable once the export permit is obtained.

PERMANENT BRADY LAW PROVISIONS:
Since Florida has an instantaneous record check procedure, we do not have a mandated federal waiting period. However, the Florida Constitution requires a three (3) day waiting period on sales of all handguns unless the purchaser is the holder of a valid Florida concealed weapons permit, or the purchase is a trade for another handgun. Fla. Const., Art. 1, section 8. Thus, there is no state-wide required waiting period for a rifle or shotgun. Whenever the purchaser is a Concealed Permit holder, you need to note his permit number on the Form 4473.

The Florida Constitution was changed in 1998, and a county may now pass an ordinance requiring up to a five (5) day waiting period on sales of any firearm to non-permit holders on public property -- ie: gun shows. This will vary county-to-county. Concealed Permit holders are not affected. The constitutional change was a completely dupe on the Florida public, allegedly to "close the loophole" on a non-existent myriad of illegal gun show sales. Another reason never to vote for a constitutional amendment! Even if there was a problem, the exact same thing could have been accomplished by passage of a statute — but there wasn't any problem, and the anti-gun lobby couldn't get it through the legislature, so they spent money frightening the public, and got it passed as a constitutional amendment. Now, we're all stuck with it, forever.

SALES OR DISPOSITIONS FROM PERSONAL COLLECTION:
First, I repeat my previous words of warning about an issue that seems to get confused far too many times -- if you are selling firearms as a business, and the business is in the form of corporate

ownership -- no individual is the "FFL" -- instead, the "corporation" is the FFL. Thus, any firearm you obtain from the business inventory that goes off-premises must be logged out to you in the disposition book just like any other disposition, together with a Form 4473, and NICS check. This applies equally to any employee, manager, corporate officer, or stockholder. On the other hand, if the business really is in your personal name, then you (and only you) may take firearms out of the business inventory, and off-premises without doing NICS or the Form 4473, and even add them to your "personal collection", so long as you have marked them into your FFL disposition book.

If you are then selling or transferring a firearm from your "personal collection" that you obtained from your business inventory as the FFL, and a year has passed since taking possession -- you may sell or transfer the firearm as if it was your personal property without doing the Form 4473 or NICS check. However, you must log the disposition into a personal bound book, which you must keep for ATF. On the other hand, if the sale or disposition is prior to the year's time, then the firearm is treated, for ATF record-keeping purposes, as still being the property of the licensed business (ie: FFL), must be re-entered into the acquisition portion of your business records, and then into the disposition portion to record the transfer — plus, you need the Form 4473 and NICS.

If you purchased the firearm as a personal gun from anyone other than your own FFL, then sell it just like an individual, and forget having to enter it into your personal book, as it doesn't apply. Only firearms obtained from the business inventory fall into this "one year" period.

MULTIPLE HANDGUN SALES TO SINGLE INDIVIDUAL:
If you sell two or more **handguns** of any type to the same individual within five (5) consecutive business days, you must report it on a Form 3310.4 -- not later than close of business date of each such transaction. In other words, if the non-licensee buys two handguns on Monday -- you must file on Monday. If he buys another on Thursday, you must file another one, because it's now "three handguns" within five business days. The Brady law also requires reporting it to the state, or local law enforcement. 18 USC 923(3)(A).

If you somehow screwed-up by not reporting it when you should — you should still report it as soon as possible, and make sure the dates are accurate, even if that may cause some consternation with ATF. My advise to any client is that "better late than never" is a rule that must be followed in all instances where you missed something. Otherwise, your friends at ATF may feel that your mistake was "knowing and willful" rather than just oversight or stupidity. "Knowing and willful" is a very bad place to be with the feds. It makes for the creation of serious felony charges! And by the way – this particular violation is one of the easier ones to screw up if you're not careful, and one of the ones most likely to get you in trouble with ATF.

LOSS OR THEFT OF FIREARMS:

If any firearm is stolen or lost from your inventory or collection, it must be reported to ATF, and to local police within 48 hours on a Form 3310.4. Likewise, just having a firearm "missing" from inventory qualifies – even if you're sure you're gonna find it. Assuming you somehow screw-up the 48 hour reporting period, I strongly suggest you file the form, and report it, even if late. Filing the form is necessary because federal law has made theft of firearms from a federal licensee, a federal offense. [18 USC 922(u)] If you think you can find the firearm, and that it's only "misplaced" — you still only have the 48 hour period to find it, or report it. I guess you could call it a "47 hour" period. If you're unsure whether the firearm was "misplaced" vs. "stolen" -- report it as "lost", and not as stolen. That way if you or an employee made an innocent mistake, or if it was legally sold, and the paperwork was misplaced -- the police won't arrest someone found with the firearm. This will save you a very big lawsuit for negligence once your legal, but very ticked-off customer gets out of jail. ATF has determined that many times a "misplaced" gun was actually legally sold by the FFL, and there was a paperwork mix-up.

ANTIQUE FIREARMS:

In an earlier chapter I noted the differences between the current Florida definition of an antique firearm, and the federal definition. Then I noted that a new case, Bostic v. State, 902 So.2d 225 (Fla. 5DCA 2005), held that an antique firearm also had to be a "reasonably exact reproduction", of a firearm manufactured before 1918, etc., or it was still a "firearm" for all purposes, and not an "antique firearm". The case wrongly mentioned that plastic grips might be a factor in invalidating such a replica from being a "reasonably exact reproduction", and since this case screwed-up the definition of an "antique firearm", probably nobody knows what a "reasonably exact reproduction" is – until the Legislature changes Florida law to follow the federal.

Anyway, the problem nobody in the Fifth District realized was that if a muzzleloader wasn't an "antique firearm" – then Florida law requires the NICS background check and Form 4473 per F.S. 790.065. Moreover, if you're selling a muzzleloader that is not "a reasonably exact reproduction" at a gun show – you now may have a 3-5 day county "wait period" to contend with.

Tell your legislator to fix this mess. Just plain stupid!

PAWNBROKERS:
Pawnbrokers who buy, sell, transfer, or hold firearms as security for a loan must be federally licensed. While filling out the Form 4473 is not needed when the firearm is pledged for security, the receipt of such must still be entered into your bound volume. However, the Form 4473 must be completed when the firearm is redeemed -- as that is considered a "disposition" of the firearm. The NICS check must also be done.

On the other hand, if the disposition is to the same person who pledged the firearms with you, and more than one firearm is involved -- it need not be reported as a multiple sale on the Form 3310.4.

Even if the person who pledged the firearm is the same person seeking to redeem it -- it cannot be returned to an underaged person, or any other disqualified person, and should only be returned to person who pawned the firearm, or the ticket holder. If it's a handgun, you could not legally return it to an out-of-state resident, even if he was a Florida resident at the time of the pawn. Nor could you return it to him if he was under 21 years of age -- even if he was the person who legally pawned it.

SELLING TO PERSONS WITH OBVIOUS IMPAIRMENTS:
Several years ago K-Mart was ordered to pay $12.5 million dollars for selling a rifle to an intoxicated person, who then went out, and shot someone. Technically, this sale violated no law, although it came awful close. The problem was that the jury felt it was negligent to sell a firearm to an obviously intoxicated person, and most juries would probably agree. [172] This should warn you that if you sell to someone who appears mentally imbalanced, appears to be using illegal drugs (even marijuana), or appears to have had too much to drink -- don't make the sale unless you have a spare twelve-and-a-half million!

Florida law doesn't allow an intoxicated person to use a loaded firearm except in necessary self-defense. That means there's a loophole if it's unloaded. The loophole applies only to the criminal violation -- negligence and recklessness are still civilly actionable, and that's where the money is -- or will go. In sustaining that 12.5 million verdict, here's what the Florida Supreme Court said:

"One who knowingly sells an article to a person incompetent in its use, with reasonable foreseeability that injury to others may occur as a result of such use, can be held accountable in tort to others for the injuries sustained thereby."

If the guy gets drunk, or shoots cocaine after he buys the firearm, you should be off the legal hook -- unless you knew, or reasonably should have known that he was an alcoholic, incompetent, illegal drug user, or was planning to do something criminal. If you do -- you're in for lots of problems. So, be forewarned.

SELLING TO KIDS:
I know, we've been over this several times. It's easy when you talk about firearms -- 21 for a handgun -- 18 for a rifle or shotgun. But, what about other weapons?

Well, if the kid is 18 years old he can buy anything he wants from a dealer except a handgun, and illegal weapons. No permission needed.

If the kid is under 18 years of age -- you can't sell anything but a common pocketknife without the permission of mom or dad, and the sale (money exchange), and delivery should be with the parent, not with the kid. Don't be cute, and hand junior the purchase Dad just bought for him -- give it to Dad, and let him hand it to junior. If you don't take my warning, and you deliver a firearm, bowie knife, dirk, brass knuckles, or electronic weapon -- it's a second degree felony. [173] Any other weapon is a third degree felony. An airgun may be considered a weapon. Generally, that depends on its use, or intended use. I would say a bow and arrow is always a weapon, because that's what it was traditionally used for. But, why take the chance? Just sell the darn thing direct to Dad, and skip all the possible legal hassles.

Another quirk is that although you can sell a person under 21 years, but at least 18 years of age a shotgun or rifle — a shotgun with a pistol grip in lieu of a shoulder stock does not qualify as a "shotgun" because a shotgun, pursuant to 18 USC 921(a)(5) is a weapon "intended to be fired from the shoulder." When the shoulder stock is missing, it is no longer intended to be "fired from the shoulder", hence — it's not a shotgun. The legal way around this is to sell the gun with a shoulder stock. If done that way, even if the stock is not attached — the sale is legal. See, FFL Newsletter, February 1999, page 3. 27 CFR 478.99(b).

SALE OF AMMUNITION TO MINOR:
Florida law does not make it a crime for a non-federal licensee to sell ammunition to a minor. A federal licensee could not. However, the loophole has been somewhat covered in the 1994 Crime Bill by making it illegal for anyone to sell or transfer handgun ammunition to a juvenile under the age of 18 years, except under very precise exceptions. Thus, a federal licensee can't sell handgun ammunition to anyone under 21 years of age, and a private citizen can't sell it to anyone under 18 years of age.

As I already pointed out in a footnote, Wal-Mart got socked with a substantial civil jury verdict for causing the death of an individual because they sold handgun ammunition to an under-aged youth who then used it to shoot the decedent. The appellate court held that this was exactly the conduct that the federal statute tried to prevent, thus a violation of the statute was negligence, and the cause of the misfortune.

A warning to the wise is sufficient!

CHART ON PERMITTED WEAPON SALES TO MINOR:

under 18	only common pocketknife – sell anything else to guardian or parent only!
18	shotgun, rifle, any legal weapon except NFA or handgun.
21	any legal weapon or firearm

REQUIRED FLORIDA WARNING NOTICES UPON SALE:

It is a second degree misdemeanor for any retailer to fail to provide the following written warning in letters no less than 1/4 inch in height to the transferee when you sell or deliver a firearm.

> IT IS UNLAWFUL, AND PUNISHABLE BY IMPRISONMENT AND FINE, FOR ANY ADULT TO STORE OR LEAVE A FIREARM IN ANY PLACE WITHIN THE REACH OR EASY ACCESS OF A MINOR UNDER 18 YEARS OF AGE OR TO KNOW-INGLY SELL OR OTHERWISE TRANSFER OWNERSHIP OR POSSESSION OF A FIREARM TO A MINOR OR A PERSON OF UNSOUND MIND.

A similar warning must be posted at each purchase counter (including gun shows) in block letters at least 1" inch in height. This written warning must be given to the purchaser, even if he is 70 years old, has no kids, doesn't know any kids, and has no desire to. It must be in block letters at least one quarter inch high. If you think this is no big deal -- remember the verdict in K-Mart. What do you think a jury will do if some kid gets hold of the firearm, and the jerk who bought it from you says he didn't know he had to keep it in a safe place away from the child? I bet you can guess!

> IT IS UNLAWFUL TO STORE OR LEAVE A FIREARM IN ANY PLACE WITHIN THE REACH OR EASY ACCESS OF A MINOR UNDER 18 YEARS OF AGE OR TO KNOWINGLY SELL OR OTHERWISE TRANSFER OWNERSHIP OR POS-SESSION OF A FIREARM TO A MINOR OR PERSON OF UNSOUND MIND.

This means at gun shows, and at your place of business. True, it's only a second degree misdemeanor. But then, there's that silly verdict in K-Mart popping-up again. Get the point?

REQUIRED FEDERAL WARNINGS :
        Federal law also requires a posted notice both on the licensed premises, and at gun shows regarding the requirements of the Youth Safety Handgun Act. These posters are available through ATF, and repeat the restrictions set forth on ATF Form I 5300.2. You may order this through the ATF Distribution Center at (703) 455-7801, or download it through the web site. You must also deliver a copy of the form with every handgun delivered to any non-FFL. The form may be included within a brochure supplied by the manufacturer or importer, or any document. 27 CFR 478.103.

STUFF YOU GOTTA SELL:
        The Omnibus Appropriations Act of 1999 requires that all FFL's now sell, and have in stock, secure gun storage devices. As of 2005, 18 USC 922(z), also makes it unlawful for an FFL to transfer or sell any **handgun** to a non-FFL unless the handgun is delivered with a secure gun storage or safety device. It does not apply to a long gun, or a curio or relic. It does not apply to a rental or loan that is kept on the FFL's business premises for the duration of the rental/loan. Other exceptions are transfers FFL's, to law enforcement officers or rail security officers for on duty or off duty use in their profession; to government purchasers. This means trigger locks, gun locking devices which render the firearm unable to discharge, lock boxes with locks, or gun safes. If such a device is temporarily not available – it must be delivered to the purchaser within ten (10) days. Mailing it is OK, if it comes to that.

        If a firearm is consigned to the FFL, or pawned – a device must be included at the point of return unless the owner supplied one of his own. The law does not apply to estate sales conducted by the executor or auctioneer on the estate's behalf - as it only applies to FFL's. If multiple handguns are sold, a lock box that fits all the handguns would be OK.

STUFF YOU JUST CAN'T SELL IN FLORIDA:

It's illegal to manufacture, sell, or try to sell any weapon commonly known as **brass knuckles**, or a **slungshot** to anyone, even an adult. Under F.S. 790.09, this would be a second degree misdemeanor. On the other hand, it's not illegal to own them. Now, you know what brass knuckles are (calling them a "paper weight" is bull) , but a "slungshot" , "billie", or "slapshot" -- is a weighted material fixed on the end of a flexible handle or strap, to be used as a weapon. By the way, calling a slungshot a "tire tester" is not going to work -- it's still a slungshot. While a telescoping "tactical baton" may act in a similar fashion, it's not the same animal, and in my opinion is perfectly legal.

Another problem is "hoax bombs". Under federal law a dummy shell or grenade is not a destructive device or weapon -- it's just a dummy grenade. They make great paper weights! Many of my friends have one. The problem is that under Florida law -- they appear to be illegal due to some really crummy drafting of a statute, F.S. 790.165. If you want to be on the safe side, as silly as it may sound, you should not sell, transfer, or possess these little gems.

Since I'm sure you'd like to know what a "hoax bomb" is -- it's any device or object that by its design, construction, content, or characteristics appears to be a destructive device, or appears or is represented to contain an explosive. So much for "dummy dynamite" clocks in those nifty gag catalogs! People just can't have any fun with these stupid laws!

Anyway, the real bad news is that it's a third degree felony to make these things, sell them, possess them, or deliver them unless you're a member of a theatrical company utilizing them as a prop -- or if you're a security person in an airport using them within your duties as you try to sneak them past detectors to see if anyone notices. Of course, we all know that this law makes no sense, as written. On the other hand, I think the statute would have a hard time withstanding a constitutional attack, unless the "hoax bomb" was being used with criminal intent. Test case time, again.

SELF-PROPELLED, BALLISTIC, OR "SPRING" KNIVES:

Lastly, you can't own, sell, possess, or transfer a self-propelled, ballistic, or "spring knife". Violation under Florida law is a first degree misdemeanor .[174] A self-propelled, or ballistic knife, or "spring knife", is a device that propels a knifelike blade as a projectile by means of a coiled spring, elastic, or compressed gas. They used to make them as belt buckles. In Florida, it's a no no. In Federal land it's a lot more serious — it's a ten year felony. [15 USC 1245]

GUN SHOWS:

We've gone over them already, but I've got a paragraph or two I need to kill, so here's the unofficial addendum. Gun shows have come under great criticism, primarily by people who don't want you to own guns. For the most part, the criticism is totally unwarranted. However, there is one thing about gun shows that poses a potential problem -- and that's non-FFL's having tables where they sell firearms out of their "private" collections. These "private" sales are often being conducted as a regular weekend business by persons who are   not following the law, and are hurting the industry as a whole by doing so. ATF has already sent warnings to some of these people, and has cracked down on others. I have handled some of these cases. I think you should think seriously about it if you are a non-FFL, and are basically conducting a weekend business in firearms. ATF is watching!

Moreover, if you're a private citizen selling firearms from your collection – my personal opinion is that unless a firearm is in your ownership for at least a year, you could have a problem if you were regularly selling as a non-FFL. The reason I give a "year" as the magic number is because that is the same period for an FFL who places a firearm from inventory into his own personal collection. Thus, if you really just like to buy and sell so you can try out various firearms, or play around with your collection rather than try to "make money" – this is the relatively safer way to do it. For good measure, make sure you keep records that document the date you purchased any firearm you're selling. Likewise, if you're selling at a gun show, you may be required to run a records check, and even have a waiting period to sell the gun legally depending on county ordinances in the county the show is held.

RELOADING AS A BUSINESS:

The same warning applies to reloaders who do not have an FFL. Since they are reloading as a business, they are "manufacturers", and need to be federally licensed under 18 USC 923. If all you are doing is "selling" legal ammo, even reloads, and not personally reloading the stuff for resale — don't worry about it, you don't have a problem.

FIREARM INSTRUCTORS:

Firearm instructors don't have much to worry about other than those who certify students for concealed weapons permits, as of July 1998, must now maintain records which certify that he or she observed the student "*safely handle and discharge*" the firearm. F.S. 790.06(2)(h)(7). That should mean using a real firearm with live ammo – not blanks, and certainly not an Airsoft! The NRA requires that of its certified instructors – and some instructors have actually been prosecuted because they certified students for the CWP application without using real guns or ammo.

As far as record keeping goes for your "student list" – this may be as simple as a list of the students names, and date observed., but you keep the records for two (2) years. You should also remember that any certificate you send up to Tallahassee should have your NRA identification number, or K license number.

As a personal note, you're gonna be asked legal questions by students. Beyond the most basic of them – I think you should try to steer away from giving legal advice. Remember, you're not an attorney, and if you give the wrong legal advice you're opening yourself to a lawsuit. That's one of the reasons the book was written, plus it's something everyone who owns a gun really should have. So, instead of giving the wrong advice, or incomplete advice — do your students a favor, and just sell them book, and let the student find out for themselves so they also remember it. The law is far too complicated to cover in a class, and quite frankly -- you're really not qualified to do it. Spend your time on safety, firearms handling, proper ammunition, and emergency situations. Push advance classes for students, such as stress-fire situations, combat and cover, low light, and the myriad of other situations that students really should be trained in.   It can't be covered in one class!   Make sure your students understand that, and understand the importance of furthering their training and knowledge. That's part of being a good instructor!

FFL OPERATING OUT OF HOME:

I know! We've already covered this, however, let me once again emphasize that an FFL can't sell and deliver from a location not on their license other than an actual gun show in their home state. A violation is a definite federal no-no.   Such was the case in U.S.v. Bailey, 123 F.3 1381 (11th Cir. 1997), where Mr. Bailey got convicted of the federal offense of "dealing without a license" because the license covers only specified business premises, and Mr. Bailey was actually working out of his home. Be warned! Serious stuff! Also remember that assuming your home is going to be listed as your licensed premises – it must be zoned for such use. ATF won't issue the FFL unless you are complying with "all state and local laws". [27 CFR 478.47]

In closing,   please remember that being a firearms dealer is not the easiest task in the world.   Moreover, just because you may know what you're doing -- there's a very good chance that your employees don't have a clue.   You need to train them, and you need the personal knowledge to be able to access if they are operating properly. If they screw up – it's your license that will be lost, irregardless. You can't leave it up to somebody else -- and if you can't figure out exactly what you're supposed to do, call up ATF, and ask!   Or, you could even hire an attorney, assuming you can find one who knows anything about this area.   Remember that you must take this stuff seriously,   otherwise you can get hit with criminal, as well as civil penalties.

ABBREVIATIONS & BOUND BOOK:

ATF has made clear that they don't particularly care for abbreviations on the Form 4473 except for approved postal abbreviations for the state's, and d/l for driver's license.

Also, if you're using a computerized bound book – back the damn thing up regularly, and print out the entire inventory twice yearly.

This is an area where I see lots of problems. These systems crash and lose info – and now it's your butt on the line. ATF doesn't like the excuse that "it was the computer's fault".

RESPONSIBLE PERSON:
The Safe Explosives Act defined the phrase "responsible person", and in the March 2006 edition of the FFL Newsletter, ATF adopted this definition across the board to apply to all FFL's. I therefore reprint that portion of the Newsletter, as I could not do it any better:

"A "responsible person" is defined as an individual who has the power to direct the management and policies of the business entity for which the Federal firearms license is being applied. Neither the Gun Control Act (GCA) nor its implementing regulations define the term "responsible person." However, historically the term "responsible person" was deemed to have the same definition in the firearms context as Congress has now incorporated into the Safe Explosives Act (SEA): a person who has the power to direct the management and policies of the firearms activity. Now that Congress has specifically defined the term in the explosives context, ATF will interpret the SEA definition to also apply in the firearms context. A determination of whether an individual is a responsible person may depend on his or her ownership interest in the business, the management structure of the business, and their ability and authority to direct the management and policies of the firearms business.

"Some examples of different types of business organizations include sole proprietorships, partnerships, corporations, and associations. The owner of a sole proprietorship would be a responsible person. In a partnership, each partner would be a responsible person. In a corporation or association, only the directors and officers who direct the management and policies of the corporation or association with respect to firearms would be responsible persons. In most firearms businesses, the store manager would be a responsible person. Each business entity may have a different business structure, so determining who is a responsible person must be made by referring back to the statutory definition: the individuals who direct the management and policies of the entity pertaining to firearms. It should be noted that not every individual at the management level is a responsible person for the purposes of Federal firearms laws. For example, a human resources manager who does not otherwise direct management and policies relating to firearms would not be a responsible person.

"Finally, every applicant for a license or permit must designate at least one local responsible person for the business. Applications alleging there is no person in the organization responsible for the firearms business will be returned for additional information. Clearly, one or more individuals must be responsible for keeping track of inventory and records. Without denoting a responsible person on the application, a license will not be issued."

SALE OF UNFINISHED RECEIVERS:

I've become aware that ATF has threatened prosecution in some sales of unfinished AR-15 type aluminum lower receivers as being the sale of an actual "firearm". The letter was dated January 29, 2004, and stated that when the machining accomplished a magazine well, trigger slot; cavity for the trigger/hammer/disconnector/safety selector; initial opening for the buffer tube; slot for magazine catch; slot for bolt carrier; right hand and center relief cuts for forward takedown pin – it had reached "the stage of manufacturing whereby they are identifiable as the frame or receiver." ATF advised a solid AR–15 type receiver casting was fine, but with a machined magazine well and central area for fire control components – the machining had gone too far, and it had become a "firearm" because a "receiver" is defined as a "firearm". Obviously, in these instances, you need to be an FFL if you're in the "business" of selling it, and you need the 4473 for the purchaser unless he or she is another FFL. Just a word of caution.

(this page reserved)

CHAPTER TEN

MISCELLANEOUS PROVISIONS

THE ASSAULT WEAPONS BAN:

In 1994 the Congress bowed to media pressure, and anti-gun advocates, and passed certain portions of the Crime Bill that redefined what an "assault rifle" was, and made the manufacture, import, and possession of such firearms, as well as "large capacity ammunition feeding devices" (ie: magazine capable of holding over ten cartridges) manufactured or imported after that date illegal. That law ended on September 13, 2004, and hopefully is only history. In case you don't already know, these firearms were never a real problem, and are rarely used in crimes. Even the FBI admits that in its statistics. However, the newest b.s. reason anti-gun politicians are using is that guns are being run across our border to Mexican drug cartels. While it's true some guns are getting there ATF records show that illegal arms sales from the United States account for only 17% of illegal firearms brought into Mexico.[175]

Most, and the more serious, of these weapons are coming from China, Russia, and South Korea thru Guatemala, and the ones from the U.S. don't include any automatic weapons - which are the ones the cartels really like. Likewise – it's already a very serious crime to run guns across the border – so don't expect any of these criminals to be deterred by reinstatement of the assault weapons law – as usual, it will just prevent honest citizens from getting them. So, when remembering back on the defunct assault weapons ban, maybe this quote from Thomas Jefferson will put it in perspective:

"Those who would sacrifice a little freedom for a little order, will lose both, and deserve neither."

In case you have any questions about the ban, I am going to reprint a portion of the September 2004 ATF bulletin that explained the sunsetting of this Act:

Q: What was the semiautomatic assault weapon (SAW) ban?

A: The SAW ban was enacted on September 13, 1994, by PL 103-322, Title IX, Subtitle A, section 110105. The ban made it unlawful to manufacture, transfer, or possess SAWs. The law defines SAWs as 19 named firearms, as well as semiautomatic rifles, pistols, and shotguns that have certain named features. The ban was codified at 18 U.S.C. § 922(v). SAWs lawfully possessed on September 13, 1994 were not covered by the ban. There also were certain exceptions, such as possession by law enforcement.

Q: Was the SAW ban permanent?

A: No. The law enacting the ban provided that it would expire 10 years from the date of enactment, which was September 13, 1994. Therefore, effective 12:01 a.m. on September 13, 2004, the provisions of the law will cease to apply.

Q. What was the Large Capacity Ammunition Feeding Device (LCAFD) ban?

A: The LCAFD ban was enacted along with the SAW ban on September 13, 1994. The ban made it unlawful to transfer or possess LCAFDs. The law generally defined a LCAFD as a magazine, belt, drum, feed strip, or similar device manufactured after September 13, 1994 that has the capacity of, or can be readily restored or converted to accept, more than 10 rounds of ammunition. The ban was codified at 18 U.S.C. § 922(w). As with SAWs, there are certain exceptions to the ban, such as possession by law enforcement.

Q: Was the LCAFD ban permanent?

A: No. The LCAFD ban was enacted by the same law as the SAW ban. Therefore, like the SAW ban, it expires 10 years from the date of enactment. Therefore, effective 12:01 a.m. on September 13, 2004, the provisions of the law will cease to apply.

Q: Does expiration of the ban affect records maintained by licensed manufacturers, importers and dealers?

A. Yes. Federal firearms licensees are no longer required to collect special records regarding the sale or transfer of SAWs and LCAFDs, however, existing records on SAWs and LCAFDs must still be maintained for a period of 5 years, and records of importation and manufacture must be maintained permanently.

Q: Are SAWs and LCAFDs marked "Restricted law enforcement/government use only" or "For export only" legal to sell to civilians in the United States?

A: Yes. SAWs and LCAFDs are no longer prohibited. Therefore firearms with the restrictive markings are legal to transfer to civilians in the United States.

Q: Does the expiration of the SAW ban and the LCAFD ban affect importation?

A: LCAFDs are no longer prohibited from importation but they are still subject to the provisions of the <u>Arms Export Control Act</u>. An approved <u>Form</u> 6 import permit is still required. Non-sporting firearms are still prohibited from importation under sections 922(l) and 925(d)(3) of the GCA. Because the vast majority of SAWs are nonsporting, they generally cannot be imported.

Q: Does the expiration of the SAW ban change laws regarding assembly of nonsporting shotguns and semiautomatic rifles from imported parts?

A: No. The provisions of section 922(r), and the regulations in 27 CFR 478.39 regarding assembly of non-sporting shotguns and semiautomatic rifles from imported parts still apply.

Q. Does the expiration of the SAW ban affect firearms under the National Firearms Act?

A: No, except it is now lawful to possess NFA firearms that are also semiautomatic assault weapons, if NFA approvals are obtained.

MODIFICATIONS TO ASSAULT RIFLES:

Before you go modifying your SKS , or other assault type rifle, let me warn you that this is one confusing area of law! I have read this stuff over and over — and still had to call the Firearms Technology Branch of ATF to explain it to me. The law does not mean what it says unless you studied at "Alice In Wonderland University". Were it not for some letters from ATF published in the American Rifleman in 1994 in response to some questions from the NRA, and some great insight from the Firearms Technology Branch of ATF — I would never have included this section.[176]

To begin, you start with 18 USC 922 (r), which states:

"It shall be unlawful for any person to assemble from imported parts any semiautomatic rifle or shotgun prohibited from importation under section 925(d)(3) of this chapter as not being particularly suitable for or readily adaptable to sporting purposes . . . ."

18 USC 925(d)(3) pertains to those firearms and types of ammunition which the Secretary of Treasury allows to be imported -- they are on a list which includes most SKS type firearms. Thus, subsection (d)(3) allows importation:

"of a type that does not fall within the definition of a firearm as defined in section 5845(a) of the Internal Revenue Code of 1954 (ie: any NFA weapon), and is generally recognized as particularly suitable for or readily adaptable to sporting purposes . . . ."

In conjunction with all this, you need to know the federal regulation that implements the law, and deals with the modification or "assembly of semiautomatic rifles or shotguns", to wit: 27 CFR 478.39. The pertinent parts of that regulation read as follows:

(a)   No person shall assemble a semiautomatic rifle or any shotgun using more than 10 of the imported parts listed in paragraph (c) of this section if the assembled firearm is prohibited from importation under section 925(d)(3) as not being particularly suitable for or readily adaptable to sporting purposes.

(b)   The provisions of this section shall not apply to:

    (3)   The repair of any rifle or shotgun which had been imported into or assembled in the United States prior to November 30, 1990, or the replacement of any part of such firearm.

(c).   For purposes of this section, the term imported parts are:

(1) Frames, receivers, receiver castings, forgings or stampings

(2) Barrels

(3) Barrel extensions

(4) Mounting blocks (trunions)

(5) Muzzle attachments

(6) Bolts

(7) Bolt carriers

(8) Operating rods

(9) Gas pistons

(10) Trigger housings

(11) Triggers

(12) Hammers

(13) Sears

(14) Disconnectors

(15) Buttstocks

(16) Pistol grips

(17) Forearms, handguards

(18) Magazine bodies

(19) Followers

(20) Floorplates

So, what the heck does all this mean? Well, you still need to read   58 Federal Register 40587 (July 29, 1993). That somewhat explains the application of 27 CFR 479 and 18 USC 922 (r). It states that it was to implement the Crime Control Act of 1990 by prohibiting the circumvention of the ban of nonsporting rifles and shotguns on domestically manufactured weapons thereby preventing the assembly of what are essentially foreign made firearms that would otherwise not be importable. So, if a rifle has more than half of the twenty essential parts listed in the regulation made from imported parts (ie: more than **ten**) — it is banned from assembly or further modification in the United States.

Now, remember — the unlawful part here is "assembly". To you, we mean "modification".   Or, to put it another way — sale, possession, and purchase of these weapons, even if illegally modified, is not illegal! Only making of the modification is illegal! Also, if you hired someone to make the illegal modifications for you — you're just as guilty as he is under the law as an accessory.

So, back to the question of what you can legally do to modify your SKS?   Here's the safe list:

1.   Replace the existing stock and handguard with a non-folding wooden or synthetic stock having either a Monte Carlo or thumbhole design.

2.   Attach a muzzle-mounted recoil compensator that is <u>not</u> also designed as a flash suppressor.

3.   Replace the fixed magazine with a detachable magazine — so long as you also replace the standard stock with a Monte Carlo or thumbhole design, and remove the bayonet mount completely from the firearm.

4.   Replace the existing ten round fixed magazine with a five round fixed magazine, or install a block in the well of the ten round magazine limiting it to five rounds.

5.   Replace the existing receiver cover with a cover having telescopic sight bases or rings.

6.   Replace the front and/or rear sights.

7.   Install an ambidextrous safety.

Adding a folding stock, bipod, flash hider, is not allowed, nor is adding a detachable magazine (unless you also have the Monte Carlo or thumbhole stock without a bayonet lug), because your federal government says that this renders it as "non-sporting", and thus would be banned from import pursuant to 18 USC 925(d)(3). Same thing about the bayonet on those imported after 1989, unless they are the Russian SKS on the curio and relic list.

QUESTION: Why can you have a bayonet mount on the Russian SKS?

ANSWER: Because it's on the curio and relic list issued by the Secretary of Treasury, and thus can be imported with the bayonet under 18 USC 925 (e)(1)

"Notwithstanding any other provision of this title, the Secretary shall authorize the importation of, by any licensed importer, the following: (1) All rifles and shotguns listed as curios or relics by the Secretary . . ." 18 USC 925(e)(1)

I hope this has been of some help to you. It is not the final word on modifications, and I didn't intend it to be. This is not my area of expertise, and I don't want to give you any bad advise. If you decide to modify your SKS, or anything else — good luck!

LAW ENFORCEMENT OFFICERS SAFETY ACT:

In July 2004 Congress passed the   " **Law Enforcement Officers Safety Act** of 2004".   This Act permits a current, or retired law enforcement officer to carry a concealed firearm in any state or U.S. territory under certain conditions. The Act is found in 18 USC 926B & C – here's the scoop:

Pursuant to 18 USC 926B, a currently qualified law enforcement officer employed by a state or any of its political subdivisions (county or municipality) who is carrying his government issued photographic law enforcement identification may carry a concealed firearm off duty anywhere in the United States, except this does not apply to a machine gun, silencer, or destructive device. However,   it does not limit or restrict any State law that:

1.   Allows a private person or entity to restrict or prohibit such possession on the private property of that entity or person, or

2.   restricts or prohibits possession on government property

The term "qualified law enforcement officer" means an employee of a governmental agency who:

1.   is authorized by law to engage in or supervise the prevention, detection, investigation, or prosecution of, or the incarceration of any person for, any violation of law, and has statutory powers of arrest;

2.   is authorized by the agency to carry a firearm;

3.   is not the subject of any disciplinary action by the agency

4.   meets standards, if any, established by the agency which require the employee to regularly qualify in the use of a firearm;

5.   is not under the influence of alcohol or another intoxicating or hallucinatory drug or substance; and

6.   is not prohibited by Federal law from receiving a firearm.

If all the conditions are met – concealed carry is legal. Open carry would still be illegal. Only a State law that restricts carry on government or private property would be effective. Likewise, any federal restrictions anywhere – still apply. Only Municipal and County ordinances would not overcome the federal legislation. Thus, the 3 day wait for purchase of a firearm would still apply in Florida unless you had the CWP. Furthermore, it is likely you could not carry concealed on private property where the owner/person in authority did not permit it; or other places banned by Florida law from concealed carry unless part of your duties.

Likewise, 18 USC 926C , permits the carrying of a concealed firearm by a retired law enforcement officer under the same conditions except:

1.   Said person must be retired in good standing from service with a public agency as a law enforcement officer, other than for reasons of mental instability;

2.   before such retirement, he or she was authorized by law to engage in or supervise the prevention, detection, investigation, or prosecution of, or the incarceration of any person for, any

violation of law, and had statutory powers of arrest;

3.   A.   before such retirement, he or she was regularly employed as a law enforcement officer for an aggregate of 15 years or more; or

       B.   He or she retired from service with such agency, after completing any applicable probationary period of such service, due to a service-connected disability, as determined by such agency;

4.   He or she has a nonforfeitable right to benefits under the retirement plan of the agency;

5.   During the most recent 12-month period, has met, at the expense of the individual, the State's standards for training and qualification for active law enforcement officers to carry firearms;

6.   Is not under the influence of alcohol or another intoxicating or hallucinatory drug or substance; and

7.   Is not prohibited by Federal law from receiving a firearm.

       The identification required by this subsection is:

(1)   a photographic identification issued by the agency from which the individual retired from service as a law enforcement officer that indicates that the individual has, not less recently than one year before the date the individual is carrying the concealed firearm, been tested or otherwise found by the agency to meet the standards established by the agency for training and qualification for active law enforcement officers to carry a firearm of the same type as the concealed firearm; or

(2)   (A) a photographic identification issued by the agency from which the individual retired from service as a law enforcement officer; and

       (B) a certification issued by the State in which the individual resides that indicates that the individual has, not less recently than one year before the date the individual is carrying the concealed firearm, been tested or otherwise found by the State to meet the standards established by the State for training and qualification for active law enforcement officers to carry a firearm of the same type as the concealed firearm.

As of March 3, 2008, Florida has implemented this Act thru Florida Statute 943.132, and Florida Administrative Code 11B-27.014. Thus, retired law enforcement officers who are qualified under the federal law may now be issued a Florida identification card once they pass the range requirements. The requirements are per the Florida Administrative Code section, and the range requirement "course of fire" (ie: proficiency test) must be given by a firearms instructor certified by the Criminal Justice Standards Training Commission. (minimum score of 80% – ie – 32 of 40 rounds in the scoring area on B-21E target). Cards are valid for one year (actually 365 days), and are consecutively numbered, and are therefore unique to the holder. If lost - the card cannot be replaced. The retired officer must be retested. Likewise, since federal law requires proficiency testing on a yearly (every 365 days) basis as a prerequisite for issuance and validity – so does Florida law. Thus, as a practical matter – a retired officer will have to arrange for retesting and reissuance before the year expires so that his or her authority does not lapse.

The cost of obtaining the testing and certification is purely upon the retired officer. Likewise, since federal law requires a photographic identification from the retired officer's agency be carried – both the Florida Firearms Proficiency Verification Card (Form CJSTC-600), and the retired officer's agency photographic identification card should be carried.

The instructor giving the test must keep the test information for a period of two years, which is subject to review and inspection by the Criminal Justice Standards Training Commission. Documentation should include the following information on the person tested: name, address, type firearms used, proficiency score, Verification Card number that was issued, date of testing, location of testing, range requirements for test.

As a footnote, federal law still forbids you to carry in the airport sterile area, on aircraft, etc., unless it's in your jurisdiction, and part of your duties. And, the law does not permit carrying machine guns, silencers, or destructive devices.

(this page reserved)

(this page reserved)

CHAPTER ELEVEN

SELF DEFENSE, AND THE LAWFUL USE OF FORCE

Your rights to defense of self, family, and property all have different rules. Understanding the rules are important if you are a responsible individual. If not, understanding the rules are still important to avoid criminal prosecution, or civil liability.

One thing I must say at the beginning of this chapter is a word on the practicality of using self-defense. The criminal always has the advantage, because he is not afraid to use his weapon illegally. Moreover, you may fall into the trap of trying to decide if your use of the weapon is legal, or not. If you miss, or not. If you get sued, prosecuted, or not. All of these things, and more will be going through your mind, and all are unfortunately to your disadvantage from a standpoint of survival. However, they are the law, and must be followed to whatever extent you reasonably can.

When people ask me when they can use a firearm, I tell them that from a practical, and not necessarily legal standpoint -- the only time anyone should know you have a weapon, or ever see the weapon -- is when you're ready to use it, sure you can use it, and can legally pull the trigger.

Why?

For one thing, it gives you the advantage of surprise. This split second advantage is often the difference between who is lying dead on the ground -- you or him. If you chose not to fire the weapon, and hope that by displaying it the other person will desist in his felonious conduct (you can never use a deadly weapon to stop a misdemeanor) -- good luck. At least you still have a momentary advantage.

But whatever the situation -- as soon as the weapon is displayed, or you threaten to draw it, whether you are justified or not -- you have probably escalated the situation. There is no real way of turning back once it comes out. The situation tends to intensify, rather than get better -- unless the guy runs, backs down, or surrenders.

The real question then becomes whether the other person is willing to push his luck -- or whether you are willing to take another life to protect your own, to protect the life of your loved ones, or in certain instances, to protect your property. Don't think you can just wound him, or shoot the knife out of his hand. It doesn't work that way. Modern thinking in the instructional area of self-defense is to keep shooting until your opponent falls to the ground, incapacitated. Moreover, until the assailant falls, it is almost impossible to determine if you've even hit him. Until that happens, and the attacker is disarmed, he's still a very lethal threat, and one shot is rarely enough to stop an attack -- even if it's enough to kill him. An attacker who dies in a hospital three hours after you shoot him, still has two hours and fifty minutes to kill you, and your family before he dies. If you think I'm kidding you -- don't! It happens all too often. Ask any police officer.

Obviously, if you get into one of these predicaments, and misjudge the situation, you will either be dead, or be prosecuted. Neither alternative seems very fair, and it rarely is. However, these are some of the facts of real life, and let me assure you that no honest, responsible citizen wants to carry a weapon or firearm. Unfortunately, it's just come to that point if you want to survive. On the other hand, you must somehow manage to keep your cool, and act responsibly. Certainly, in this type of circumstance -- that will be a very difficult, if not an impossible task.

On this happy note we start the most important chapter in this book -- your current right to self-defense under Florida law. The first part of this is understanding some basic definitions which are essential to having the slightest idea of what your rights or liabilities are. Here goes:

FORCIBLE FELONY

Before you learn anything else, you need to know what a "forcible felony" is.[177] Knowing this is very important because it defines when you can use a deadly weapon in self-defense, when you can use deadly force, and when you can't. Of course, a "deadly weapon" is one that by use or design is likely to cause death or great bodily harm.[178] A "deadly weapon" doesn't need to meet the typical classification of what you'd think a weapon would be — thus, the courts have held that where there is proof a person intended to use an object (broom stick; blow gun; cinder block; screwdriver; lawn mower blade; box cutter; beer bottle; BB gun; etc.) as a "deadly weapon", and the object was capable of inflicting such harm, a jury is entitled to find that the object is a "deadly weapon".[179] Thus, the only time you can use a firearm, or any other deadly weapon in self-defense is when it is used to stop or prevent a "forcible felony."[180]

The list of forcible felonies in Florida is as follows:[181]

1. Treason

2. murder

3. manslaughter

4. sexual battery

5. robbery, including carjacking & home invasions

6. burglary

7. arson

8. kidnaping

9. aggravated assault

10. aggravated battery

11. aircraft piracy

12. unlawful throwing/placing or discharging of a bomb or destructive device

13. aggravated stalking

14. unlawful discharge/placing/throw destructive devices

15. any other felony (not misdemeanor) which involves the

use, or threat of physical force or violence against any person (not animals -- persons!)

Now, the list of forcible felonies may seem all very clear on paper, but I can assure you that it's not as simple as you may think. You still cannot just shoot someone for the heck of it, even if they are committing a forcible felony. Your use of deadly force must still be "reasonable", or you wind-up using excessive force, and facing possible manslaughter or aggravated battery charges.[182] To help you along on this rather varying system of what is legal or not, we'll move on to the specific statutes that define the parameters of lawful self-defense, but before we do, I think you should also be aware of a few more important definitions:

DEADLY WEAPON:

A "deadly weapon" is one that is likely to produce death or great bodily harm depending on its designed use, or the way it is used.[183] [184] If you're wondering what a just a "weapon" is – it's defined as an instrument of attack or defense in combat. State v. Houck, 652 So.2d 359 (Fla. 1995). A firearm is always a deadly weapon according to the law,[185] however, it's use may not always constitute the use of "deadly force". More about that later. A baseball bat, or any other instrument capable of inflicting death, or great bodily harm can also be a deadly weapon -- depending on its use, or intended use.[186] For instance, a stone could be a deadly weapon depending on size, and circumstances of its use. Same thing for an ice pick, or screwdriver. And certainly, a bow and arrow would be a deadly weapon, because it would then be an instrument that was designed to inflict death or great bodily harm. Obviously, it all depends.

You should know that the terms "deadly weapon" and "dangerous weapon" are synonymous. Jones v. State, 885 So2d 466 (Fla. 4DCA 2004).

IMMINENT:

The next important definition is a word used all the time in self-defense statutes, to wit: "imminent". What does it mean? [187]

It means something that is about to happen on an <u>immediate</u> basis. Not an hour from now, not a month from now, but usually within seconds, and if not -- it is so immediate that there is no way to reasonably avoid it.[188]   Before an aggravated assault can take place there must be a well founded fear of imminent violence perceived by the alleged victim. <u>McClenithan v. State</u>, 855 So.2d 675 (Fla. 2DCA 9/03).

"Imminent" is also used to define many situations where deadly force can be used. In those situations the danger must also appear imminent. From reading the case law I think the correct definition of "imminent" most closely resembles "an immediate threat that is unavoidable unless something intercedes to stop it".[189]

REASONABLE BELIEF ("reasonably believes"):

What you reasonably believe the facts to be, and/or what you need to do to protect yourself, family, or property -- means just that. It must be objectively and subjectively <u>reasonable</u> under the particular circumstances, as they "reasonably" appeared to you at the time, even if you were mistaken. "Subjectively" means what you think. "Objectively" means how others will analyze your actions later on based upon reason. In other words, if you make a mistake, it must be a mistake that a "reasonable person" could also have made knowing the same facts as you did at the time of the incident. This is not an easy definition since the reasonableness of your actions will be judged by others, rather than yourself, at a point in time well after the event has transpired. This after-the-fact analysis needs a real good lawyer, and sympathetic jury to assure your legal survival. A sympathetic police officer, and prosecutor wouldn't hurt, either.

So remember, that while you may have a personal belief that your neighbor, Herb, is from the Andromeda Star System, and is preparing an invasion of earth -- it is doubtful that the rest of your neighbors, judges, lawyers, and juries will go along with this. Thus, when you read the words of wisdom enacted by your Legislature that have limited your once God-given right to self-defense, try to remember that you must act within the terms of normal reality -- rather than the reality you'd like things to be.

The classic real example of this was when some elderly woman heard noise outside her house during the daylight hours, and decided there was a criminal outside who was going to burglarize her house and attack her. When she heard the guy make some noise immediately outside her front door, she grabbed a shotgun and shot it through the door. It killed him dead. Unfortunately for both, it was her milkman, and all he was doing was leaving her some milk. Yeah, it was reasonable to her -- she was scared of everything that moved. Shows you what watching T.V. can do to you. However, it had nothing to do with objective reasonability -- and she was convicted of homicide.

Just about the same thing happened not too long ago in another state where that poor Japanese kid got shot during Halloween by an over-reactive homeowner. The homeowners fears were real. That's what happens when you watch the news everyday, and start to take it too seriously. You can really lose perspective.

The homeowner had a good jury, and great lawyer in that case, and got off. But he still stands to lose everything if he gets sued civilly. Mistakes happen, huh?

A great quote on this subject is found in a Florida appellate court case decided in 1958, Harris v. State, 104 So.2d 739, 744 (Fla. 2DCA 1958). It succinctly states the philosophy of today's court in easy to understand terms:

> "Men do not hold their lives at the mercy of unreasonable fears or excessive caution of others . . . ."

DEADLY FORCE:

Deadly force, like a deadly weapon, is force <u>likely</u> to cause death or great bodily harm.[190] It doesn't legally matter whether either of these result from your actions -- it is legally enough that such might have caused, and was likely to cause death or great bodily harm. Great bodily harm can be a permanent or incapacitating injury, a non-trivial scar, or any other injury of a serious nature. A nosebleed is not a serious injury. A broken arm is.

Use of a firearm, baseball bat, metal pipe, ax handle, knife, etc. -- all are <u>likely</u> to be classified to involve the use of deadly force. Display of these items, combined with the threat of imminent violence, may constitute the felony of aggravated assault, or at least the first degree misdemeanor of improper exhibition of a dangerous weapon, unless there is a <u>legal</u> justification. Legal justifications are not necessarily what you'd like them to be, or think them to be. That's one of the problems.

From a legal standpoint only the **discharge** of a firearm always constitutes the use of "deadly force".[191] Whereas **pointing** a gun to ward off an attack is, as a matter of law, not greater than the use of **"non-deadly force"**. <u>Rivero v. State</u>, 871 So.2d 953 (Fla. 3DCA 2004).[192] On the other hand, it's still usually a jury issue on whether it constitutes aggravated assault,[193] and there is also an open question whether it is the "use" of any "force", at all.

Remember, that lawfulness of the use of force is determined on whether your subjective belief was "reasonable" under the "reasonable man" standard.[194]

JUSTIFIABLE USE OF FORCE -- NON-DEADLY FORCE:

OK, we've been discussing some concepts that relate to the use of deadly force, but what about non-deadly force? Actually, this area will give you considerably more leeway in what you can or cannot do. The problem, as with any use of force, is that it can <u>escalate</u> whatever situation you're in. In other words, anytime you use force, the likelihood is that the other party will use equal or greater force against you. Sooner or later this may get way out of proportion to the incident. However, since all you really want to know about is the law, rather than my silly interruptive comments, here it is:

A person is justified in using force, <u>except</u> deadly force, against another person, when and to the extent he <u>reasonably believes</u> that such force is necessary to defend himself or another from the other person's <u>imminent</u> use of <u>unlawful</u> force. (sounds familiar, huh?) <u>F.S.</u> 776.031. This will normally apply to misdemeanors, and non-violent felonies that fall short of a "forcible felony".

A person may use non-deadly force to stop the commission of a misdemeanor or non-violent felony upon himself, or property which he has an ownership or possessory interest in, or a legal duty to protect. <u>F.S.</u> 776.031. "Legal duty to protect" does not usually extend to neighbors protecting a neighbors property. A person may also have the right to use non-deadly force to stop a "breach of the peace".[195] A "breach of the peace" is a tricky phrase, can get real technical, and is asking for a problem. Unless you're a security guard hired to protect the property, or an employee on the premises, I think you better just call the police. There may be an exception where a neighbor or friend has actually agreed to protect his neighbor's property – but I haven't found any case law on this. An employee should have an equal right to protect his employer's property as he is an "agent", and the law says he or she "stands in the shoes of his employer". In other words – if the employer could do it, the employee should be able to, as well.

QUESTION: Is that a good idea?

ANSWER: Very hard to say! What if you get hurt – who's gonna pay your off time, medicals, and rehabilitation? Whose gonna hire you if you become permanently disabled? If you think Workmen's Compensation will do it – you'd better read that statute, first. You're not that well protected!

Examples of the legal use of non-deadly force? A trespasser who refuses to leave your premises after being asked to leave, a person attacks you with fists, someone tries to steal something from you short of a robbery or burglary, a person who is committing a criminal mischief on your property, a person who deliberately and unlawfully blocks you from the use of your property, a person who is so disorderly as to be committing a breach of the peace in your presence and who will not desist, a person you have lawfully arrested (very "iffy") who resists your lawful arrest. If the criminal conduct involves only a trespass to real property -- then you must be a person who has a right or duty to protect it. If you don't -- then go call the police because your legislature seems to have screwed-up this law, too. It used to be that anyone could protect the property of anyone else, but this may not be the law today. I guess that's just part of where being a good neighbor has gone to.

QUESTION: How about the use of pepper spray, a stun gun, or a Taser. These are "non-deadly force", right?

ANSWER: They are certainly non-deadly force,[196] but could still be "excessive force" which we'll be discussing soon. If the crime about to be perpetrated upon you involves physical violence -- it's my opinion that you should have an absolute right to use a non-deadly weapon to prevent harm to yourself, rather than having to battle-it-out with your hands.[197] If it involves a trespass, or property damage, I personally still feel the same way, but believe it becomes more "iffy", only because excessive force is usually a question of fact. Therefore, my opinion is of little use if somebody else disagrees -- especially if they're a judge or jury.

QUESTION: Is there anything else other than pepper spray, a Taser, or a stun gun, that is non-deadly force?

ANSWER: Well, knives and firearms are almost always deadly weapons, as are nun-chuks. There are some risky exceptions. Anything else depends on how it's being used. I mean, a full swing with a baseball bat is the use of deadly force -- but using it as a pole, to push someone away should not be. Fists, and kicking are not deadly weapons,[198] although they can constitute the use of deadly force depending on the injury. The flat part of a shovel, or the flat part of a machete might not be a deadly weapon, but then again, it might be real hard convincing a jury on that. The machete would be a real tough sell -- because most people think of it as a weapon, rather than as a tool. Obviously, in the hands of someone skilled, it can be used in a non-deadly manner. But, I think I'd rather pass on that particular trial. Brass knuckles might be. Anyway, you've got the idea.

QUESTION: What about waving a firearm in warning without firing it?

ANSWER: Very risky! While it is non-deadly force, it is still a "deadly weapon", and there is a question whether it is an "imminent" threat, a "conditional" threat, mere display, or a simple warning[199]. Unless it's a clear-cut self defense issue where you had the right to use deadly force, an arrest is likely, and you'll have to battle it out in court. Therefore, I recommend against it, unless you are reasonably in fear of your life, or if needed to stop a forcible felony.

QUESTION: Do I have to retreat before using non-deadly force?

ANSWER: Nope. The retreat rule, to the extent it may still exist, only applies to the use of deadly force. On the other hand, sometimes retreat is prudent even if you could use force. Being "macho" is out in today's world, and isn't worth a mistaken arrest because the police can't determine who's telling the truth.

JUSTIFIABLE USE OF DEADLY FORCE:

So, the bastard deserves to get shot. At least that's the way you feel. The real question is: how will the police and State Attorney feel about this course of conduct? What if it goes to a jury, and you're facing a mandatory prison sentence? This is the real crux of the problem! The law basically states that deadly force shall be used only if you reasonably believe that such force is necessary to prevent the imminent commission of a forcible felony, or prevent imminent death or great bodily harm to yourself or another.[200] If you'd like to see how this really works in a court of law, here's part of the 2004 version of the Standard Jury Instruction that's read in a self-defense case. Whether this instruction survives the new 2005 "Protection of Persons and Property" law, remains to be seen:

"In deciding whether the defendant was justified in the use of force likely to cause death or great bodily harm, you must judge him by the circumstances by which he was surrounded at the time the force was used. The danger facing the defendant need not have been actual; however, to justify the use of force likely to cause death or great bodily harm, the appearance of danger must have been so real that a reasonably cautious and prudent person under the same circumstances would have believed that the danger could be avoided only through the use of that force. Based upon appearances, the defendant must have actually believed that the danger was real." SJI 3.04(d).

No matter what the instruction is – get a good jury -- you win. Get a bad jury, and you've got real serious problems. And we are not just talking criminal law here, because people are getting sued all the time for the excessive use of force -- which, by the way, is not covered by your Homeowners Insurance Policy. (Gads! How did that ever happen? More on that later)

Moreover, if you are the initial aggressor, or if you are in the process of perpetrating a forcible felony -- you may not have any right to use deadly physical force, at all, even in self-defense, since you are the initial wrongdoer. Also, if you were not the initial wrongdoer, but he changes his mind and breaks-off the illegal act/attack -- your continuing the attack makes **you** the initial attacker in the eyes of the law. Beware! Just because he started the thing, doesn't necessarily give you the right to finish it. Moreover, when we get to the new law – it won't change this paragraph.

QUESTION: Hey, you're really getting me nervous. You mean that if I use a firearm to defend myself, I may get arrested?

ANSWER: Unfortunately, that's always a possibility, unless you have a responding police officer who also believes in your God-given Right to self-defense. On the other hand, you will be alive. Your wife will be alive. Your kids will be alive. The other alternative (lying dead on the ground) sure leaves a lot to be desired.

EXCESSIVE FORCE:

As usual, the use of non-deadly force, and the lawful use of deadly force, is limited to that amount you reasonably believe is necessary to prevent or terminate the other persons criminal conduct, or to reasonably protect yourself from harm. If you exceed this imaginary "reasonable" amount, your excess of force becomes "unrea-sonable" because it's "unnecessary", and becomes a criminal act to that extent, even if the initial use of force was otherwise legal.

NEW "PROTECTION OF PERSONS & PROPERTY" LAW:

In April 2005 the Florida Legislature passed Senate Bill 436, which was a substantial revision of Chapter 776 of the Florida Statutes. Here's a synopsis of the legislation written by the Senate Committee on Criminal Justice:[201]

"The bill permits a person to use force, including deadly force, without fear of criminal prosecution or civil action for damages, against a person who unlawfully and forcibly enters the person's dwelling, residence, or occupied vehicle. Additionally, the bill abrogates the common law duty to retreat when attacked before using deadly force that is reasonably necessary to prevent imminent death or great bodily harm.

"The bill creates a presumption that a defender in his or her home, in a place of temporary lodging, as a guest in the home or temporary lodging of another, or in a vehicle has a reasonable fear of imminent death or great bodily harm when the intruder is in the process of unlawfully and forcibly entering or enters. It also creates a presumption that the intruder intends to commit an unlawful act involving force or violence. These presumptions protect the defender from civil and criminal prosecution for unlawful use of force or deadly force in self-defense.

"These presumptions about the intent of the intruder, however, do not apply when the intruder:

- Has a right to be in the home, place of temporary lodging, or vehicle, unless there is a domestic violence injunction or written pretrial supervision order of no contact against that person;

- Is seeking to remove a person lawfully under his or her care from a home, place of temporary lodging, or vehicle; or

- Is a law enforcement officer, acting lawfully, and the defender knew or had reason to know that the intruder was a law enforcement officer.

"Additionally, a defender is not entitled to the benefit of the presumptions created by the bill if the defender was engaged in unlawful activity at the time . . . or was using his or her home, place of temporary lodging . . . or vehicle to further unlawful activity. The bill does not require any connection between the unlawful activity and the unlawful and forcible entry.

"This bill expands the castle doctrine by expanding the concept of what is a "castle" and by expanding the group of persons entitled to the castle's protection.

"Under the castle doctrine, a person has no duty to retreat from his or her "castle" (a person's home or workplace), before resorting to deadly force necessary for self-defense. The bill expands the concept of the castle to include attached porches, any type of vehicle, and places of temporary lodging, including tents.

"Under the castle doctrine, only persons lawfully residing in a dwelling have no duty to retreat before resorting to deadly force necessary for self-defense. Under the provisions of the bill, invited guests in another person's "castle" will have the same rights to self-defense as a resident . . . .

"Under Florida common law, a person has a duty to retreat, if outside his or her home or place of business, before resorting to deadly force reasonably believed necessary to prevent imminent death or great bodily harm. A person attacked within his or her home by a co-occupant or invitee must also retreat, if possible, within the home, but not from the home, before resorting to deadly force. Under the bill, a person will no longer have any duty to retreat, as long as the person is in a place where he or she is lawfully entitled to be.

"The bill provides that a person who acts in self-defense in accordance with the provisions of the bill is immune from criminal prosecution and civil actions. This provision is slightly different than the defense to civil actions under s. 776.085, F.S., in that the bill does not require proof that the intruder was attempting to engage in a forcible felony. Under the bill, the intruder's actual intent is irrelevant. The bill, in effect, creates a conclusive presumption of the intruder's malicious intent."

Anyway, now you know what the Legislature was trying to do. Whether the courts interpret the law exactly as the Criminal Justice Committee envisioned will be determined over time. However, one thing that should be perfectly clear is that the Legislature was not very happy with the "retreat rule", and had great concern about people being prosecuted for using legitimate self defense. To try to remedy the situation the Legislature enacted some new laws, and amended some old ones. Here's my analysis of what they did:

CHANGES IN 776.012:

Florida Statute 776.012 is entitled "Use of Force in Defense of Person". In a nutshell, the first part of this statute is pretty much a rehash of the law on self defense as it's always been, plus the elimination of the retreat rule (ie: "Stand Your Ground"). I'll get technical here for a moment in describing it. This law has a prefatory part followed by two distinct numbered sections. The prefatory part states that a person is justified in using (non-deadly) force to the extent that the person <u>reasonably believes</u> such conduct is <u>necessary</u> to defend himself or another against another's <u>imminent</u> use of unlawful force. It then goes on to authorize the use of deadly force, and abolishes the retreat rule if certain predicates exist as set forth in section (1). The predicates in section (1) for using deadly force (without retreating) are that the person reasonably believes such force is necessary to prevent imminent death or great bodily harm to himself or another, or to prevent the imminent commission of a forcible felony. As mentioned before – this is Florida's previous self defense law with the "retreat rule" removed. Of course, there has never been a requirement to retreat when using non-deadly force.

Section (2) of 776.012 is important because it basically says that the same rules apply in any of the circumstances permitted in Florida Statute 776.013. While that's probably not real important for a layman to understand, it is really important for a lawyer handling a self defense case - because it should mean that a person charged with a crime who claims self defense has a choice of relying on 776.012, and/or 776.013. Since 776.013 has more predicates, and can be more complicated to use – that can be a really good thing. Plus, if the predicates in either section 776.012, or in 776.013 are met – then you should get "immunity" by virtue of another section, 776.032, which we will discuss later in this chapter.

<u>HOME PROTECTION UNDER F.S. 776.013</u>:

Completely new to the statutes is Florida Statute 776.013. Although it's title is "<u>Home Protection; Use of Deadly Force: Presumption of Fear of Death or Great Bodily Harm</u>", it encompasses several different self defense situations, and in those situations creates some very important presumptions. The first set of situations involve the use of deadly force against a person who "unlawfully and forcibly" enters or attempts to enter a "dwelling, residence, or occupied vehicle"; or who removes or attempts to remove another person against their will from such a location. The presumptions form sort of a "<u>safe haven</u>" for the use of deadly force, in that these are the situations most protected by the statutes – and would be very difficult to prosecute successfully.

The **first presumption** is:

A person who uses deadly force under certain conditions is conclusively presumed to have a "reasonable fear" of "imminent" death or great bodily harm to themselves or others when an intruder (1) has unlawfully **and** forcefully entered, or is unlawfully and forcibly attempting to enter, a dwelling, residence, or occupied vehicle, or (2) the intruder has removed or is attempting to remove another person against their will from such place or occupied vehicle.

The **second presumption** is:

A person who unlawfully and by force enters or attempts to enter a person's dwelling, residence, or occupied vehicle is doing so with the intent to commit an unlawful act involving force or violence.[202] (F.S. 776.013(4))

NEW DEFINITIONS IN 776.013:

Since the presumptions in 776.013 only apply to a dwelling, residence, or occupied vehicle – it's important to know exactly how those words are defined in the statute. The statute redefines a "**dwelling**" as a building or conveyance of any kind, temporary or permanent, mobile or immobile, including an attached porch, so long as (1) there is a roof over it, and (2) it is designed to be occupied by people lodging there at night. It includes a tent. Obviously, it should also include a house trailer or recreational vehicle, and case law should extend the definition to include attached carports.

A "**residence**" is defined as a dwelling where a person resides either temporarily, permanently, or is visiting as an invited guest. This will include a motel room, hotel room, or even a friend's home.

A "**vehicle**" means a conveyance of any kind, motorized or not, which is designed to transport people or property. Bicycles are likely excluded, and possibly excluded are mopeds, and smaller non-motored boats where sleeping space is not provided as manufactured, as these are generally not considered a "conveyance".[203]   However, a vehicle does not receive the protections of either of these two presumptions UNLESS it is also occupied.

The word **"forcibly"**, although not defined in the statute, should mean any use of force, even if slight, according to the case law. Thus, in Cappetta v. State, 162 So.2d 309 (Fla. 3DCA 1964), the appellate court in discussing a "breaking" in a burglary case held that even the "slight" force of pushing open a closed and unlocked door was an "act of physical force." Thus, climbing thru an open window or walking thru an open door would not constitute "forcibly", while pushing a window open should.

HOW DOES SECTION, 776.013, WORK?

According to the Senate Staff Analysis[204] the presumptions in this section are absolute (ie: a "conclusive" presumption)[205], and cannot be controverted or rebutted in a court of law. The case law agrees,[206] so long as the facts relevant to the presumptions are not materially disputed.

In application, the law says that in order to use deadly force you must have a reasonable fear of imminent death or great bodily harm, or reasonably believe it is necessary to stop or prevent the imminent commission of a forcible felony.[207]   However, if you fit the sections in Florida Statute 776.013 that create the presumptions – the presumptions conclusively establish this level of fear, establish your fear was reasonable, establish the "imminent" factor, and establish that the intruder was involved in a forcible felony with the object of doing physical harm to you or another occupant of the home, residence, or occupied vehicle.

If you have the right to use deadly force – excessive force should generally not be an issue, because deadly force is the "most" force you can use.[208]   On the other hand, if you've incapacitated your assailant, he surrenders, or runs, or you're using dad's surplus WWII flame-thrower, I think there are some real serious problems with your pulling the trigger.

Why?

Well . . . under those conditions there is an excellent possibility that you and your family are out of any imminent danger, and/or the forcible felony has ended. If that occurs it is rare you would have a "reasonable" fear of an "imminent" anything. Such a situation occurred in State v. Heckman, 993 So.2d 1004 (Fla. 2DCA 2007), where the appellate court held that the presumptions did not apply to protect a homeowner who had shot a burglar, because the burglar was outside, and retreating from the residence at the time he was shot. Thus, the homeowner was successfully prosecuted for aggravated battery – a crime that carries a twenty to twenty-five year mandatory minimum sentence because a firearm was discharged. F.S. 775.087 (actually 25 years because the victim in the Heckman case was also shot)

IMMUNITY AND 776.013:

Anyway, aside from the limitations mentioned in the last paragraph, and since section (1) of this statute creates a conclusive presumption that an attacker who unlawfully uses "force" [209] to gain, or who (with the use of "force") attempts to gain entry into your dwelling, residence, or occupied vehicle is doing so with the intent to injure you or another person[210], and likewise, since the statute creates a conclusive presumption that under these circumstances you also have a legitimate and reasonable fear of imminent death or great bodily harm to yourself or another – you would seem to be "**immune**" from prosecution according to the new immunity statute, F.S. 776.032(1).

That section states:

> "A person who uses force as permitted in s. 776.012; 776.013; or s. 776.031 is justified in using such force and is **immune** from criminal prosecution and civil action for the use of such force, unless the person against whom the force was used is a law enforcement officer, as defined in s. 943.10(14) . . . . As used in this subsection, the term "criminal prosecution" includes arresting, detaining in custody, and charging or prosecuting the defendant."

Now, don't take the "immunity" literally. Immunity is a legal issue that is subject to proof, and hence controversy. If the material facts are in dispute, you might still be arrested and prosecuted, although this new section is designed to lessen your chances of this. At worst, if your use of force was due to an intruder's unlawful and forceful entry, and you raise a defense pursuant to F.S. 776.013 – it appears that the only issues in such a case will be: (1) whether the person against whom the force was used was engaged in an unlawful attempt or unlawful entry into one of these places (ie: residence, dwelling, or occupied vehicle); (2) if the person using the force knew or had reason to believe this unlawful event was happening; and if so, (3) whether any of the statutory exceptions (*explained in the next section*) applied.[211]

Furthermore, it seems clear that these presumptions apply to guests, residents, lawful occupants, and those who have a present right to enter the dwelling, residence, or occupied vehicle. It's also possible that it may extend to anyone else who is defending such a structure or vehicle under the same requisites as an occupant – but I think the safer view to follow, at least until we have some case law on the subject – is to interpret the presumptions in this section to apply only to occupants, guests, owners, lessors, and those with a right or some type of invitation to be inside. Unfortunately, the drafting of the law leaves a number of open questions, and is going to foster litigation to resolve those issues.

QUESTION: Just in case there are problems with the statute, what should I do?

ANSWER: Always make sure you're acting reasonably before using deadly force. Don't think it's "open season" on anyone who breaks in your home unless your fear is real. Moreover, if the culprit is fleeing the premises – I would strongly suggest not using deadly force unless such is an immediate attempt to make a citizens arrest of the assailant, and the crime involved was **ex-**

tremely serious in the sense of forcible rape, murder, forcible kidnap, or the forcible attempt of any of these. Otherwise, it becomes legally risky. Plus, I think I'd make darn sure I gave a very loud warning that everyone around would hear before I ever thought of pulling the trigger.

EXCEPTIONS TO THE PRESUMPTIONS IN 776.013:

Now, remember – when you are defending your dwelling, residence, or occupied vehicle there are definite exceptions to the presumptions and protections of the statute. In the following situations [212] there are no presumptions or immunity:

A.   The presumption in F.S. 776.013(1), that you had a reasonable fear of imminent death or great bodily harm to yourself or another does not exist if used against a person who is a lawful resident, owner, lessee, titleholder, or person with a right to be in such home/residence/occupied vehicle, unless

     i.   There is an active injunction for protection from domestic violence against them, or

     ii.   There is a written Court order of pretrial supervision of "no contact" against them.

Interestingly, although committee and staff reports say the presumption in F.S. 776.013(4) also disappears under these circumstances, the actual subsection that became law is not drafted that way. So, it's very likely that an appellate court may one day say that the second presumption survives (ie: intruders intent to do physical harm), even to this protected class, whenever a person "unlawfully and forcefully" enters or attempts to enter. Test case time, again.

B.   The same loss of presumption analysis applies to the use of deadly force against a parent or grandparent trying to remove their child or grandchild, or any other person who has lawful custody or guardianship of the child.

C.   The same loss of presumption analysis applies when the person **using** deadly force is engaged in an unlawful activity, or is using the residence, dwelling, or vehicle to further unlawful activity.

D.   There are no presumptions or immunity in favor of the use of deadly force when the person using deadly force knows or should know the person it is used against is a law enforcement officer; or in situations where the officer enters or attempts to enter after identifying themself while in the performance of his or her legal duties.[213]

QUESTION: You mean if grandpa decides he wants to kidnap my kid, I can't stop him?

ANSWER: No – you can stop him, and maybe you can even use deadly force – but if you do the first presumption in 776.013 doesn't apply, and maybe the second. However, you may still have "immunity" under different sections of the law because you have the right to use deadly force to stop an actual   forcible felony –   no matter who is involved.

QUESTION: What if it's my landlord, he kicks in the door and he threatens to shoot me unless I pay the rent?

ANSWER: I think I'd pay the rent. However, since he is the "owner" or "titleholder" to the property the first presumption of F.S. 776.013 doesn't apply, and maybe the second. On the other hand, he is committing a forcible felony, and you may have the right to use deadly force. If so, the "immunity" in F.S. 776.032(1) should apply. Get a receipt before pulling the trigger.

QUESTION: What if I'm smoking a joint at home when somebody tries to break in?

ANSWER: Well, you shouldn't be smoking a joint because it's unlawful and stupid, and will likely be a federal felony if you also possess a firearm. Moreover, since you are acting illegally, the presumptions will disappear – although you will likely still have "immunity"if you acted reasonably because your actions might still fall under F.S. 776.012 or F.S. 776.031.

DUTY TO RETREAT UNDER THE NEW LAW:

Well, as already mentioned, the new Protection of Persons and Property Law (also known as the "Stand Your Ground" law) has made major changes by virtually eliminating the retreat rule when lawfully using deadly force. Prior to the new statute the case law made it clear that unless you were inside your home or business, you had to **retreat** before using deadly force if you could do so without increasing the danger to yourself. In your home or business premises there was no obligation to retreat except against a co-occupant, or person with a legally equal right to be there. It's crystal clear from the Committee Reports and Staff Analysis that the Legislature wanted to totally undo the retreat rule to residents, occupants, and guests in a dwelling, residence, or occupied vehicle against an outside attacker. Likewise, F.S. 776.012 also eliminated the retreat rule in favor of being able to "stand your ground" for all lawful instances set out in F.S. 776.013; and F.S. 776.031 also eliminated the retreat rule the same as 776.012(1), except it added the predicate that you also had to be in a "place where you have a right to be".

Unfortunately, the drafting of F.S. 776.013 is a bit confusing on this issue because subsection (3) seems to apply only to places not covered by subsection (1). In other words, subsection (3) applies to "any other place" than an occupied vehicle, dwelling, or residence. Furthermore, to use subsection (3) you have the additional requirements of needing to be in a "place where they have a right to be"; and, of course, you need to meet the standard that the defender reasonably believes such is necessary to prevent imminent death or great bodily harm, or to prevent or stop (the imminent commission of) a forcible felony:

> "A person who is **not engaged** in an unlawful activity and who is attacked **in any other place** where he or she has a right to be has no duty to retreat, and has the right to stand his or her ground, and meet force with force, including deadly force if he or she reasonably believes it is necessary to do so to prevent death or great bodily harm to himself or herself or another, or to prevent the commission of a forcible felony." [F.S. 776.013(3)]

So, what happened to the retreat rule? Well, to rehash it somewhat: if you start with the amendment to F.S. 776.012 [Use of Force in Defense of Person], that section states a person has no duty to retreat if they "reasonably believe the force is necessary to prevent imminent death or great bodily injury to themselves or another, or prevent the imminent commission of a forcible felony. If taken literally, you can use deadly force anywhere and anytime, co-occupants be damned, so long as there's a reasonable belief of imminent death or great bodily harm, or if you reasonably believe it's necessary to stop the imminent commission of a forcible felony.[214] On the other hand, while I don't believe there should be limitations read into this section because of the way the law was drafted, still, an appellate court might conceivably construe all these sections of Chapter 776 together, rather than independently.

If so, the most probable limitation, assuming it will be limited at all, is by reading in the amendments to F.S. 776.031, which abrogates the retreat rule in defense of property – so long as you are **"in a place where you have a right to be"**? Sounds somewhat possible when you consider that "in a place where you have a right to be" is also a requirement of F.S. 776.013(3).

QUESTION: If that's true, where are those places you "have a right to be"?

ANSWER: Darned if I know! Another drafting oversight by the Legislature that will have to be resolved by the courts! However, I'll give you my best guess in the following section:

PLACES WHERE YOU SHOULD HAVE "A RIGHT TO BE":

So, assuming we want to play it safe on the meaning and application of this new law – where are these places you "have a right to be"? My best guess is arrived at by figuring out all the places you "**don't**" have a right to be in. That would seem to make the most sense, and follow the intent of the law. These "forbidden places" should include anywhere you would need permission to be where you don't have it; anywhere you've been told to keep off by the owner or a person with authority (ie: trespass); any place where you would be violating the law by being there; any place of nuisance such as a crack house or house of prostitution. What's left is probably where you have a "**right to be**". Again, no case law on this so far, and only my best guess. However, if you want to play it even safer, go to my second guess.

My second guess is a lot more restrictive on where you can be without worrying about the retreat rule, and would seem to defeat the broad purpose of the new law. However, sometimes playing it safer is better. In that   respect, you have a "right" to be on your own property, property lawfully in your possession, property you have a legal duty to protect, and all public property such as roads, parks, etc., where the law does not restrict your presence. For example, if a park closes at night, and you are still there – you no longer have a "right to be" there. Step two feet outside of the park – and you'd be legal. Trying to figure this out in the middle of a self-defense situation would be no easy task which is another reason I don't think the Legislature intended this, and a reason why I don't think the courts will be so restrictive. Still, this is just my opinion, for now, and a "test case" scenario.

Thus, if you want to take no chances until the courts sort this mess out, here's my third, and **safest interpretation** of where you should be able to "stand your ground" and use deadly force without retreating, so long as you have a reasonable belief that deadly force is necessary to prevent the: (a) imminent death or great bodily harm to yourself or another, or (b) prevent the imminent commission of a forcible felony:

a.   Your dwelling or residence (ie: where you live), even if it is only temporary. (eg: motel, hotel, rental, home, tent). This includes everyone who resides there with you, and all invited guests.

b.   Other places you lease, rent, or pay money to belong to and are current on, or have an invitation (eg: farm, club, golf course, pool, health club, restaurant for dinner, etc.).

c.   Public places that are then open to the public (roads, streets, side walks, parks, etc.).

d.   Your occupied vehicle, and all invited passengers.

Unanswered in all these situations is what happens to the "guest" status when a person with superior authority orders them to leave the premises, or they commit a forcible felony in the dwelling, residence or occupied vehicle against a person with superior authority. Based on prior case law, I assume they lose any protected status.

Anyway, by reading all these amendments and new sections in the new law together it appears that the retreat rule is dead in almost every circumstance where it's reasonable to use deadly force to prevent imminent death, great bodily harm, or a forcible felony, [215] with the possible qualifier – you may have to be "in a place where you have a right to be", as well. If you don't, and you're somewhere you shouldn't be, or would technically need permission to be (like a neighbor's yard) – my advice is to retreat if you can do so without increasing the danger to yourself. Of course, I once again warn you this is only my opinion at this point, but it's buttressed by the new F.S. 776.032(1), which clearly states that the "immunity" from arrest and prosecution applies across-the-board to each of the revised sections (ie: 776.012; 776.013; 776.031). So, if it applies to "each" instance – it should cover the totality of what they allow, combined!

SOME QUALIFIERS TO THE NON-RETREAT RULE:

Still, when relying on these new "Stand Your Ground" provisions of the law, you probably can't be engaged in any unlawful act yourself, and cannot be the initial aggressor. [F.S. 776.041] That is what the prior interpretations of self-defense law said, and should still apply.

Also, unless you are acting under the protections of F.S. 776.013 (ie: dwelling, residence or occupied vehicle against unlawful and forceful intruder); F.S. 776.013(3) and F.S. 776.012 say before using deadly force you must still retreat unless you **reasonably believe** your use of deadly force is **necessary** to prevent the imminent commission of a forcible felony, or prevent imminent death or great bodily harm. This is pretty much a rehash of the law as it existed before except the elimination of that portion of the previous "retreat rule" which required you to retreat if you could do so without increasing the danger to yourself.[216]   However, under these last two sections, since there are no presumptions, if you fail to retreat, and the State Attorney takes the position that your belief in the need to use deadly force was not "reasonable", you will likely be prosecuted.

WHAT WILL HAPPEN TO THE BURDEN OF PROOF:

However, the "million dollar question", yet unanswered, is since F.S. 776.032 states you are "immune" if you acted pursuant to any of these new or amended statutes (ie: 776.012; 776.013; 776.031), what happens if you are somehow arrested and prosecuted? Will it be the State's burden at trial to <u>disprove</u> you acted reasonably from the beginning of the trial, will it be your initial burden just to raise it, or will it be your burden to prove otherwise? Very critical question!

Based upon the current case law on immunity, and from a purely legal standpoint, my opinion is that the burden would have to be on the State from the inception so long as you put the court on notice that you were raising this issue.[217] There are a number of recent cases on these issues, and I've placed them in the endnote section if you're interested, as they are primarily of interest only for an attorney, and are somewhat in conflict with each other.[218]

RETREAT RULE – BUSINESS PREMISES:

There is nothing in any of the new or amended sections of the law that specifically discusses retreating or not retreating on business premises. However, if you're on the property of your employer you should have the right to defend it as if it were yours, and thus qualify for being **"in a place where you have a right to be"**. Same thing if you were a security guard. F.S. 776.031. Of course, this means you reasonably believe that such force is necessary to prevent the imminent commission of a forcible felony; or as per F.S. 776.012, you reasonably believe that such force is necessary to prevent imminent death or great bodily harm to yourself or another person. In other words, if you fit these circumstances you should have immunity under the new law, and not need to retreat.

Well . . . I've explained this as far as anyone can at this point in time. For now, all I can say is "good riddance" to the old retreat rule, which in my opinion was hugely unfair, and caused numerous convictions of innocent persons who were merely trying to protect themselves or their families. My heartfelt thanks to the Legislature, and all the sponsors of these new laws! That being said, let's get back to self-defense, and the use of deadly force:

DEADLY FORCE -- USE TO PREVENT ESCAPE:

A citizens right to prevent an escape is not as broad as a police officers. It is a dangerous area to get into since a mistake can lead to criminal, and civil repercussions. Basically, you can use any <u>reasonable</u> force that you <u>reasonably believe</u> is <u>necessary</u> to prevent the escape of a person who is under arrest, and was in your <u>custody</u>.[219]   This presumes you made a "lawful" citizens arrest! If it was unlawful – big problems!

I wouldn't suggest that it's a reasonable use of force to shoot somebody who is trying to escape from a non-violent felony or misdemeanor. Even if it were legal, the hassle that you'd probably go through afterwards would rarely be worth it. And remember, that once this guy is running in the other direction, you are rarely in physical danger, nor is there much of "imminent" anything! If you shoot him, and a jury decides that was the use of "excessive force", you've just committed an aggravated battery, or manslaughter.[220]

QUESTION: So, when could I use deadly force involving an escape?

ANSWER: Unless you're a police officer, it's a tough question, and likely best to avoid. However, my opinion is that anytime it's a rape, armed robbery, homicide, arson of an occupied dwelling, non-parental kidnaping, or bombing, (or the attempt), and the guy refused to stop after a warning. These situations are so serious that society would have a hard time faulting you.[221] As to these, and anything else -- it's gonna depend. Play it on the side of caution, and only in the most extreme cases take the chance!

QUESTION: How about non-deadly force, like a Taser, stun gun, pepper spray, or something similar?

ANSWER: If it involves a felony, and you're willing to take the chance, I personally feel this would be a "legally" better method, although not necessary a "safer" method. Still, I'd personally avoid a stun gun since it requires very close contact — and I don't want to get hurt. If it's a misdemeanor, I really don't know, and would probably advise to stay away from it altogether, just because of the civil liability side, no matter what the law is.

LESS THAN LETHAL AMMUNITION:

Law enforcement and correctional officers were granted an exception from the definition of "deadly force" where they use "less-than-lethal munition" in good faith, and within the scope of their duties. This is a 1999 amendment to F.S. 776.06. Less than lethal ammunition is defined as a projectile that is designed to stun, temporarily incapacitate, or cause temporary discomfort to a person without penetrating the person's body. Thus, the good faith use of such ammunition by an officer will be considered the use of "non-deadly force", and an officer using such ammunition in good faith during the performance of his or her duties is not liable for that use, civilly or criminally. This statute does not apply to a citizens use of such ammunition, although it raises the question.

USE OF FORCE BY LAW ENFORCEMENT:

Law enforcement officers need never retreat in the lawful pursuit of their duties. They have no retreat rule. Moreover, they may use any non-deadly force they reasonably believe is necessary to defend themselves from bodily harm when taking a person into custody. This is the "reasonable man" standard. [F.S. 776.05]. The degree of force must be both reasonable and necessary, or it may constitute the use of "excessive force". However, the use of any force is technically illegal and excessive where the arrest or custody would be unlawful. [F.S. 776.051(2)].

A law enforcement officer may use deadly force to arrest a fleeing felon or person who escapes from his custody only where the officer reasonably believes the prisoner or fleeing felon poses a threat of death or serious physical harm to the officer or others; or reasonably believes the fleeing felon committed a forcible felony involving the infliction or threatened infliction of death or serious bodily harm to the officer or others.   In such instances a warning must be given before using deadly force, if the making of such a warning is feasible. [F.S. 776.05(3) & F.S. 776.07].   While the statutes are worded in terms that could be interpreted as allowing deadly force any time it was "reasonable" – constitutional limitations have been placed on what is, or what is not reasonable.   Thus, the use of deadly force to stop a non-violent felony, or a misdemeanor – will always be considered unreasonable unless the suspect uses or attempts to use deadly force against the officer. Tennessee v. Garner, 471 U.S. 1 (1985).

CRIMES & PENALTIES FOR USING EXCESSIVE FORCE:

Uh, oh! Here comes the real bad news! What happens when you screw-up, make a mistake, or are just an unfortunate victim of circumstances. The name of the game is punishment. You and your legislators are screaming for penalties and jail time -- but everybody forgot to put some protections in for those of us who are using self-defense, and who mistakenly go over the line, however slight.   A person who is justified in using force, but goes too far should not ordinarily be facing the penalties that exist today, but he or she does. Here's the scoop.

MANSLAUGHTER:

Manslaughter is the killing of another human being by culpable negligence, without lawful justification. It also occurs when there is a use of excessive force.   Manslaughter is a second degree felony which is ordinarily punishable by up to fifteen years in the prison system. Add a firearm or deadly weapon to the charge, and it increases to a first degree felony with a likely mandatory sentence. F.S. 775.087.

Since this legal definition of manslaughter may be somewhat confusing, let me explain it a bit simpler by breaking it into its components. Basically, I meant that manslaughter happens one of two principal ways. Method one is called "culpable negligence". Culpable negligence is more than simple negligence, it is conduct so gross and flagrant that it amounts to a reckless disregard of human life, or is conduct done with such a want of care as to raise the presumption of a conscious indifference to the consequences. It must be of such a nature that the defendant knew, or reasonably should have known that the act or <u>inaction</u> was likely to result in death or great bodily injury to another.

The second way it occurs is where you misjudge the law or the facts involved in self-defense or legal justification. If you do, and you also wind-up killing someone -- the crime is manslaughter. One way this happens is if you do have the legal right (ie: "justification") to use force, but in doing so you "unnecessarily" kill another. What do I mean by "unnecessarily"?

Well, that is kind of self-explanatory. It means that you acted in a manner disproportionate to the act, or took a life where there was no reasonable necessity for doing so. I use the word "<u>reasonable</u>" necessity, because deciding what is reasonable doesn't always mean you were right. You may have been wrong to use the degree of force you did, but if this your belief was objectively reasonable under the circumstances -- you would still be legal, and should not be subject to prosecution. However, if it was not objectively reasonable under the facts known to you, and thereby your use of force exceeded the amount of force that was reasonable or could have been reasonable – and a death resulted – it's manslaughter.

By the way, although manslaughter is generally a felony of the second degree (15 year maximum prison sentence) it becomes a first degree felony (punishable by up to 30 years prison) when a weapon or firearm was used or carried by the perpetrator during the commission of the crime. <u>F.S.</u> 775.087(1).

AGGRAVATED ASSAULT:

The most common case I defend is generally related to a self-defense situation that has gone wrong. That crime is aggravated assault.[222] Aggravated assault is a third degree felony that carries a three (3) year mandatory minimum prison sentence if a firearm or destructive device was involved. F.S. 775.087(2). By mandatory prison sentence -- we mean that if convicted, you've got to serve the prison portion, even if the judge doesn't feel you deserve it. He just has no choice.

I've seen cases (not mine, thank God) where judges have actually apologized to citizens they are sentencing to jail telling them that the facts of the case don't justify prison — but they have no choice. They have to sentence the poor guy to three years! It's not a pretty picture!

So, what is an aggravated assault? Well, to understand, you first have to know the definition of an assault.

An assault is an intentional, unlawful threat done by word or act, to do violence to another person, coupled with the apparent ability to do so, and by doing some act that creates a well-founded ("reasonable") fear in the other person that the violence is "imminent" (ie: "immediate"). To make an assault "aggravated" -- the assault must be committed with a deadly weapon, without any intent to kill, or must be done with an intent to commit a felony. F.S. 784.021

Thus, the key elements of an assault are:

An intentional threat

a.   That is unlawful

b.   To do violence against another

c.   By doing some act

d.   Which act creates a reasonable fear in the other person

e.   That the violence is imminent (ie: "immediate").

224

Some cases illustrate these elements. Thus, in <u>Butler v. State</u>, 632 So.2d 684 (Fla. 5DCA 1994), the appellate court held that a threat to do violence in the future lacks the essential element of "imminent" – and therefore falls short of an assault. It's only a "conditional threat". Another case made it clear that the **intent** of the defendant as to the "threat to do violence" element is crucial, rather than the reaction of the victim. <u>Benitez v. State</u>, 901 So.2d 935 (Fla. 4DCA 2005). Of course, reaction of the alleged victim is still essential as to another element – "reasonable fear of imminent violence". Thus, holding a gun without pointing it may, or may not constitute a threat depending on whether there was some overt act in aid of a threat. <u>Turner v. State</u>, 771 So.2d 1286 (Fla. 4DCA 2000). However, where the defendant only had a knife, made no indication of any attempt to throw it, and there was a vehicle and distance between his victim, the appellate court held that the threat was not yet imminent as it was "two steps re-moved". <u>Sullivan v. State</u>, 898 So.2d 105 (Fla. 2DCA 2005). My opinion is that this was a lucky decision for the defendant, and if a firearm had been involved the decision probably would have gone the other way. Another case held that a mere verbal threat generally requires an additional "overt act" to elevate it to an assault. <u>O.D. v. State</u>, 614 So.2d 23 (Fla. 2DCA 1993).

So, how does an aggravated assault typically happen in a self-defense context?

Well, let's say your neighbor's kid keeps running over your lawn with his truck at high speed. This is dangerous. This is a breach of the peace. This is a trespass. This is criminal mischief. This stinks! Every time you call the cops -- they arrive twenty minutes after all is done and over, and they can never catch the kid. Plus, they can't arrest him for a misdemeanor not done in their presence. That's the law, and it really stinks! It also needs to be corrected.

You're frustrated as hell. You're also rightfully worried that your dog, kid, wife, etc. -- will eventually get run-over by this nut. You're probably right.

Rather than call me for innovative legal advice,[223] you decide to save a buck, confront the stupid bastard, and make an impression he won't forget. Surely, who could blame you? Being an avid movie-goer, you reason: "If Clint Eastwood can do it – so can I!"

The magic day arrives, and as junior begins to zero-in at high-speed, you raise your mighty 12 gauge in his direction, and utter the magic words of your silver screen hero: "Well, Punk. Are you feeling lucky?"

Apparently not, because suddenly, an amazing change in attitude is noticed, and junior turns his truck in the opposite direction as fast as he can. However, since he hates your guts, anyway, he calls the cops. Maybe he calls daddy or mommy -- who can't understand why anyone would point a gun at dear, darling junior -- but the end result is always the same -- you're charged with aggravated assault!

Unless you find an understanding prosecutor, a super jury, a really good attorney, or a combination of all the above -- you're going to jail for three years!

Incredible, isn't it? I mean, we all know who should be going to jail -- and it sure aien't you -- but that's the way it goes. Moreover, even if you get the charge reduced -- you stand a very good chance of losing your right to own and possess firearms ever again!

ROAD RAGE PROBLEMS WITH AGGRAVATED ASSAULT:
Another typical example of how you can get yourself into big trouble is good ol' road rage. But before starting, let me personally thank all of you who carry a gun in your vehicle, and think that by displaying it to the nut who is tailgating you – you are acting properly. If it were not for that attitude, my yearly net as a criminal trial attorney would be significantly lowered, and I would be forced to reduce my already insignificant lifestyle.

You should know that display of a firearm in a road rage incident, even if the other driver is the "real nut" – is likely to get you arrested for aggravated assault. As I warned before, aggravated assault carries a three (3) year mandatory minimum prison sentence if you get convicted Bye, Bye!   Have a nice stay!

Now, you'll probably say – "I was in fear of my life!"   Maybe you'll even say: "I wasn't really trying to threaten him!   I was just trying to scare him away so he'd stop!"

Interesting response, and a fairly standard argument – and I actually agree with you! Unfortunately, this is usually a jury question, and there is no case law in Florida that has settled the issue whether merely holding a gun skyward is a "threat", a "conditional threat", or "just being ready if something happens".   Sure, the Turner case I discussed a few paragraphs ago might apply, but what if the court says your pulling the gun out in anger was the "overt act"?

The argument from the defense side is that holding a gun without pointing it is at worst a "conditional threat" that doesn't constitute aggravated assault because the threat of violence isn't "imminent". (by "imminent" we mean usually mean "immediate") It's only conditional.   The other argument is that it wasn't really a "threat" at all, but only a warning that if necessary, you could protect yourself if things got worse, or that you were in fear that things were going to get worse, and just wanted to be ready if it got to that point. A third innovative theory is that you were doing anything but displaying it, just in case you needed to have it.   Assuming the jury buys it – you're a free man or woman.   Assuming the jury goes the other way – you've got very big problems, and are going to be praying real hard that some appellate court will extend the Turner case to your situation. If not, you've got a three year stay in the slam to think about it.

Sure, there are other scenarios.   There's always a chance at a misdemeanor charge of getting a "careless display" under F.S. 790.10. Get a good lawyer, sympathetic prosecutor – and anything is possible. Many times a prosecutor can (rightly) be convinced that the misdemeanor is the better way to do things. Other times, you can plea to the felony – but the prosecutor will agree to do it without the mandatory minimum. However, going to trial is a really brave act since an adverse verdict kicks in the mandatory minimum prison sentence without exception! At that point – if convicted – you're probably going to be more than willing to pay the "test case" price for an appeal on whether holding a gun skyward is a threat or something else.

On the other hand – and here's the bad part – almost every case I take has the other driver swearing you pointed the gun at him or her regardless of whether this really happened. Pointing a gun is an "imminent" threat, and hence aggravated assault! People who tailgate and deliberately cut you off are not really the highest quality human beings we have out there. Many times they have a problem which they'd like to resolve at your expense. Getting even with you, the world, or themselves – even if that means lying, and seeing you rot in prison over something they caused – is a satisfying thing for these folks, and they're usually good liars, besides. These are the tough cases, and seem to be the ones I get all too often.

So, what's the answer?

Well, I thought I made that crystal clear by now, but if not – here we go! Don't take out your firearm over a road rage situation. Leave it in the console or glove compartment. Pull over or slow down, dial 911 or *FHP, and let the fuzz know what's going on. I know that means you've backed down – but macho isn't really the smart thing to do in this day and age, and quite frankly – prison sucks! If the nut approaches you after you've stopped your vehicle, that's completely another situation, and maybe you really will need your firearm. That's something I can't answer without lots of additional facts. But the safe way to avoid arrest is not to get in the situation in the first place. I know you always wanted me to represent you – but heck – save your money! Stay out of harm's way. Nobody should want to be arrested to prove their point, and being prosecuted, rightly or wrongly, is not an experience anybody should ever look forward to.

A NEEDED SELF-DEFENSE STATUTE:

Is there no justice? Probably not -- but that's your fault for not pushing the Legislature to protect you more. The 2005 "Stand Your Ground" – "Protection of Persons and Property" law is a good start, but we still need more! What we really need is a statute that amends F.S. 784.021 by adding a new subsection (3), and says something to the effect of:

> "No person who is convicted or found guilty of aggravated assault, shall be subject to a mandatory minimum sentence, where said person establishes by a preponderance of the evidence that (1) the display of such weapon was made upon the actual belief, even if unreasonable, that the other person was engaged in the imminent commission or attempt to commit a forcible felony, and (2) if the weapon displayed was designed to expel a projectile, that said projectile was not discharged."

A statute so worded would avoid mandatory sentences in almost all situations where it would be unfair, and would thereby allow a sentence to be imposed within the applicable guidelines. If you agree -- write your state senator and representative. Do something you can be proud of. Heck, that's what being a citizen is all about!

EXCUSABLE HOMICIDE:

Excusable homicide is not a crime. It is a defense.[224] You can't be convicted of manslaughter or murder if the homicide is legally excusable.[225]

> QUESTION: You mean there are actually times when I can kill somebody, and legally get away with it?

> ANSWER: Well, the answer is that "accidents happen", and as tragic as it may be, if a death results from an accident that falls short of culpable negligence -- it's not considered murder or manslaughter, as the conduct is legally excusable.

> QUESTION: Why?

ANSWER: Probably because our Constitution has a requirement that the punishment must not be disproportionate to the act being punished, and con-
victing somebody of murder or manslaughter for
a total accident, or simple negligence, is a bit too
much for most courts. That doesn't mean that
that's the end of it, because I can guarantee you
that somebody is gonna get sued in civil court --
and the suit will be for "big time" damages. But,
at least there shouldn't be (the key here is
"shouldn't be") any criminal charge for a homicide.

If you'd like some examples of excusable homicide, I'll pick a
few from the law books that actually happened. The classic case is two
kids cleaning, or looking at a loaded weapon. It drops, and somehow
goes off. Another scenario is a hunting accident where culpable
negligence is not involved.

However, the definition of excusable homicide is much broader
than this, and can act as a total, or as a partial defense (which could
allow a homicide to be downgraded to a lesser charge). In order to
understand this, you need to know the legal definition of "excusable
homicide.[226] The definition follows:

Homicide is excusable when:

(1)   Committed by accident and misfortune in doing any
lawful act by lawful means with usual ordinary caution,
and without any unlawful intent; or

(2)   When done by accident or misfortune in the heat of
passion, upon any sudden and sufficient provocation; or

(3)   When done upon a sudden combat, without any dangerous weapon being used, and not done in a cruel or

unusual manner.

Subsection (1) we've already discussed. Subsections (2) and (3) are actually pretty similar in execution. They both involve situations where a fight or heavy duty verbal argument is (usually) occurring. In subsection (2) the death must be accidental upon a sudden and sufficient provocation. In subsection (3) it is upon a sudden combat, without any dangerous weapon being used, and not done in a cruel or unusual manner. Thus, the third section protects a person who becomes involved in a fight which accidentally leads to the death of the other party, if the other conditions are met.[227]

There aren't a lot of examples of these cases around. In fact, most of the court decisions explain why the facts do <u>not</u> constitute an excusable homicide. However, I will give you the few examples that have managed to be decided. Please remember, that if you change the facts in these cases only slightly, the result could be just the opposite of what occurred.

Typical, are two people in a normal fist-fight, and a normal blow causes an unexpected death to the other. Another example is one man pushing another in a verbal dispute, and the other man suffering a heart attack, and dying. Last, but not least, is one man pushing another, with the other falling, and unexpectedly landing on an object that killed him.

Obviously, these cases could be decided differently if you change the facts only slightly. For instance, if you knew the other guy had a bad heart -- you might have a real problem. So too, if you saw that pointed object on the ground, and gave him a push in the right direction. And, if you were a karate expert looking for a vital spot that could cause such a result? Anyway, I think you get the point -- and the point is: Don't get involved in these things in the first place. Buy a large, intelligent dog, and have <u>him</u> take care of things for you.

DEFENSES TO CIVIL LIABILITY:

It is a complete defense to any civil action for damages against you if you prove that the injured person was injured during the commission or attempted commission of a forcible felony (not the escape from). F.S. 776.085. This defense can alternatively be shown by proof that the injured person was convicted of the forcible felony.

QUESTION: What if you use excessive force?

ANSWER: Darn if I know, although my guess is that you will still be OK, unless the other guy surrendered, and you shot him, anyway. That's because the crime would be over — and you'd be the new aggressor. Again, there are no reported Florida cases on this question, and it's a hard one to answer. Time for that exciting test case, again.

Likewise, under the 2005 "Protection of Persons and Property" law, specifically F.S. 776.032, a person who used force (deadly or non-deadly) in conformity with sections 776.012; 776.013; or 776.031, is immune from civil suit unless the person the force was used against was a law enforcement officer who was acting in the performance of his/her official duties and the officer identified himself/herself in accordance with law, or the person using the force knew or reasonably should have known that the person was a law enforcement officer. If the court finds you were immune, then the court shall award reasonable attorney fees, all expenses involved in defending the suit, and any lost income due to the suit against the plaintiff.

OTHER CIVIL PROBLEMS — INSURANCE:

The first thing you need to know when you use self-defense is that you are probably not covered by your insurance policy for anything that involves self-defense, defense of property, or preventing a forcible felony. Your Homeowners insurance does not cover it because your act is generally not one of negligence -- but instead is an "intentional" act which is normally <u>excluded</u> in almost all insurance policies. This probably won't apply if the weapon goes off <u>accidentally</u> in a struggle, because an accident would imply "negligence" or an "unintentional act" that should be within your coverage.[228]

Now, you may say that a jury would never award damages against you for defending your life or property -- but in a 1989 in a Florida Supreme Court case, <u>State Farm v. Marshall</u>, the Supreme Court affirmed a $575,000.00 verdict in favor of a person who broke into the Defendant's home and attacked him.[229] In its Opinion, the Court not only upheld the jury verdict, but also held that the Homeowners policy did <u>not</u> cover any part of this since the act of intentional self-defense was involved.

Incredible! How the heck a jury could ever come up with this result is beyond me, but it happened! And, you'd better be aware that if it happened once, it can happen again. Anything is possible in the law!

So, what can you do about it? You can try the impossible, which is finding an insurance company that will accept a rider to your policy that states something to the effect of: "Despite any wording to the contrary, this policy covers any act by any insured performed in self-defense on or immediately about the insured property." However, don't bet on finding one that will do it.

On the other hand, the NRA now offers insurance that reim- burses self defense cases up to $50,000.00 — if you beat all the charges. That means that you have to pay for the lawyer, and win <u>everything</u> to get reimbursed. But, it's the only thing out there, for now that I know of.

DAMAGE CAUSED BY YOUR KIDS:

Believe it or not there's a statute, <u>F.S.</u> 741.24, that makes the parents of any child liable for the damage caused by that child. The only requirements are that the child lives with the parent(s), is under the age of 18 years, and that the child maliciously or willfully destroys or steals property.   Damages are limited to the actual loss, and any court costs.   There are other theories of liability that might be usable. Negligent supervision. Negligent entrustment of a weapon or firearm. Etc.

If you wonder why I put this here rather than in the section about children – it's because I thought it was important to know that if your kid is shooting up the neighbor's place – you might want to know that besides your kid being arrested – you can get sued. On the other hand, if you live next to the Beverly Hillbillies – you now know you can legally get even!

A SUMMARY ON THE USE & DISPLAY OF WEAPONS:

On a technical note, remember that there's a distinction between "deadly force", and a "deadly weapon".   There is also a difference between the "display" and "use" of any weapon, deadly or not.   Thus, the "display" of a deadly weapon, <u>without its discharge</u> is considered the use of "non-deadly force",[230] and can be argued as the use of "no force", at all.   In other words, just because it's a deadly weapon doesn't mean it's also the **use** of deadly force – unless it's also discharged.   While that may not seem real important -- it is.

Why?

Well, since you only have the right to use any <u>reasonable</u> "non-deadly force" against a misdemeanor -- you may have a defense to the mere "display" of a deadly weapon. Obviously, a very important question if you're charged with aggravated assault, and are facing a three year mandatory prison sentence. Likewise, you can "stand your ground" if the other person is committing a crime against you, or such crime is imminent.

QUESTION: How is it possible to use deadly force without a deadly weapon?

ANSWER: Well, I'll give you an example. If you were trying to stop a person from committing a grand theft, and grabbed him by the throat until you choked him to death -- there would be no deadly weapon involved -- but you certainly would have used deadly force. Obviously, lots of other examples could be thought of.

QUESTION: Using that last example -- is there any way that that might be legal?

ANSWER: Well, let's try the example method, again. Let's say that the guy refuses to let go of whatever he's stealing, and you keep choking him until he stops struggling. Unfortunately for him, he dies. It should be excusable homicide, or justifiable use of force in that circumstance. Test case time.

QUESTION: So, when should I use a deadly weapon?

ANSWER: This is opinion time. In my opinion, you should only display it when it appears "reasonably" necessary to stop the commission or attempted commission of a felony. If you're going to use it, then make sure the felony is a "forcible fel-ony" and its commission is imminent, or you have a reasonable fear of imminent death or great bodily harm. Otherwise, the risks are too great, even if you are legal.

QUESTION: What if three guys surround me, and say they're gonna beat me up?

ANSWER: It depends. If their motive is robbery, or another forcible felony -- you're legal. If they just want to do some bodily damage, the answer is "no", unless they've made it clear that you'll be hospital material afterwards, and you believe it. Same thing if they don't tell you their motive, but it's reasonable to believe it's hospital or felony time. If you've got a weak heart, and won't survive -- I'd warn them of your condition before I did anything. If you don't know what the hell they want -- maybe. However, don't get "macho" just because you have a gun. This is why some people who use guns go to jail -- and should. Moreover, the legal consequences of using deadly force, no matter how justified you were, are just not worth it, if it's avoidable.

QUESTION: Didn't you just tell me that I could legally display a firearm if I didn't discharge it?

ANSWER: No! I said that you might be able to do it, and it might be legal — because mere display, even coupled with a threat to use it, is normally the use of "non-deadly force". But — you also might get arrested. You also might have a jury decide that the display was not reasonable. In other words, "might" doesn't necessarily mean "right", in this scenario. It's always better to be on the safe side unless you're sure that the alternative is death, great bodily harm, or a serious felony!

QUESTION: What other situations do you see where people get in trouble?

ANSWER: Well, there are several types of cases that seem
           to come up, again-and-again, with slight factual
           variations — I'll give you a few in the next
           section.

SELF-DEFENSE EXAMPLES – GOOD & BAD:

Situation Number One -- Road Warriors:

The worst place to display a weapon is in the heat of a traffic
jam, or somebody cutting you off. Tempers seem to flare, and as he
cuts you off, tailgates you, or whatever — you do it right back.
Eventually, it escalates to the point of you taking out your handgun,
and displaying it — usually without pointing it. You've shown him
that you're armed — and not to push his luck.

Whether justified or not -- it's usually a **very bad decision**! You
should have used the cellular, backed-off, and realized this guy was a
low-life, hateful, egg-sucking, moron — instead, you're now the moron.
What's worse is that the jerk now has the opportunity to "really" get
even, and will call the police, and lie about what happened. He'll say
you pointed the gun at him, and that he was in fear of being shot.
I've seen this happen time and time again! I handle a minimum of one
case a year exactly like this. Moreover, once he says that to the police
— he's stuck himself to the story, or he may get in trouble for a false
police report.   He'll also leave out the fact that he almost killed you
several times with his car, and that your gun was pointed skyward. In
fact, he'll probably get immense satisfaction from your unjustified
arrest, and prosecution. If you're real lucky, he may realize somewhere
down the line that you don't deserve a three year mandatory sentence,
and may tell the truth — or may tell the prosecutor that he doesn't
mind if they "plea bargain" the case to something less.

So remember, rarely will you be in a position that displaying a
firearm in a vehicle is anything but a really bad move. Only if you
reasonably think you're about to be highjacked, or robbed is this
advisable. I guess if he was trying to ram you, and you weren't trying
to ram back, the same would apply. But otherwise, remember that you
can normally pull over, and let him go by.   If you can avoid it,

you should.   And,   assuming you're involved in such a situation, I highly recommend that you call 911 or *FHP, and let the police know what's going on. Whatever you do, don't lie to the police — even if you have to admit that you were involved in some improper driving. Better to admit you gave the other guy the "finger" than to have the police think you're the instigator, and a liar.

Situation Number Two -- "What's that gonna do against this?":

Remember what I told you about escalation?   It tends to get worse and not better. Typical scenario is you get in a verbal confrontation with someone, and rather than walk away — you take out your pepper spray. The next thing you know — the guy has his gun out saying: "What's that gonna do against this?" Very serious situation. An apology, or back-off is usually the safer method of conduct, even if you were in the right, and do have to swallow your pride.   When the guy is gone, call the cops, and thank God you're alive.

Situation Number Three -- "Get the hell off my property":

This usually is justified, but nobody believes you. You have a trespasser, or somebody on your property who doesn't belong there. You take your gun with you for "just in case". This is totally legal when you're on your property. You never point the thing at him, but you make darn sure he knows it's there. He, being the wonderful person that he is, makes that 911 call telling the police that you pointed the gun at him, and threatened to blow him away unless he left your property. The police arrest you.

Sometimes this guy honestly believes you pointed the gun at him., even though you didn't. I've seen it happen many times. Sometimes it's a pure crock of you-know-what. Sometimes you overreacted. But, usually, you were well within your rights. Whatever, you now have a problem if he didn't tell the complete truth. If he did, then the police shouldn't be arresting you because you do nothing wrong by going armed on your own property. I mean . . . if you were right . . . what are you gonna do?   Ask the armed robber to wait while you go and get your gun? On the other hand, let's hope you didn't threaten to shoot him if he didn't leave. This would not be a real good move

unless he was in the commission of a forcible felony. I guess you just
need to use good judgment. Personally, if I were in this situation, I'd
try to hide the gun in a pocket, or under a jacket so the other person
didn't know it was there. That way, I'd have the element of surprise
if I needed it, and be totally legal. I'd also have my cellular with me,
and call 911 right there if the guy refused. Make sure it's in your
hand so he can't say you were reaching for a gun. In this day and
age, I advise people that the cellular phone is your best defense against
anything. Make sure it's programed to 911, and also to *FHP for
when you're on the highways.

Situation Number Four -- South Florida Armed and Ready:

Well, I've given you all the bad scenarios -- here's the other one
that I've heard over-and-over that always works out for the best. It
happens in driveways, in shopping malls, and in gas stations. Nobody
reports it to the police because they're scared as heck that they'll get
arrested. It goes something like this:

You pull into a gas station late at night. Suddenly, a car pulls
up next to you, and three or four very scary looking dudes appear ready
to do you in some very serious fashion. You calmly display your
handgun, pointed upwards — and they drive away just as suddenly as
they came. You wipe away the sweat, and thank God for the handgun.
You think about calling the police, and then think better of it. Very
typical. You did the right thing all around — especially in South
Florida.

There are other cases I see — but these are the most common.
I hope the examples can be of some help, but every situation is
different. There are no set answers for anything, and like everything
else, there is always the danger that the cops could be called against
you, even if you were totally legal. You really have to weigh each
situation against life and death, and hope your decision was the right
one.

A SUMMARY ON SELF-DEFENSE LAW:

In summation of this chapter I repeat the same old major warning as before. Was your action reasonable?   Was it necessary? Maybe to you it was -- but what will a police officer, prosecutor, or jury say later? Hmmmm! That's the problem! That's why these laws are dangerous to the average citizen.   Moreover, if you are only permitted to use non-deadly force, and possibly exceed that by displaying and threatening the use of a deadly weapon, or engaging in the use of deadly force -- you may be charged with of aggravated assault, even if you don't fire a shot, shoot an arrow, or throw that hatchet.

So, to summarize this section, when can you use deadly force? Hmmm, tough question. The answer? Well, truthfully -- whenever you're not prosecuted for it.

And when will that be, you ask?

Probably, if it's a life or death situation, or it looks like it. Probably, if somebody is already using a firearm or deadly weapon against you, and escape could be hazardous or risky. Almost certainly, if someone breaks into your house or tries breaking into your home, and you just don't want to take the risk of telling him to drop the weapon, because if you do -- he's got the drop on you. Probably in any kidnap situation by a stranger. And probably, if there is a robbery of your business involving the display of a firearm or other deadly weapon by one of the perpetrators.

These are classic cases of where people are usually not prosecuted -- and also where the "immunity" in the 2005 "Protection of Persons and Property" Law will kick in. But, as I said before: There are no guarantees!

WHAT TO DO AFTER THE POLICE ARRIVE:

I've done a lot of speaking engagements since I first wrote this book, and everybody seems to ask me the following question: "What should I do if I've shot someone in self-defense?"

Well, first of all -- take my business card, you're gonna need it -- and call me, or another qualified criminal attorney before you make any detailed statement to the police. However, if it happened outside don't drag the body inside, like everyone tells you to. That's the worst thing you could possibly do. With modern crime scene technology, you'll already be branded a liar, and it will go downhill from there. Don't disturb the scene, to whatever extent that is possible. Don't get rid of, or destroy evidence. That will also go against you.

Next, remember that "anything you say can, and will, be used against you." While many attorneys tell their clients not to say anything, I go along with a modified version of that. I think it's extremely important that the police realize that the body on the floor in the pool of blood is NOT the victim! You're the victim! In order to make sure the officer knows this, something akin to the following statement is extremely pertinent:

"Officer, I was attacked by this man, and thought he was armed.[231] I was in fear for my life, and was forced to shot him in self-defense."

Once you've said this, and you're sure he's heard it -- you don't generally want to go into any specifics until after you've spoken to a really good lawyer who knows this stuff. Specifics can get you into deep trouble, even if your act was one hundred per cent perfectly legal. I've seen this happen again and again, where the citizen thought they couldn't say anything that could cause them trouble – but got arrested, instead.

Why?

Well, obviously, you're nervous as hell, and fourteen million different thoughts are racing through your head, all at the same time. If ever you're gonna screw something up, get it twisted and out of place, or leave out an important detail -- this is it! Moreover, even though you know what happened, you haven't gotten your thoughts together, yet -- and you don't know how to say what happened in the "right way".

Now, I don't mean that by the "right way" you've made something up. That's not the way I do business. On the other hand, you can say the same thing ten different ways -- and only one of them is gonna walk you out of that courtroom. That's why you want to speak to your lawyer. So he can go over the entire thing with you, and make sure you know what to say -- and more importantly -- what not to say.

Yes, you want to make sure the police know that it was self-defense; that you were in fear of your life; that he was the attacker, and that he was armed -- or you thought he was. But, saying anything beyond these generalizations is dangerous, and anything you say (other than wanting an attorney) will probably seriously screw your case up, later.

Most police officers who are on your side will not push the point, and will almost lead you into saying it was self-defense, you were in fear for your life, and you want to talk to your lawyer before you say anything else. However, if they want details -- beware! Tell them that you'll be glad to talk to them once you've had a chance to calm down, and have spoken to your lawyer. If they're on your side -- that will normally satisfy them. If it doesn't satisfy them, they're probably looking to make an arrest -- and that's certainly not on your side. If they try pushing you as to why you don't want to talk to them, remind them that you're really nervous, need time to calm down, and time to speak to an attorney -- and then remind them that even police officers are normally given a 24 hour period before they can be questioned about a shooting they're involved in so that they can calm down, get the facts straight in their mind, and have a chance to talk to their F.O.P. representative, and attorney before responding to an investigator.

Remember "Gutmacher's famous truism" about arrests:

"If they're gonna arrest you -- they're gonna arrest you!"

Giving them a detailed story isn't going to change anything -- you'll still wind-up in a cell, and will have created a **real problem** for you and your attorney. So, if you followed my advice, at least you won't have screwed it up for yourself later on.

There is a slight modifier to all of this due to the "Stand Your Ground" law. Again, you don't want to go into details before talking to an attorney, but if there was a break-in or attempted break-in – and you know the intruder broke a window, door latch, etc. – it would be wise to show the police that place. If asked – you may also respond the intruder was not a member of your household or invited guest. Beyond that – stick to my previous advise on what to say. Remember, with the new law the less you say, probably the better – because once the police have evidence that an intruder had forcefully entered, or forcefully tried to enter a residence, dwelling, or occupied vehicle – your actions in using deadly force are **presumed** legal! Unless the police have evidence this didn't happen, they can't legally arrest you. That means that the more you say, the more chances you have of screwing it up.

Last, if you're going to hire an attorney – make sure the attorney is a gun owner, and actually believes in your right to self-defense. There are a lot of attorneys out there who really aren't into this stuff, and the last thing you want is somebody who is philosophically anti-gun, no matter how good they're supposed to be. Make sure your attorney belongs to the NRA, Gun Owners of America, or similar organization. If they don't – he or she is probably not the right person for this particular type case.

911 — USE IT!

The best thing you can ever do if you think you're being attacked, broken into, or about to be attacked, etc. -- is call 911, or *FHP if you're on the Turnpike. Tell them you're frightened! Tell them you think the guy may be armed (even if you're not sure -- it's certainly not a lie in this day and age). Tell them to hurry up and send somebody!

All this is being recorded! It's gonna be used as evidence in your favor! If the police don't get there in a few minutes, call 911 again! It's gonna be recorded again! The jury is going to wonder what the heck the police were doing while you're panicking out trying to defend home and family. Moreover, when the police do get there they already know that you're already the victim! They're going out there to rescue you! The dead son-of-a-bitch on the floor in the congealing pool of blood is the "bad guy" -- you're just the poor victim who luckily managed to save himself . . . and in the process, you performed a valuable civic service. Now, they have one less criminal on the street! Good job!

So, thank heaven for 911 -- if you use it.

One word of warning. These calls are routinely erased by law enforcement after a certain period of time, the least being 30 days, and the most being one year. It varies from department to department. You need to get a copy of the tape before it's been destroyed, and should personally obtain it, or have someone obtain the copy for you before it's too late. The usual method is calling up the communications division, and finding out the procedure they require. Many times it's a certified letter return receipt requested to the Chief of Police, or Supervisor of Communications. If done by letter, call a few days later and make sure they got it! The charge is generally less than fifty bucks, and is well worth the trouble. Once it's destroyed — it's too late -- it's gone forever!

CELLULAR PHONES — YOUR BEST DEFENSE:

Of course, if you're on the road, the same thing goes for cellular phones. When in a vehicle, or anywhere where a regular phone is not handy -- they are your best defense against the nut-cases that inherit our streets and highways. If someone is doing strange things, dial 911 or *FHP, just so you have a record of your fear -- in case it really happens.

If you're lucky, they may send a unit to check it out before it happens. If not, at least we know who the victim is, and who the bad guy is. Very important factors in analyzing who gets sued, who gets arrested, or both.

On the other hand, please don't say that "I'm gonna shoot him if he tries anything" -- even if you intend to. That's just asking for trouble. You want to make sure that they know you're scared. If you aren't, then there's something wrong with you, no matter how controlled you may be. Moreover, you certainly don't want to give the 911 operator the impression that you're gonna blow this guy away no matter what happens. That just sounds like you're looking for trouble, and want to perform a "legal execution".

That's not what you want to do, in fact, you really want to give the impression that you'll only use your weapon as a "last resort". Try remembering that.

GETTING STOPPED BY THE POLICE:

What are your rights when the police stop you? Do you have to tell them you've got a gun on you, etc.? Interesting questions.

As a general rule — you have no obligation to tell a police officer you have a gun or weapon on you, or in your vehicle. However, if you lie about it, and he finds out, you will probably have a very displeased police officer, and a heap of trouble. My personal rule of thumb is to never volunteer that information unless the officer is about to look into the glove compartment, etc. — where he will obviously find it. Other than that — keeping your mouth shut on the issue is probably the best approach.

However, if asked — you need to make a decision on whether to answer the question directly — or not. You could legally, and truthfully say: "Officer, I have absolutely nothing illegal on me, or in my vehicle." However, this might not be an appropriate response in all situations. Moreover, if this doesn't satisfy him, I do **not** suggest lying.

I think the best approach on being specifically asked is usually to say something that "legalizes" your position — ie — "Officer, I have a legal firearm 'securely encased' in my vehicle." Or — "Officer, I have a concealed permit in my wallet. I also have a 'legally concealed' firearm. Would you like to see the permit?"

On the other hand, if the officer discovers or is informed that you have a weapon or firearm — he has the absolute right to temporarily take it into custody during the encounter to protect himself/herself from harm. Totally legal. The officer may even unload the weapon, and place it in his unit until the encounter is over.

After the encounter — unless you're being arrested, you're supposed to get the firearm or weapon back. Probably unloaded with the cartridges separate from the firearm — until you or he leaves. Again — totally legal. Police don't want to get shot — that makes perfect sense to me.

Whatever the situation, I would rehearse my suggestions just in case they ever happen. If you've actually verbalized them several times, it won't be as awkward if the situation actually materializes. Otherwise, you'll probably screw it up. Murphy's Law in action!

Whatever you do, remember a very important point in how to handle yourself: Police officers are creatures of "respect", and quite frankly, they deserve your respect.   If they perceive your response as "disrespectful" — you're probably in for trouble.   Therefore, don't argue.   Don't challenge his authority (that's what lawyers are for). Don't threaten to "fight it in court", "get a lawyer", or make a complaint with the police agency.   Even if you're right, even if your "rights" are being violated — saying anything like that is sure to get you in more trouble.   Those are things you discuss with a lawyer, and do **afterwards** -- assuming they're advisable.

Use the words **"yes, sir"** and **"no, sir"** a lot.   If you're unlucky enough to get an officer who likes to make trouble, or give a hard time — trouble it will be, and you need to try to minimize it.   So, use your best judgment under the circumstances .   If you have to give up some of your constitutional rights to avoid jail — maybe that isn't the worst choice.   I've handled lots of false arrest cases, and I don't think anything is worth going to jail for, no matter what damages you might get awarded later on.   You'll obviously have to make your own decision on this.   On the other hand — let me tell you — jail sucks, no matter how short the visit is.

USE OF FORCE AGAINST ANIMALS:

We all know, or think we know, what our rights of self defense are against another person.   But, what are your rights when it comes to an attack or trespass by an animal?

I guess the starting point begins with F.S. 828.12 which is titled "Cruelty to Animals".   That section makes it a crime to "unnecessarily kill" or cause an animal "unnecessary pain or suffering".   The key word here is "unnecessary".   What does unnecessary mean?   Well, that's a long question, and to answer it I think I'll first explore some Florida statutes.

Let's begin with Chapter 767 of the Florida Statutes which discusses dogs.   Read it, and you find out that one defense to killing a dog is that the dog was killing or had been killing any domestic animal or livestock. (F.S. 767.03). If you read further in F.S. 828.24, you find out that if you must kill any animal, it must be done by a "humane method". According to another statute, a humane method is any method whereby the animal is rapidly and effectively rendered insensitive to pain, and includes an arrow bolt or gunshot with proper caliber and placement.

So, how do we apply these statutes, and is there any case law out there on the subject that further defines it? Well, there's no case law in Florida on these exact areas, but other states have had more than their fair share. Typical example is what can you do when someone else's dog, cat, chicken, etc. wanders on your property? The answer is basically "not much". You could capture the animal, and inform the owner so he/she can pick it up. You could try to shoo it away. I guess you could even turn the water hose on the critter if you didn't intentionally injure it. But, the case law makes it clear that just because an animal wanders onto your property – no matter how annoying you find it – it is usually a minor matter that does not justify any injury to the animal.

Why not?

Well, the damage to you is relatively minor. It's got to be fairly serious before the law starts thinking that killing an animal is "necessary". Furthermore, if worse comes to worse, you can always sue the owner for any damage caused. Even if it's a dog chasing your precious cat – unless there is a real threat to the cat's life that can't be avoided without killing or injuring the dog – the remedy is calling the authorities, capturing the dog or animal for the owner or authorities, or trying to scare it away. In these cases killing or injury is "unnecessary" – hence, 'cruelty to animals". Same thing if the dog is chasing a wild animal. All that amounts to is a "nuisance".

Now, remember the statute, F.S. 767.03? It said you could kill any dog that was killing, or had been killing another domestic animal or livestock. But, don't take that section literally! Although it certainly applies if you shoot the critter in the act, still you couldn't track the dog to the owners property, and kill it. That would get you in big trouble. Likewise, there's quite a few cases that indicate that once the attack is completed, and the attacking animal is wandering away – you generally don't have a right to kill or injure it because – there are other reasonable alternatives.

Of course, they'll be some exceptions. One exception that is described in various appellate decisions occurs when the same animal has attacked (and killed or seriously injured) your domestic animals more than once, you've been unsuccessful in stopping it by other means, and you've notified the owner who hasn't restrained his critter from further attacks. In those case the courts usually indicate it's a jury question whether shooting the dog/cat/hog – was reasonable and necessary. (Sounds a lot like self defense law, doesn't it?)

What about when the animal is attacking you, or another human being?

Well, that's a more serious issue! Again, it's always going to be a question of was it "unnecessary"? Was it "reasonable"? Could you escape with safety? Could you take safe refuge somewhere? Was there a reasonable way to avoid a dangerous and immediate confrontation? If not, you may certainly protect yourself and others, and I think law enforcement would likely see it your way. Still, it could wind-up as a jury question if there was doubt. Add to this equation the new "Stand Your Ground" law in C. 776 of the statutes – and you have a really interesting legal question popping up for some court to resolve. My guess is that you don't have to retreat from an animal – if you don't have to retreat from a human. But – that's a pure guess since there's no case law on it for now!

Next question – could you pursue a vicious or rabid dog? Again, a very "iffy" issue. The issue there is whether the danger is real, and was there also an immediate danger to others if you didn't act? If calling the authorities would work just as well, that may be a real fact to consider. If failing to take immediate action means the critter(s) will escape, and continue their rampage – it makes your response more reasonable and necessary. Again, a possible jury issue if you were charged.

That raises another interesting issue.   What happens if the animal is on a "protected" list?   We're not talking about "cruelty to animals" here – we're talking pure game protection laws.

The few cases where this happened involved bears killing sheep, or moose and horse herds wiping out valuable grazing areas. As a general rule the courts are very unsympathetic to the citizen where human life isn't at stake. Protected animals stay protected, and only state or federal authorities are permitted to remove or destroy them. How does that apply to your favorite dog or cat being attacked by a gator?   From a "cruelty to animals" standpoint – my personal opinion is that it would be legal since you're saving a life. Again – just my opinion, because there is no case law. If it was a bear, I'd really try a warning shot first, if I had a chance, because more intelligent animals will frequently flee. As to a Florida panther – I'm really not sure, because Florida's Constitution might allow a defense – however, the case law from other states and the federal courts would likely be on the side of the panther. On the other hand – if it's a human being that's about to be attacked by the critter – fire away – as long as you don't have any other reasonable recourse. The one case I came upon made it a jury question whether there really was a necessity, or whether the defendant just wanted an excuse to shoot a bear. In other words – if there's a reasonable alternative – you've got to take it.

I wish there were some Florida cases here to give you a more definite answer – but I think the parameters are clear. You can't shoot or injure an animal just because it's a nuisance. It's got to be a real and immediate threat to something substantial. Even then, there are possible exceptions. Hope that helps.

NANOSECONDS TO REACT:

I've thought very hard about including this particular section in the book. As a trial attorney I read lots of cases, every day of the week. Many of these cases are frightening. They don't involve self-defense. They involve people who didn't use self-defense. People who didn't have time to defend themselves, didn't know how, or didn't have the weapons or knowledge to defend themselves. These people, for the most part — are now dead. They are murder victims, and worse. The excerpts I've taken from just a few of these cases are not for the weak of heart — but it's instructional. Maybe, they will not have died totally in vain if you read it, and learn something from it. Again, it's not a pretty sight. It's sad — and if you shed a tear, it's OK. I do, every time I read them.

Heynard v. State, 689 So. 2d 239 (Fla. 1996):

Around 10 p.m. on January 30, Lynette Tschida went to the Winn Dixie store in Eustis. She saw Henyard and a younger man sitting on a bench near the entrance of the store. When she left, Henyard and his companion got up from the bench; one of them walked ahead of her and the other behind her. As she approached her car, the one ahead of her went to the end of the bumper, turned around, and stood. Ms. Tschida quickly got into the car and locked the doors. As she drove away, she saw Henyard and the younger man walking back towards the store.

Ms. Lewis noticed a few people sitting on a bench near the doors as she and her daughters entered the store. When Ms. Lewis left the store, she went to her car and put her daughters in the front passenger seat. As she walked behind the car to the driver's side, Ms. Lewis noticed Alfonza Smalls coming towards her. As Smalls approached, he pulled up his shirt and revealed a gun in his waistband. Smalls ordered Ms. Lewis and her daughters into the back seat of the car, and then called to Henyard. Henyard drove the Lewis car out of town as Smalls gave him directions. The Lewis girls were crying and upset, and Smalls repeatedly demanded that Ms. Lewis "shut the girls up." As they continued to drive out of town, Ms. Lewis beseeched Jesus for help, to which Henyard replied, "this ain't Jesus, this is Satan." Later, Henyard stopped the car at a deserted location and ordered Ms. Lewis out of the car. Henyard raped Ms. Lewis on the trunk of the car while her daughters remained in the back seat. Ms. Lewis attempted to reach for the gun that was lying nearby on the trunk. Smalls grabbed the gun from her and shouted, "you're not going to get the gun, bitch." Smalls also raped Ms. Lewis on the trunk of the car. Henyard then ordered her to sit on the ground near the edge of the road. When she hesitated, Henyard pushed her to the ground and shot her in the leg. Henyard shot her at close range three more times, wounding her in the neck, mouth, and the middle of the forehead between her eyes. Henyard and Smalls rolled Ms. Lewis's unconscious body off to the side of the road, and got back into the car. The last thing Ms. Lewis remembers before losing consciousness is a gun aimed at her face. Miraculously, Ms. Lewis survived and, upon regaining consciousness a few hours later, made her way to a nearby house for help. The occupants called the police and Ms. Lewis, who was covered in blood, collapsed on the front porch and waited for the officers to arrive.   As Henyard and Smalls drove the Lewis girls away from the scene where their mother had been shot and abandoned.   Jasmine and Jamilya continued to cry and plead: "I want my Mommy," "Mommy," "Mommy." Shortly thereafter, Henyard stopped the car on the side of the road, got out, and lifted Jasmine out of the back seat while Jamilya got out on her own. The Lewis girls were then taken into a grassy area along the roadside where they were each killed by a single bullet fired into the head. Henyard and Smalls threw the bodies of Jasmine and Jamilya Lewis over a nearby fence into some underbrush.

The moral to this case is what police experts will tell you — in an abduction, you stand a better chance doing anything but getting in the car.   Criminals who are out to rob you, are normally not going to abduct you.   Abductions are usually reserved for murderers. Cooperation only places you in a remote area where help is impossible. Better to be shot where somebody may call an ambulance — than dead in the middle of a field. If you're alone — break and run. If you're armed — use your weapon once you're free of being grabbed, and possibly disarmed.   Too many police officers have lost their lives because they tried to grapple with dangerous offenders — rather than break away, and distance themselves, first. You won't be of any help to anyone if you're disarmed, bound, gagged, stuffed in a trunk, and then murdered.

James v. State, 695 So. 2d 1229 (Fla. 1997):

Pearson stated that when the two met, James was on his way to visit Tim Dick, the victim's son, and his girlfriend, Nichole, who also lived nearby.   They stopped and talked for about ten minutes and Pearson watched James ingest about ten "hits" of LSD on paper. James told Pearson he had been drinking at Todd Van Fossen's party, but he appeared sober to Pearson.   After briefly visiting Tim Dick and Nichole where he drank some gin, James returned to his room at Betty Dick's house. When he entered the house, James noticed that Betty Dick's four grandchildren were asleep in the living room.   One of the children, Wendi, awoke briefly when James arrived. She observed that he was laughing and appeared drunk.   James went to the kitchen, made himself a sandwich and retired to his room.   Eventually, he returned to the living room where he grabbed Betty Dick's eight-year-old granddaughter, Toni Neuner, by the neck and strangled her, hearing the bones pop in her neck. Believing Toni was dead, he removed her clothes and had vaginal and anal intercourse with her in his room.   Toni never screamed or resisted.   After raping Toni, he threw her behind his bed.   James then went to Betty Dick's bedroom where he intended to have sexual intercourse with her.   He hit Betty in the back of the head with a pewter candlestick. She woke up and started screaming, "Why, Eddie, why?" Betty's screaming brought Wendi Neuner to the doorway of her grandmother's bedroom where she saw James stabbing Betty with a small knife. When James saw Wendi he grabbed her, tied her up, and placed her in the bathroom.   Thinking that Betty was not dead, James went to the kitchen, grabbed a butcher knife and returned to Betty's room and stabbed her in the back.   James removed Betty Dick's pajama bottoms, but did not sexually batter her. Covered with blood, James took a shower in the bathroom where Wendi remained tied up and then threw together some clothes and belongings.   He returned to Betty's room and took her purse and jewelry bag before driving away in her car.   James drove across the country, stopping periodically to sell jewelry for money.

What do you say about this one?   First — if she had a gun, she could have used it. Nothing else would have worked. Other than that, if you associate with people who use drugs and alcohol — disaster may occur. Be forewarned!

Campbell v. State, 679 So.2d 720 (Fla. 1996):

Campbell rang the doorbell to the Bosler home at 2:15 p.m. on December 22, 1986, and when Billy Bosler answered the door, Campbell stabbed him a number of times.   Billy's adult daughter, Sue Zann Bosler, heard the commotion and came to her father's aid, and Campbell stabbed her. Billy died, Sue Zann lived. Sue Zann's testimony about the murder began with her describing what happened when she came out of her bedroom at the parsonage, which was the home of her father, mother, and sister:

Q.   You're indicating that your dad was in the doorway, a man was stabbing him?

A: Yes.

Q.   What, if anything, did you do?

A.   By the time I got, I was walking out towards him to help him. He was being stabbed so many times that he was collapsing to the floor.

Q.   And what did you do as you approached this scene?

A.   As I approached the scene I went forward to help and I must have screamed because he turned around and he was going to stab me in the front.

Q.   When you say he, Sue Zann, who are you talking about?

A.   The man who was stabbing my father.

Q.   You turned around and he goes to stab you in the front?

A.   Yes.

Q.   What do you do?

A.   I turned to the right like this and he stabbed me three times in the back.

Q.   Where on your back did he stab you?

A.   Once in my shoulder, the knife went approximately four inches into my flesh, once below my shoulder in the back and three inches in and right by my spine approximately two inches.

Q.   After you were struck those three times, what did you do?

A.   I was knocked to the floor on my knees.

Q.   Okay. Did he continue stabbing you?

A.   No.

Q.   What was your father doing?

A.   He was trying to get up on his knee to try to help me.

Q.   When you last saw him, he was on his knees in the hallway?

A.   He was trying to get on his knees.

Q.   So he was trying to lift himself up?

A.   Yes.

Q.   Was he able to do that?

A.   No.

Q.   Did he start to crawl toward you?

A.   No, he couldn't.

Q. And you're stabbed over here?

A. Yes.

Q. Your father starts to move towards you or tries to get up?

A. He is trying to still get up.

Q. What happens to him next?

A. After I was stabbed to the floor, dad was trying to get up and the man turned around and start stabbing dad in the back many times.

You know the answer to this last case, and so do I. Sue Zann needed a firearm, and needed to use it before she did anything else. Nanoseconds to react!

In fact, private citizens firearms use guns in self-defense 800,000 to 2.5 million times a year according to a study by Professor Gary Kleck, a noted criminologist at the Florida State University. In 80 or 90 percent of these cases no shots are fired — because the criminal flees! According to the study, at least half a million cases of lawful self-defense happen a year where the crime is stopped! [232]

Next time your legislators – especially those in Congress, try taking away your firearms or firearm rights — tell them to get real. Only criminals benefit by firearm regulations! It protects them from honest citizens like you and I. They don't obey the laws, and don't really care about them. That's why we call them "criminals".

MANDATORY SENTENCES FOR FIREARM OFFENSES:

Be careful when you vote for a candidate who promises to pass more laws for mandatory sentences. Remember that every time such a law passes you are taking the discretion out of the sentencing, and basically saying you don't trust the judge or the jury to do the right thing. To me, that's a sacrifice of the liberty your forefathers died for over the generations.

Why?

Well, because we already have so many laws that we've passed the area of sensibility, and are turning a once free society into a totalitarian state where almost anything you do can constitute a crime. If anything, we need to back-off on some of the laws we already have.

So, get ready for the bad news — mandatory sentences of draconian proportions. Sheer fright — for anyone with any degree of insight or commonsense. The Legislature doesn't trust judges or juries – and unfortunately doesn't understand how things really work in the courtrooms. Unfortunately, these sentences have no exceptions, even when justice calls for it. Make a mistake on a self-defense issue — and you are literally fighting for your life before the court. Here goes:

F.S. 775.087(2) & F.S. 775.087(3) requires a judge to impose a "mandatory minimum" sentence on any of the following crimes or their attempt where a firearm or destructive device is possessed: murder, sexual battery, robbery, burglary, arson, aggravated assault, aggravated battery, kidnaping, escape, aircraft piracy, aggravated child abuse, aggravated stalking, drug trafficking, unlawful throwing/placing/discharge of a destructive device, possession of firearm by convicted felon, etc.) where the person charged is in possession of a firearm or destructive device. Use of the firearm or device is not necessary – it's possession is sufficient. A "mandatory minimum" sentence means that if found guilty — the judge has no discretion to impose a lower sentence, even if he or she thinks the mandatory sentence is totally unfair, under the particular circumstances! The mandatory minimum sentences are found on the chart that follows:

CHART OF MANDATORY FIREARM SENTENCES:

3 years	aggravated assault; possession of firearm by convicted felon; burglary of conveyance
10 years	firearm/destructive device possessed in any listed felony except aggravated assault; possession by felon; burglary of conveyance
15 years	possessed semi-automatic firearm with high capacity detachable box magazine (ie: capable of holding more than 20 centerfire cartridges); or machine gun, during any of the listed felonies or their attempt
20 years	discharged a firearm or destructive device during any of listed felonies or their attempt
25 - life	same as previous, and as a result death or great bodily harm was inflicted on any person

FIRING A WARNING SHOT:

Remember, if a firearm is discharged — then the mandatory sentence is twenty (20) years in prison. This applies even to aggravated assault! So, if you fire a "warning shot" in a self-defense situation, and you somehow get prosecuted -- you're facing a mandatory twenty year sentence unless you take a plea bargain, or are found "not guilty"! If a person suffers death or great bodily harm on any of these — the mandatory sentence is a minimum of twenty-five (25) years to a maximum of life. If you possessed a machine gun, or firearm with a magazine equipped with a magazine that is "capable" of holding 20 or more centerfire cartridges — and commit one of the enumerated felonies — you have a fifteen (15) year mandatory minimum sentence.

QUESTION: What are all the problems, you talk about?

ANSWER: First, if you misjudge a self-defense situation you've probably committed an "aggravated assault". Three year minimum mandatory. Kiss the wife and kids goodbye unless you've got a sympathetic detective working the case, and a pro-self defense prosecutor, to boot. If you didn't want to hurt the varlet — and fired a warning shot — you're now facing a twenty (20) year mandatory sentence.   Kiss the wife and kids goodbye.   Also kiss any grandchildren goodbye.   If you hit the bastard, and wound him — twenty five years to life.   Probably a good point to consider suicide.

One thing you should notice immediately from this is — firing a warning shot is no longer a very good idea — even if it is a very good idea. What I mean by this is that sometimes — firing a warning shot is the act that saves both your lives — yours, and the stupid bastard's who was about to attack you.   But, the Legislature doesn't want to know about that. If firing a warning shot is reasonable, and did not cause damage to persons or property – I don't feel it should be labeled as the use of "deadly force", and certainly shouldn't carry an additional mandatory sentence. I know that will never pass – but I also know of too many instances where it really was the deciding factor in saving lives or preventing a felony.

THE AFTERMATH OF MANDATORY SENTENCING:

Again — that's why these mandatory laws are absolutely awful! They're fine if the guy is really a criminal — but for the marginal case, or the case of mistaken judgment — it's tragic!   The judge has no discretion. The mandatory sentence must be imposed!   And if the other side are a bunch of good actors, or are out to get even — you're gonna pay the price, guilty or not.   This is sad stuff.

What really makes it sad is that the person who just tried to break into your home, or threatened to club you when you came out will probably tell the cops that he was just walking across your lawn when you came after him with a gun. You were a "crazy man". All he was doing was cutting across the lawn, and you held a gun on him saying he was trying to break in your house.   If this is a neighbor you've been having a problem with, I almost guarantee this is what he'll say — and sometimes the police aren't real concerned about who really did what -- they just want that felony arrest, and let the system "sort it out".[233]

Now, you're suddenly facing three years in prison.   Never did anything illegal before in your life.   The prosecutor offers you a deal. No jail — just probation.   Are you gonna take it?

You bet you are!   When you look into the eyes of your wife and kids — they'll be no doubt what you're going to have to do. Innocent or not — the odds are usually with the State.   If the alleged "victim" is a good liar, and really wants to get you — it's even worse. He may even bring some of his buddies in to lie.   Again, I see it all the time, and many times if anti-gun, the State is not concerned about what the real truth is, or if the prosecutor is unsure and concerned with doing justice — the best he or she will usually do is offer you probation in return for a plea bargain.   Go to trial -- you face the maximum sentence!

And hey, and what if you fired a warning shot as he came at you with the club?   Now, it's twenty years!   Are you really thinking you're going to take this to a jury if they offer you a deal with two years in prison?   Even if you go to trial, and win — how much has it cost you in money, stress, and sleepless nights?   Have you lost your job?   Will you lose it?   Have you had to mortgage the house to pay the legal fees?   Has the wife left you after two years of trials and appeals?   Very heavy duty stuff -- make no mistake about it.

MORE EXAMPLES & JURY PARDONS:

Situation number two — also quite common.   You have an absolute right to keep and carry a firearm anywhere on your property. You hear something outside, grab your firearm just in case, and walk outside.   Your nosey, antagonistic neighbor sees you, says what are you doing with a gun, you tell them mind their own damn business — and they call up the police saying you threatened them with a gun. And the police, who probably don't have much choice at that point, are forced to arrest you.

Doesn't happen?

I see it all the time.   One neighbor trying to "get even".   The fact that you'll go to jail for something you didn't do — is not even a real concern.   Life in America!   God Bless this Country!

Want another example more on the lines of a real criminal? Fine!   Here's the typical example:

Some stupid kid drops off a friend who commits a residential burglary.   The kid waits for his buddy not knowing what he is about to do, but soon finds out when he sees him break in the house.   The kid has a firearm legally in the glove compartment, and now knowing what is happening, waits for his buddy to come out.   He hears a police car coming, and when his buddy gets in the car they try to escape, but are caught.   This kid is just an accessory, but he faces a ten year minimum prison sentence for having possession of the gun. For a career criminal — very good.   For somebody in between — perhaps a total injustice.   Hard to say — it depends.   But there again, is the problem.   Judges don't have discretion.   The sentence is mandatory.   If you fall one inch within the statutory definition of the crime, no matter what the degree of your involvement — you are in deep trouble.   The fact that a jury has the right to come back anyway they want isn't real comforting when you know the Florida Supreme Court has <u>forbidden</u> juries from being told what the possible sentence is that might be imposed, and has forbidden lawyers from telling the jury that they have the inherent right under the law to "jury pardon" a defendant no matter what the evidence is, or come back with a guilty verdict on a less serious charge as part of this pardon power.

So, juries that used to do the "right thing" — have been severely hampered by the law, today.   They aren't allowed to be told about the power they actually possess.

Same problem with judges.   The Legislature doesn't trust them to be fair -- so they've imposed   a mathematical set of "Sentencing Guidelines" which a judge must follow in most instances. This is where we are currently at.   I think it's a damn shame because I see how it operates, first hand.

A NEEDED CONSTITUTIONAL AMENDMENT:

As much as I dislike amendments to the Florida Constitution, what we need is a constitutional amendment that would guarantee that a jury be told about any mandatory penalty that might be imposed. If that happened, and they were also told they had a "jury pardon" power where they could acquit, or come back with a lesser crime in situations where they felt they should exercise that discretion – terrible sentencing laws would be counter-balanced by the commonsense of the jury. Until that happens — or unless the Legislature gives us some real relief from mandatory sentences in self defense situations – we're still in a lot of trouble.

(this page reserved)

CHAPTER TWELVE

MORE MISCELLANEOUS

This chapter is a collection of miscellaneous information which I feel you may find interesting. I strongly suggest you also search the internet for information using search terms such as "firearms", "weapons", "second amendment", etc. Some excellent websites I recommend include: www.nra.org (NRA site); www.gunowners.org (Gun Owners of America); www.jpfo.org (Jews for the Preservation of Firearms); www.ccrkba.org (Second Amendment Foundation); http://licgweb.doacs.state.fl.us (Florida. Dept. of Agriculture); www.atf.gov (ATF); www.world.guns.ru (Modern Firearms and Ammo).

PRIOR EDITIONS OF "FLORIDA FIREARMS":

If you own any previous version of the book other than the Sixth edition, I advise throwing it away as being substantially out of date. I'm not kidding -- too many things have changed. You should not be using it. Moreover, once you have a book that is two years old – throw it away, and buy a new one – even if you've been getting the updates off the web, or it's still the same edition. Too many things change, and we reprint this book once to twice a year. Every time we do, all updates and changes in thinking are incorporated into the new printing. Thus, the book is always changing. Even if the edition is the same things are being added to the reprints that are not in the updates.

Think of it this way – would you hire an accountant who advertised that he hadn't looked at any of the new IRS regs in the past two years? I would certainly hope not! So, why have a book that is obviously two years out of date that deals with laws equally complicated?

FREE UPDATING SERVICE:

Updates are posted free on our website at least twice yearly — www.FloridaFirearmsLaw.com.   One usually at the very end of January, and another usually at the very end of August.   Interim updates are also published on the web when I feel they're needed. You can only get the updates off the web, we don't mail them, and don't keep past updates. On the other hand, updates do not include all new materials in any reprinting of the book! They only show major corrections to the current book, and new laws and decisions of importance that would change the book. It's not that we want your money for a new book – it's just that this stuff really does change yearly, and my opinions sometimes change, especially when new cases come along.

MY BLOG:

There is a link on the website to my blog. The blog responds to many of the more interesting email questions I get, and also posts matters of interest for firearm and weapon owners on a more rapid and extensive basis than the updates. Many of these posts eventually find their way into the book. I strongly suggest you check the blog at least every two months for new material.

WEBSITE AND E-MAIL QUESTIONS:

Our website has lots of information, and is constantly undergoing change. Updates can be downloaded free off the website. I always welcome emails on weapon and self-defense related questions from the website link, and many times I use these questions for my monthly column in Rods N Guns Magazine, or in book revisions. Not every question can be answered, because I only take the ones of interest to myself, or those I think I can use. However, I do try to reply to all emails, even if I am not in a position to fully answer it. I try to reply within 48 hours, however, if I have a busy schedule going on, it can be several days. Likewise, if a question is too "fact intensive" or complicated, such that you're really asking for a formal legal opinion on a case – that's something I probably won't answer other than acknowledging it. Many of these really require retaining myself or another attorney for a proper response.

ENDNOTE SECTION:

The next section of the book contains the "endnotes". These are some of the citations, statutes, cases, and other sources from which the information in this book is derived. If you want to know where the information came from, and what I based it on – this is where to go. Plus, I **strongly** recommend you read these as an independent chapter as the insight and information contained in it is absolutely essential. However, I will tell you that it contains only a fraction of the research that went into this book. If I put in all of the research – I'd have to write another book to fit it.

LIST OF PRO-SECOND AMENDMENT ORGANIZATIONS:

Well, I doubt I'll be able to name even a small percent of the many great organizations out there. Here are the most prominent I can think of:

National Rifle Association: The most influential of all firearm groups with extensive publications, activities, and political lobbying. Has the best magazine publications out there. Well worth the membership for the subscription, alone. Great website, and great organization. For all information phone: 1-800-672-3888. (dues $35.00 yearly). Join on the web at **www.nra.org**.

Gun Owners of America: Not as large as the NRA, but extremely active and influential politically. Takes a very aggressive stand on firearms issues. Newsletter, e-mail updates, automatic contact with Congress through its Web site, and other programs. Like the NRA, it's essential to belong to. E-mails will keep you advised of everything going on in Congress like nobody else can. To sign-up for membership with credit card phone: 1-800-886-8852. Join on the web at **www.gunowners.org**

Unified Sportsmen of Florida: This is the Florida State affiliate of the NRA, and is a vital organization for all Florida citizens to belong to. Heavy lobbying of the Florida Legislature, numerous newsletters, and on-line bulletins advising members of current bills, and happenings. My third "essential" membership for any Florida gun owner.

Main phone number: (904) 222-9518. You may join by phoning, and using credit card.

Second Amendment Foundation: Another fine organization. Suggested dues are $15.00 or $30.00 -- whichever you can spare. It's well worth supporting.

GETTING A SEIZED FIREARM BACK:

Let's assume your firearm was seized by the police. How do you get it back? The starting point is _F.S._ 705.105, which deals with the "procedure regarding unclaimed evidence".   According to this statute, assuming the seizure was legal, title automatically vests to the seizing agency 60 days after the conclusion of the criminal proceeding, assuming you haven't taken affirmative steps to get it back.   There is also F.S. 790.08, which concerns seizure of weapons. That section states that any weapon seized are forfeit if the person used them in a crime, and they are convicted of the offense. Whether a "withheld adjudication" would constitute a conviction for purposes of this subsection is undecided.   On the other hand, if the charges are dismissed or there is an acquittal, the citizen again has sixty (60) days to "call for" the weapon.   After that, the weapon is supposed to be delivered to the Sheriff, and if the weapon remains unclaimed for an additional six months it's forfeit — but this time to the State. The Sheriff then may then use the weapons, loan the weapons to other law enforcement, sell the weapons, or destroy them.

The usual way of getting a seized firearm back is by a motion to return property before the case has ended, and an order from the judge.   Assuming charges were never brought, you can try calling the evidence room at the agency which seized the weapons, and ask their procedure to get them back.   Sometimes, it's as easy as just making a call. Assuming the property is worth an attorney fee — you may want to engage the services of an attorney if you hit a road-block.

GEORGIA LAW FOR CWP HOLDERS, ONLY:

Georgia law permits a person holding a valid Florida Concealed Weapons license to carry in that State pursuant to the Florida license only if the person is not a resident of Georgia. [16-11-128(c)]. This allows concealed carry of a "handgun, but not any other weapons, whatsoever. Moreover, if the handgun is carried on the person, it must be in an actual holster. It is also permitted to be carried in a briefcase, handbag, or other closed container, but must still be inside a holster. [16-11-126(c)] The handgun may not be taken to any "public gathering" as well as any of the following places: athletic/sporting events; church or church functions; political rallies and functions; establishments where alcoholic beverages sold; publically owned or operated buildings. It cannot be taken onto school grounds or a school bus, and can only be on school grounds when legally kept inside the vehicle, and only where the stop is temporary to pick up or drop off a student. [16-11-127.1] These were laws as of December 2003. These apply only to a valid Florida CWP holder who is not a resident of Georgia. You should check with Georgia authorities for any possible changes thereafter. I plan to expand this section in future editions.

Hope you enjoyed the book. Hope you got some valuable information from it. If you liked it, please feel free to recommend it to others. Likewise, I also encourage you to re-read it. I'll guarantee that every time you do – you'll see something you missed the last time you read it, or you'll understand the law better.

CONCLUSION:

Well, that's it for the book. Hopefully, you'll never have to experience any of the situations I outlined in it. That's why it was written, in the first place. Good luck, and God bless.

(this page reserved)

ENDNOTES

1. That Every Man Be Armed, by Stephen P. Halbrook, Chapter 3, The Independent Institute (1984). See also, The Bill of Rights in Modern America, edited by David J. Bodenhamer, Indiana University Press (1993).

2. United States v. Emerson, 270 F.3d 203 (5th Cir. 2001), cert. denied, 536 U.S. 907 (2002), was a scholarly opinion that accurately traced the development of the Second Amendment, and should be required reading for anyone who wants to understand this important concept.

3. The problem with federal appeal courts is that sometimes judges are more concerned with their own "agenda" than truth, or the law.

4. See, Rinzler v. Carson, 262 So.2d 661,668 (Fla. 1972).

5. While the anti-gunners seem very concerned about the "one life" that your firearm might take -- they are not very concerned about the lives it will save. Moreover, armed citizens get involved in stopping crimes to a much higher degree than others, and will take the chance to assist others, only because they are armed. I hear about this all the time. So, don't swallow this "one life" garbage the anti-gunners are trying to feed you. In fact, if they put their money into firearms education like the NRA has -- they'd probably eliminate the very problem they are complaining about.

6. See, American Rifleman, Armed Citizens and Crime Control, July 1988. In fact, according to another part of the study by Professor Gary Kleck, armed citizens legally kill two to seven times the number of criminals killed by law enforcement officers, a year.

7. United States v. Lopez, 115 S.Ct. 1624 (1995)

8. The Ninth Circuit, in United States v. Stewart, Docket Number 02-10318 (9th Cir. 11/13/03), also would appear to agree that the statute is an unconstitutional exercise of power.

9. Printz v. United States, 117 S. Ct. 2365 (1997)

10. Staples v. United States, 511 US 600 (1994)

11. See, State v. Mitchell, 652 So.2d 473 (Fla. 2DCA 1995) which held that legal fireworks were not destructive devices, although fireworks which exceeded the permitted explosive weight allowed in Chapter 791, Florida Statutes, could be, if used as a weapon, or used to destroy property.

12. As of November 2003, ATF says three black powder firearms are therefore excluded from being classified as antique firearms: the Thompson Center Encore Contender, Savage 10ML, and New England Firearms Huntsman. This could change if any of these models are altered to comply with the regulations.

13. F.S. 790.001(6)

14.   Interestingly, Judge Sharp's dissent in Bostic hit the nail on the head trying to explain another case, Williams v. State, 492 So.2d 1051 (Fla. 1986).   In that case the Florida Supreme Court affirmed a conviction for a felon in possession of an antique firearm. The Opinion isn't all that clear on the basis, but the reason is obvious because the antique firearm was carried concealed.   F.S. 790.23 does not allow a convicted felon to carry a concealed weapon – and while an antique firearm may not technically be called a "firearm" for most purposes, it certainly is a "weapon" because it is a "deadly weapon". See, F.S. 790.001(3)(a).

15. A "weapon" is defined as an instrument of attack or defense in combat. State v. Houck, 652 So.2d 359 (Fla. 1995). Whereas, a "deadly weapon" or "dangerous weapon" is one, taking into account the manner of use, is likely to produce death or great bodily harm. Smith v. State, 573 So.2d 306 (Fla. 1990); Lindsey v. State, 64 So. 501 (Fla. 1914); Clemons v. State, 37 So. 647, 649 (Fla. 1904). It has also been more fully defined as: (1) any instrument which, when used in the ordinary manner contemplated by its design and construction will or is likely to cause death or great bodily harm, or (2) any instrument likely to cause death or great bodily harm because of the way it is used. J.W. v. State, 807 So.2d 148 (Fla. 2DCA 2002).

16. F.S. 790.065 (12)(a)

17. State v. Menuto, 30 Fla. L.Weekly D. 1173 (Fla. 2DCA 2005) is the case that decided a "withheld" juvenile conviction was still a conviction under F.S. 790.23. I disagree, and feel the Opinion is unfair and wrongly decided.

18. Federally Firearms Licensee or "FFL".

19. F.S. 790.17

20. F.S. 790.18

21. While there is some debate on exactly what a dirk is, it is usually defined as a long dagger. A dagger, on the other hand,   is usually defined as a weapon with a narrow, pointed, double-edged tip that is used for stabbing. Appellate courts in Florida have come up with their own "catch-all" definition for a dirk which is any straight knife worn on a person which is capable of inflicting death, except for a "pocket knife." "Dirk" and "dagger" are used synonymously, and consist of any straight stabbing weapon. McNeally v. State, 884 So.2d 494 (Fla. 5DCA 2004)

22. In Clemons v. State, 37 So. 647 (Fla. 1904), the Defendant was convicted of second degree murder for using brass knuckles, which resulted in the death of a man. The court held that brass knuckles could be classified as a "deadly weapon" in this case because anytime a weapon, as used, produces death (or great bodily harm) -- it's a deadly weapon.

23. F.S. 790.22

24. F.S. 790.22(3) & (4)(a).

25. 18 USC 922 (x)

26. F.S. 790.17

27. In U.S. v. Moore, 109 F.3d 1456 (9th Cir. 1997) the court held a purchase from a dealer for a child under 18 was an illegal "strawman" transaction even though it was not illegal under state law. I think the decision would have been different had the person been 18.

28. 18 USC 922(a)(3) & (a)(5)

29. Rentals should be restricted to dealers, since this is a business purpose, and the business of dealing in firearms is restricted to those possessing a federal license to do so.

30. 18 USC 922(a)(5)

31. 18 USC 922(a)(3)(A) & (5)(A)

32. Interestingly, F.S. 790.28, which allows a Florida resident to purchase a rifle or shotgun in any contiguous state to Florida, shouldn't really affect this interpretation in the least, because the Florida statute doesn't prohibit anything. Changes in federal laws have rendered the term "contiguous state" as meaningless.

33. 18 USC 922(b)(3)(A)

34. 18 USC 922(g)(5)

35. The "90 day" requirement comes from 27 CFR 478.11, which defines "state of residence" for aliens as requiring the 90 day period. ATF recently interpreted this as the 90 day period immediately before the purchase, without interruption as to non-immigrant aliens. [ATF Ruling 2004-1]. Resident aliens also need to establish the 90 day residency, and any travel outside the U.S., even vacation, begins the period anew.

36. U.S. v. Atandi, 376 F.3d 1186 (10th Cir. 2004), held failure of a foreign exchange student to maintain student status made him an "illegal" alien, and thus it was a federal felony to own/possess a firearm. (But he couldn't have it anyway as a non-immigrant visa holder). On the other hand, in U.S. v. Orellana, 405 F.3d 360 (5th Cir. 2005), an alien who entered the U.S.A. illegally, but was later granted "temporary protected status" is no longer an illegal alien, and if he/she otherwise qualifies - could own or possess.

37. It is not a crime to "possess" a firearm where the disability is a felony or crime of domestic violence until the "conviction" takes place. Usually this means the date the sentence is imposed by the court.

38. <u>United States v. Hansel</u>, 474 F.2d 1120 (8th Cir. 1072); <u>United States v. Giardina</u>, 861 F.2d 1334 (5th Cir. 1988); <u>United States v. Waters</u>, 23 F.3d 29 (2d Cir. 1994)

39. "Intimate partner" means a present or former spouse; present or former cohabitating partner, or parent of a mutual child. 18 USC 921(32)

40. Domestic Violence section of 1994 Crime Bill, section 110401(8); 18 USC 921 (33); 18 USC 922 (d)(8) & (g)(8).

41. 18 USC 922(g)(9)

42. In Florida, in a criminal case the judge will either "adjudicate" you guilty of the crime, or "withhold adjudication" — unless you were found "not guilty" or the case was dropped (nolle prosequi), or dismissed. Some benefits of a "withheld" are you can get your record sealed at some later point, and that the finding of guilt does not generally count as a "conviction" for many purposes.

43. <u>F.S.</u> 741.28 defines "domestic violence" as any form of assault, battery, stalking, including aggravated & sexual, or any criminal offense resulting in physical injury or death of one family or household member by another who is, or was residing in the same single dwelling unit.

44. It does apply to those who "manufacture" ammunition for sale.

45. Fla. Admin. Code 11-C 6.009.

46. <u>F.S.</u> 907.041(4) gives a list of "dangerous crimes", many of which are also "forcible felonies". These dangerous crimes include: arson, aggravated assault, aggravated battery, illegal use of explosives, child abuse, aggravated child abuse, abuse of elderly or disabled person or aggravated abuse thereof, hijacking, kidnap, homicide, manslaughter, sexual battery, robbery, carjacking, lewd, lascivious or indecent assault or act upon or in presence of child under 16, burglary of a dwelling, stalking, aggravated stalking, domestic violence under F.S. 741.28, home invasion robbery.

47. Although <u>F.S.</u> 790.065(2)(a)(3) requires that FDLE issue a "conditional nonapproval" for a withheld adjudication on a misdemeanor crime of domestic violence until 3 years after sentence, there does not

appear to be any legal authority for a denial if an appeal of the non-approval was taken.

48. United States v. Chubbuck, 252 F.3d 1300 (11th Cir. 2001), clearly indicates the 11th Circuit screwed this up, but the court was unable to correct itself. Florida law makes it clear that a "withheld" is not a "conviction" even on a guilty plea. State v.McFadden, 772 So.2d 1209 (Fla. 2000). However, the confusion the 11th Circuit had arose because a "withheld" can be considered for some sentencing purposes. McFadden, supra; State v. Freeman, 775 So.2d 344 (Fla. 3DCA 2000).

49. Obviously, the court cannot OK this if you were adjudicated guilty of a felony, or have an adjudication for domestic violence.

50. In State v. Hart, 668 So.2d 589 (Fla. 1996), the Florida Supreme Court held, in a case involving a convicted felon, that this condition of probation was a standard condition of probation. The decision would be wrong if applied to an individual with a "withheld" felony conviction or a misdemeanor (other than domestic violence), as F.S. 948.03 applies only to "firearms", and not other weapons, and still allows the court to approve possession and ownership of a firearm, with the approval of the probation officer, presumably when the case involves a misdemeanor or "withheld adjudication" felony.

51. W.J. v. State, 688 So.2d 954 (Fla. 4DCA 1997); Williams v. State, 681 So.2d 817 (Fla. 2DCA 1996).

52. Again, I caution that currently the federal court (11th Circuit) has held that a "guilty plea" or guilty verdict in a trial is a "conviction" regardless of whether there is a "withheld adjudication", and will sustain any federal conviction for felony possession or possession for crime of domestic violence . U.S. v. Chubbuck, 252 F.3d 1300 (11th Cir. 2001).

53. See the citation in the previous endnote.

54. I think the interpretation is wrong, and should only give reason for a conditional disapproval until the federal disability issue is determined, but for now, that's the way it is.

55. F.S. 790.065(12)(d)

56. F.S. 790.065(12)(a)

57. F.S. 790.065(1)(a)

58. F.S. 790.065(7)

59. F.S. 790.065(12); 18 USC 922(a)(6)

60. Fla.Admin.Code 11C-6.009.

61. 18 USC 922(t)

62. I use a few words interchangeably even if I'm technically incorrect. These are: "ATF" or "BATF" for the Bureau of Alcohol, Tobacco and Firearms and Explosives I also prefer to use concealed "permit", or CWP, rather than the more correct term of concealed weapons "license."

63. Roberto v. State, 853 So.2d 582 (Fla. 5DCA 2003); Randall v. F.D.L.E., 791 So.2d 1238 (Fla. 1DCA 2001). There was a conflict as to whether a full pardon negated guilt, that conflict has been resolved by the wording now added to a full pardon that it does not indicate innocence or expunge a record.

64. Technically, the arresting agency and other criminal justice agencies involved can keep a notation showing they complied with the expunction order – but that's it.

65. I use the terms "license" and "permit" interchangeably.

66. U.S. v. Chubbuck, 252 F.3d 1300 (11th Cir. 2001).

67. F.S. 790.061

68. F.S. 790.06(12)

69. 18 USC 930(g)(1) defines "federal facility" as a building or part thereof owned or leased by the federal government, where federal employees are regularly present for the purposes of performing their official duties. F.S. 790.115(1) differentiates between school "grounds" and "facilities" — thus, they obviously relate to different definitions.

F.S. 159.27(22) defines "educational facility" in terms similar to the federal statute recited.

70. If the legislature wanted to cover everything, they probably would have included the "grounds" of the school, just as they did in F.S. 790.115(1)(ie: "on the grounds or facilities of any school"), or they would have defined it as "school plant" per F.S. 228.041(7), or "campus" per F.S. 228.091. Research of numerous Florida statutes shows similar definitions. Compare, 18 USC 930(g)(1), as in the prior endnote.

71. F.S. 790.115 concerns school related possession of weapons.

72. Except for "securely encased" per F.S. 790.115(2)(a)(3).

73. 18 USC 930. "The term "Federal facility" means a building or part thereof owned or leased by the Federal government, where federal employees are regularly present . . . ." Postal regulations also forbid dangerous weapons and firearms in a post office. 39 CFR 232.1

74. 18 USC 2115 allows a prosecution for a burglary or robbery committed on such property, but it does not cover CCF or CCW.

75. F.S. 790.06(1)

76. "Willful" under Florida law means: intentionally, knowingly, and purposefully. State v. May, 670 So.2d 374 (Fla. 2DCA 1996). Under federal law it means that the person actually knew his conduct was illegal. Ratzlaf v. U.S., 510 US 135 (1994); U.S. v. Sanchez-Corcino, 85 F.3d 549 (11th Cir. 1996).

> "A thing is willfully done when it proceeds from a conscious motion of the will, intending the result which actually comes to pass. It must be designed or intentional, and may be malicious, though not necessarily so. "Willful" is sometimes used in the sense of intentional, as distinguished from "accidental," and, when used in a statute affixing a punishment to acts done willfully, it may be restricted to such acts as are done with an unlawful intent." Jersey v. Paper, 658 So. 2d 331 (Fla. 1995)

77. This is a chronic alcoholic whose mental process is permanently affected — not somebody who got intoxicated a few times — unless they've been convicted of two DUI's within 3 years.

78. This particular subsection allows revocation of the license in the discretion of the Dept. of Agriculture — it is not mandatory. F.S. 790.06(3).

79. In McFadden v. State, 732 So.2d 412 (Fla. 3DCA 1999), aff'd 772 So.2d 1209 (Fla. 2000), the court held that a "withheld adjudication" is not a conviction even on a guilty plea. The problem is that the federal appeals court (11th Circuit) refuses to recognize this even though they are legally bound to do so. This may be shocking to many people, but the 11th Circuit is not known for being a court that is overly concerned with citizen rights. They normally rule as restrictively as possible against the citizen, and bend over backwards for the government. That's my opinion.

80. Miami v. Swift, 481 So.2d 26 (Fla. 3DCA 1985), affirmed a jury award of $50,000 for the false arrest of a person with a gun in the console.

81. Sult v. State, 30 Fla. L. Weekly S. 470 (Fla. 2005).

82. F.S. 790.053

83. F.S. 790.01

84. In Peoples v. State, 287 So. 2d 63 (Fla. 1973), the Florida Supreme Court interpreted F.S. 790.25 as including concealed carry on residential or business premises.

85. The term "manual possession" came from former F.S. 790.05, and means that the weapon is actually in your hand.

86.   There is an unanswered legal question whether a county or municipality has the legal ability to enact valid ordinances prohibiting certain weapons not specifically permitted under C. 790, as the preemption clause technically applies only to firearms and ammunition.   From a constitutional standpoint the arguments vary from weapon to weapon, and whether the person has a concealed permit, or not.

87. <u>Dozier v. State</u>, 662 So.2d 382 (Fla. 4DCA 1995). Also, the term "ship" should be synonymous with the term "boat" in the sense of a motor boat, and a sail boat with a cabin. Since a "bicycle" has been excluded as a conveyance — I assume a canoe or similar type craft would also be excluded, but there is no case law.

88. <u>A.M. v. State</u>, 678 So.2d 914 (Fla. 1DCA 1996)

89. <u>F.S.</u> 790.001(16)

90. <u>Urquiola v. State</u>, 590 So.2d 497 (Fla. 3DCA 1991)

91. <u>Alexander v. State</u>, 477 So.2d 557 (Fla. 1985). While Velcro isn't specifically mentioned, it functions the same as a zipper, takes the same amount of effort to open, and makes a loud-ripping sound that would likely make it real clear to you, what you were doing. It fits the statutory purpose perfectly, and it also makes the bag a "closed container". Of course, that's my opinion for now, as there's no case law.

92. <u>Gemmile v. State</u>, 657 So.2d 900 (Fla. 4DCA 1995)

93. An interesting but unanswered question that the <u>Alexander</u> case presents is whether an unzipped "zippered gun case" with a weapon is still "securely encased" – because <u>Alexander</u> held that a purse with a zipper is a "zippered gun case" as a "matter of law", and the statutory language doesn't say it must be "zipped". Or, perhaps, does the Opinion stand for the fact that a quick opening and closing of the case didn't compromise its "securely encased" status?

94. <u>Bell v. State</u>, 636 So.2d 80 (Fla. 2DCA 1994)

95. <u>Cates v. State</u>, 408 So.2d 797 (Fla. 2DCA 1983)

96. Actually, this makes a lot of sense. Since the key purpose of your Florida Constitutional right to keep and bear arms is for self defense, and since this is confirmed by both the "Declaration of Policy" in <u>F.S.</u> 790.25(1), and the constructions given to <u>F.S.</u> 790.25(4) & (5) -- it would be pretty silly to require the firearm to be difficult to access in an emergency. I mean, these things usually happen in a matter of seconds -- and you can't tell the bad guy to wait while you load your gun, or unlock your glove compartment. If you did, you'd already be dead.

Moreover, you might be interested in knowing that throughout the early history of this country, and well into the mid-Twentieth Century, many States allowed travelers to keep pistols in their vehicles, even if such was otherwise not permitted to the regular populace. In some part, this was due to the dangers associated with being waylayed while on the road. Sounds familiar, doesn't it?

This was certainly the rule in Florida. See, Biennial Report of Attorney General, January 12, 1933 (p. 628) & March 20, 1936 (p. 751); and Opinion of Attorney General, 051-105 (1951).

97. F.S. 790.053

98. On the other hand, even if unsnapped, if it has a flap which must be moved to get the gun out – probably fits the Urquiloa case.

99. Remember, if you can fire the weapon or obtain the weapon without physically opening, removing, moving, or undoing the cover, flap, or restraining device -- you're not legal -- because it's not "securely encased".

100. Doughty v. State, 979 So.2d 1048 (Fla. 4DCA 2008).

101. F.S. 790.001(15) states: "readily accessible for immediate use' means that a firearm or other weapon is carried on the person or within such close proximity and in such a manner that it can be retrieved and used as easily and quickly as if carried on the person."

102. In Ashley v. State, 619 So.2d 294 (Fla. 1993), the Florida Supreme Court held that an unloaded gun under the seat was "readily accessible" where ammo was lying in open view on the passenger seat. However, in both Strikertaylor v. State, 997 So.2d 488 (Fla. 2DCA 2008); and State v. Weyant, 990 So.2d 675 (Fla. 2DCA 2008), the appellate court held an unloaded handgun under the seat with ammo in either a closed console, or closed glove compartment was not. Thus, the critical element seems to be an analogy that the ammo was "securely encased" – so the unloaded weapon couldn't be "readily accessible". Makes sense to me.

103. Boswink v. State, 636 So.2d 584 (Fla. 2DCA 1994).

104. Watson v. Stone, 4 So.2d 700, 702-703 (Fla. 1941).

105. Again, I remind you that a "bicycle" is not a conveyance - and I doubt that a canoe, single man sailboat, or a rowboat would qualify, either because they would probably be considered purely "pleasure craft", and not really a functional conveyance. However, there are no court cases defining this.

106.   Ostomy sissors with an overall length of 4" or less, when accompanied by a ostomate supply kit are legal.

107. United States v. Copeland, 2003 U.S. Dist. LEXIS 6446 (U.S. Dist. Ct. S.D. Tenn. 2003); U.S. v. Hendrick, 207 F. Supp. 2d 710 (S.D. Ohio 2002); U.S. v. Garrett, 984 F.2d 1402 (5th Cir. 1993); United States v Lee 539 F2d 606 (6th Cir. 1976).

108. F.S. 790.23 (3)(l)

109. See, Watson v. Stone, 4 So.2d 700, 702 (Fla. 1941).

110. In Brook v. State, 999 So.2d 1093 (Fla. 5DCA 2009), the court held that an employee may legally carry at his place of business even after hours when the business was closed – purely for social reasons.

111. See, Sherrod v. State, 484 So.2d 912 (Fla. 3DCA 1986), where a conviction for carrying a concealed firearm was sustained because the defendant was on his apartment unit's parking lot when arrested -- a "common area".

112. Caban v. State, 475 So.2d 968 (Fla. 4DCA 1985), held that a person's home or business in F.S. 790.25, refers to an individual's surrounding property as well as the buildings and structures situated thereon. This is not restricted to curtilage, for you can carry open or concealed, anywhere on your home or business property, although be careful if unfriendly neighbors are around due to "improper exhibition".

113. Wassmer v. State, 565 So.2d 856 (Fla. 2DCA 1990); and Turner v. State, 645 So.2d 444 (Fla. 1994).

114. <u>F.S.</u> 790.052

115. If you have a concealed permit, it's a second degree misdemeanor pursuant to <u>F.S.</u> 790.06(12). Otherwise, it's a first degree misdemeanor for a weapon, or a third degree felony for a firearm.

116. The primary case on this issue was <u>Wilson v. State</u>, 344 So.2d 1315 (Fla. 2DCA 1977), <u>reh. denied</u>, 353 So.2d 679 (Fla. 1977); which held that it was reversible error for the judge not to instruct the jury that "knowledge of the presence of the firearm" was essential to a conviction. <u>Accord</u>, <u>L.J. v. State</u>, 553 So.2d 286 (Fla. 3DCA 1989); <u>V.B.L. v. State</u>, 408 So.2d 855 (Fla. 3DCA 1982). In essence, you don't want to make a criminal out of someone who merely made a mistake, and carried it unwittingly. <u>See</u>, <u>Cole v. State</u>, 353 So.2d 952 (Fla. 2DCA 1978).

117. <u>U.S. v. Garrett</u>, 984 F.2d 1402 (5th Cir. 1993)

118. Recent studies have shown that these chemical sprays can be ineffective against people on certain types of drugs, and against mentally unbalanced persons. I would guess that this might also apply against a highly motivated assailant. It's a good reason to remember that a spray will never replace a firearm in a life-and-death situation. Also, if you're buying a chemical spray -- I highly recommend a pepper based spray rated at 1.5 million Scoville heat units (SHU), or better. The other types of sprays have limited shelf-life, and are not always effective.

119. In <u>L.B. v. State</u>, <u>supra</u>, the court held the statute to be vague, and a violation of due process of law.

120. 18 USC 930(g) excludes a pocket knife from the definition of a "dangerous weapon" where the blade length is less than 2 ½ inches.

121. 18 USC 930(g)(2) says a pocket knife with a blade <u>less</u> than two and a half inches is not a dangerous weapon, thus in <u>U.S. v. Hendrick</u>, 207 F. Supp. 2d 710 (S.D. Ohio 2002), the federal court upheld a conviction, and found a three inch blade was a dangerous weapon.

122. <u>F.S.</u> 790.01; <u>F.S.</u> 790.053

123. Actually, <u>F.S.</u> 951.22 uses the term "dangerous weapon" which should eliminate a "self defense chemical spray" from any criminal liability if brought into a county jail facility for your own use, rather than to aid an escape, etc.   Still, even if not prosecuted, I guarantee you can't get it in if they know about it, nor should you try. The other two statues apply to any "weapon".

124. Since chemical sprays do not fall under <u>F.S.</u> 790.06(1), they are excluded under <u>F.S.</u> 790.06(12). On the other hand, electric weapons are covered under the permit — so "willful" carry into a courthouse or jail is a second degree misdemeanor.   Under any circumstance, the courts have the right to set regulations on citizen access — so, a requirement of "no weapons" is totally legal.

125. Since a self defense chemical spray is not regulated by the Concealed Permit law, a licensee would have more legal leeway with the spray. Likewise, there's an untested and common sense argument that if it's allowed under <u>F.S.</u> 790.25 – you should be able to do it as a CWP holder, as you wouldn't be carrying "per your permit", but instead, would be carrying per <u>F.S.</u> 790.25, just like any Florida citizen can do.   Test case time!

126. Whether it's a misdemeanor trespass, or a felony depends on whether a self defense pepper spray or nonlethal electric weapon is considered a "dangerous weapon" under <u>F.S.</u> 810.08 & 09. Since a dangerous weapon is one that, taking into account the manner in which it is used, is likely to produce death or great bodily harm — it should be only a misdemeanor. <u>See</u>, <u>Houck v. State</u>, 634 So.2d 180 (Fla. 5DCA 1994).

127. Opinion of Attorney General, 068-103 (1968)

128. In <u>Chaungocnguyen v. State</u>, 28 FLW 2640 (Fla. 1DCA 11/03), the appellate court held that a stun gun would not ordinarily be classified as a "deadly weapon".

129. <u>F.S.</u> 790.115(1)

130. <u>Ensor v. State</u>, 403 So.2d 349 (Fla. 1981). <u>Goodman v. State</u>, 689 So.2d 428 (Fla. 1DCA 1997).

131. As previously noted, the preemption law covers only firearms and ammunition. Whether local laws concerning weapons other than firearms, ammunition, nonlethal stun guns, and self defense chemical sprays would run afoul of the Florida Constitution (ordinances may not be in conflict with general law) is an undecided question. See, Fla. Const., Art. 8, section 1(f).

132. F.S. 790.10

133. F.S. 790.115(1)

134. In an aggravated assault case mere pointing the firearm at someone else is generally going to qualify as sufficient to create an "imminent" fear of harm – although the "intent" issue would still be for the jury since it is the intent of the person with the firearm that counts – not the subjective reaction of the alleged victim (although reasonable fear is an additional element). Benitez v. State, 901 So.2d 935 (Fla. 4DCA 2005).

135. Improper display is a "lesser included" of aggravated assault. Konrath v. State, 997 So.2d 1281 (Fla. 5DCA 2009).

136. F.S. 790.15

137. An automatic firearm is one which can fire a series of "bursts" (ie: "select fire"), or can fire continuously (automatic mode) -- from a single pull of the trigger. Such firearms normally have the additional ability to fire single shots in a semi-automatic mode, as well. The mode on such firearms is controlled by a manually operated switch located on the firearm. A "semi-automatic" weapon is one which is able to reset itself for each succeeding shot, but still requires the trigger to be pulled before each individual shot can be fired.

138. F.S. 790.16

139. See, Rinzler v. Carson, 262 So.2d 661 (Fla. 1972), where the use of a registered submachine gun was condoned in a self-defense situation.

140. F.S. 790.221; 18 USC 5801-5872

141. The definition of a firearm in 27 CFR 479.11 states:

> "The overall length of a weapon made from a shotgun or a rifle is the distance
> between the extreme ends of the weapon . . . ."

142. Yeah, I know some people insist you can manufacture your own machine gun, and be legal.   In 2003in United States v. Stewart, the Ninth Circuit said that possession was not illegal where the defendant manufactured the machine gun at his home, and it was not for resale or transfer. However, the U.S. Supreme Court reversed the decision at 545 US 1112 (2005), and the Ninth Circuit then reinstated the conviction. United States v. Stewart, 451 F.3d 1071 (9th Cir. 2006)

143. F.S. 790.001(9)

144. Since the sole justification for the registration is to pay the tax, it's hard to understand why you would still have to register if there was no tax to pay.

145. An "NFA" firearm (but never a "machinegun" or "destructive device") may be placed on the list per 26 USC 5845(a). This is "Section III" of the published list, which then removes the weapon from NFA requirements. However, a machinegun that is a curio, relic, or antique — still needs the Form 4, and tax stamp. Same thing on destructive devices.

146. True, it's not the gun – it's the wallet that makes it an NFA weapon when the firearm is placed inside. Since "any combination of parts" only applies to machine guns, silencers, and destructive devices – you can legally have the wallet and gun without violating the NFA so long as you don't put them together. On the other hand, the newly sought definition of "pistol" (April 2005) will make some of the more exotic firearms an NFA weapon.

147. The Ninth Circuit, in United States v. Stewart, Docket Number 02-10318 (9th Cir. 11/13/03), held it was not illegal for an individual to manufacture a firearm for his personal use when most of the parts were fabricated by himself in his own home, and the machine gun was not for transfer or sale.   This decision is no longer the law, and has been reversed. Therefore, manufacture of any machine gun by an individual will result in serious legal consequences.

148. In <u>United States v. Burgert</u>, 116 Fed. Appx. 124 (9th Cir. 2004), the court held that use of a conversion kit did not equate to self manufacture of a machine gun, and hence it was a felony.

149. <u>F.S.</u> 790.157(2)(c) makes it "prima facie" that a person is under the influence at 0.10 per cent blood alcohol level. Between 0.05% and 0.10% is a gray area. Below 0.05% — you're presumed to be OK.

150. You might also remember that if you're not sober, you may be too intoxicated to realize you're gun is not really unloaded. Certainly, a sobering thought (no pun intended) to ponder.

151. A "felony" under Florida law is a crime that could be punished by more than a year imprisonment, regardless of the sentence imposed.

152. <u>F.S.</u> 775.087(2)(r).   Mandatory is only if actual possession proven. <u>Johnson v. State</u>, 855 So.2d 218 (Fla. 5DCA 2003). 18 USC 924(a)(2).

153. <u>F.S.</u> 790.23

154. <u>F.S.</u> 775.087(3)

155. 18 USC 929

156. <u>F.S.</u> 790.001(4); 26 USC 5845 (f)

157. A 12 gauge shotgun has a bore more than one half inch.

158. <u>State v. Darynani</u>, 774 So.2d 855 (Fla. 4DCA 2000). The case, and opinion by the court showed an incredible lack of understanding, and lack of legal research as to a century old definition that was clear in both federal law, and in numerous other states. The result was legally "sloppy", and below the standard of a Florida appellate court.

159. <u>F.S.</u> 370.08; and Fla. Admin. Code 46-4.012(1).

160. IRS Rev. Rul. 55-569.

161. <u>F.S.</u> 810.08 & 810.09

162. F.S. 493.6120

163. 18 USC 922 (x)

164. F.S. 790.174; & the 1997 amendment (C.97-234) to 790.115(2)(c)(2). See also, F.S. 790.175

165. This particular section is governed under the culpable negligence statute, Florida Statute 784.05(3), rather than the chapter on weapons and firearms, Chapter 790.

166. As stated in previous footnotes the Ninth Circuit would likely continue to hold the amended act as unconstitutional. United States v. Stewart, Docket Number 02-10318 (9th Cir. 11/13/03).

167. Chapter 97-72, Florida Statutes (1997), and 99-284 in 1999.

168. F.S. 790.33 wisely preempted firearms and ammunition laws (not other weapons) from local governments. However, local government is still restricted on weapons if they pass laws that conflict with C. 790. See, Rinzler v. Carson, 262 So.2d 661,668 (Fla. 1972).

169. 18 USC 930(g)(1) defines "federal facility" as a building or part thereof. F.S. 159.27(22) defines "educational facility" in similar terms. And, F.S. 790.115(1) differentiates between school "grounds" and "facilities" making it obvious that the Legislature recognizes the terms mean different things.

170. Authority to support an FFL receiving/purchasing (not selling) firearms out of state can be found in 27 CFR 478.29 & 478.29a. 18 USC 922(a)(3).

171. 18 USC 922(y);   27 CFR 478.32 & 478.99

172. K-Mart v. Kitchen, 662 So.2d 977 (Fla. 4DCA 1995) was reversed by the Florida Supreme Court on July 17, 1997 in Kitchen v. K-Mart 697 So.2d 1200 (Fla. 1997), which reinstated the jury verdict. Also, in Wal-Mart v. Coker, 742 So.2d 257 (Fla. 1DCA 1997), Wal-Mart was found liable for the death of a person when it sold handgun ammo to a minor who then used it to shoot the decedent. Big bucks!

173. <u>F.S.</u> 790.18

174. <u>F.S.</u> 790.225. The real bad news is that federal law can make possession, manufacture, distribution a ten year felony per 15 USC 1245:

> "Whoever in or affecting interstate commerce, within any Territory or possession of the United States, within Indian country (as defined in section 1151 of title 18), or within the special maritime and territorial jurisdiction of the United States (as defined in section 7 of title 18), knowingly possesses, manufactures, sells, or imports a ballistic knife shall be . . .imprisoned not more than ten years. . . ."

175. It was established that 90% of "traceable" firearms came from the United States – but since most of the firearms being smuggled into Mexico weren't traceable – the overall total was 17% of total firearms.

176. American Rifleman, "<u>You, Your SKS & The Law</u>", by Michael R. Irwin, May 1994.

177. These are listed in <u>F.S.</u> 776.08.

178. <u>Clemons v. State</u>, 37 So. 647, 649 (Fla. 1904). <u>See</u>, endnote 12, <u>supra</u>, for a full definition.

179. <u>Williams v. State</u>, 727 So.2d 1062 (Fla. 4DCA 1999). On the other hand, a cigarette lighter that looks like a firearm is not usually a "deadly weapon" even if the victim believes it is — because it is not designed to cause death or great bodily harm. <u>J.W. v. State</u>, 807 So.2d 148 (Fla. 2DCA 2002).

180. <u>F.S.</u> 776.012 & 776.013.   However, pursuant to <u>F.S.</u> 782.02, deadly force may be justifiable to stop the commission of <u>any</u> felony upon your own person, or to stop the commission of a felony upon or in any dwelling house in which you may be, so long as you did not "unnecessarily kill" the perpetrator by using excessive force, per <u>F.S.</u> 782.11.

181. <u>F.S.</u> 776.08

182. Use of force is found in Chapter 776, Florida Statutes, in numerous subsections that delineate what can, and cannot be done.

183. A "deadly weapon" is either an instrument which will **likely** cause death or great bodily harm when used in the ordinary and usual manner contemplated by its design and construction, or an object which is used, or threatened to be used in such a way that it would be **likely** to cause death or great bodily harm. Butler v. State, 602 So.2d 1303 (Fla. 1DCA 1992). In Dale v. State, 22 FLW 670 (Fla. 10/97) the Supreme Court of Florida held that whether an unloaded BB gun was a deadly weapon was a jury question. This is a rather awful decision that makes little sense, and seems to allow a jury to decide if a weapon is deadly from the perception of the victim, rather than from the standpoint of reality or logic. See also, Mitchell v. State, 1997 Fla. App. Lexis 7870 (2DCA 7/29/97), where the court also held an **unloaded** BB gun could be a deadly weapon.

184. F.S. 790.001(13); L.B. v. State, 681 So.2d 1179 (Fla. 2DCA 1996).

185. Heston v. State, 484 So.2d 84 (Fla. 2DCA 1986)

186. Similar to a firearm is a nunchaku, or nun-chuks, which is also considered a deadly weapon. Why? Because "unlike common objects which may be deadly only because of their use or threatened use, the sole modern use of nunchaku is to cause ." R.V. v. State, 497 So.2d 912 (Fla. 3DCA 1986). On the other hand, in the case of Heston v. State, 484 So.2d 84 (Fla. 2DCA 1986), the court held that an unloaded crossbow was not a deadly weapon as it could not have inflicted injury upon another person without arrows.

187. In Sullivan v. State, 898 So.2d 105 (Fla. 2DCA 2005), the court held that a threat was not "imminent" where there was a distance of 30 feet between the defendant (armed with a knife) and the victim, and there was also a car between them. This is a critical case for an attorney to read on how to defend an aggravated assault, and what "imminent" means.

188. In Gaffney v. State, 742 So.2d 358 (Fla. 2DCA 1999), the court quoted from the American Heritage Dictionary that "imminent" was defined as "about to occur". Likewise, before an aggravated assault can take place there must be a well founded fear of imminent violence by the alleged victim. McClenithan v. State, 855 So.2d 675 (Fla. 2DCA 2003).

189.   I got the idea from <u>White v. Godwin</u>, 124 So.2d 525 (Fla. 1DCA 1960), a negligence case where the court said "When the on-coming car reached a <u>point</u> so close that a head-on collision appeared imminent . . ." Likewise, when you read cases such as <u>Lane v. State</u>, 32 So. 896, 899 (Fla. 1902), you see this immediate threat element:

> "if the circumstances are such as to authorize a reasonably cautious man to believe his life to be in immediate danger, or that he was in immediate danger of receiving great personal injury , it will suffice."

190.   <u>F.S.</u> 776.06

191.   <u>Howard v. State</u>, 698 So. 2d 923 (Fla. 4DCA 1997).

192.   Unresolved is whether pointing a gun skyward, or towards the ground is the use of force, at all? I can't find any cases on this, and my personal opinion is that no use of force is involved. However, there's no case law to back me up. Test case time. I think that such a situation is, at worst, an "improper display". To me, the act in a confrontation is either a conditional threat, or just letting the other folks know I am armed if it ever comes to that. On the other hand, I'm not suggesting it unless you think there is a reasonable possibility of a forcible felony about to occur.

193.   <u>Stewart v. State</u>, 672 So. 2d 865 (Fla. 2DCA 1996); <u>Deluge v. State</u>, 710 So. 2d 83 (Fla. 5DCA 1998); <u>Howard v. State</u>, <u>supra</u>.

194.   <u>Hernandez v. State</u>, 842 So. 2d 1049 (Fla. 4DCA 2003); <u>Reimei v. State</u>, 532 So. 2d 16 (Fla. 5DCA 1988).

195.   <u>B.A.A. v. State</u>, 333 So.2d 552 (Fla. 3DCA 1976), defines "breach of the peace" as "the violation of any law enacted to preserve peace and good order." In <u>City of St. Petersburg v. Calbeck</u>, 114 So.2d 316 (Fla. 2DCA 1959), the court defined breach of the peace as:

> "In general terms, a breach of the peace is a violation of public order, a disturbance of the public tranquility, by any act or conduct inciting to violence or tending to provoke or excite others to break the peace, or, as sometimes said, it includes any violation of any law enacted to preserve

peace and good order. The term disorderly conduct has been construed as embracing all such acts and conduct as are of a nature to corrupt the public morals or to outrage the sense of public decency, whether committed by words or acts. Disorderly conduct may in many cases be a breach of the peace, but it is not necessarily so."

196. A stun gun is not a deadly weapon. Jones v. State, 885 So.2d 466 (Fla. 4DCA 2005)

197. Even though you have no duty to retreat, I would strongly advise that you make it very clear that you want no part of any physical altercation, no matter what your legal rights are. This is because you want to make sure that it's understood you're not participating in any consensual form of mutual combat, nor are you looking for a fight. These are factors which could turn a police officer, prosecutor, or jury -- against you. So, avoid it if you can, and make it clear that you want no part of it. That way, there will be no doubt that you were the victim.

198. Dixon v. State, 603 So.2d 570 (Fla. 5DCA 1992).

199. A "warning" would seem to be a "conditional threat", and not "imminent" because it's saying "if you do something, then I'll do something".   However, that's only my interpretation, for now.   In United States v. White, 258 F.3d 374, 383 (5th Cir. 2001) the court stated: "A threat imports "[a] communicated intent to inflict physical or other harm" and is "distinguished from words uttered as mere . . . idle talk or jest."

200. F.S. 776.012 & F.S.776.031.

201. 2005 Senate Committee Reports, Summary of Legislation Passed, page 105-106, SB 436, "Protection of Persons/Use of Force".

202.   This new subsection should not apply to "curtilage". Curtilage is the yard area immediately around your dwelling where that portion of the yard is fenced, has shrubs, or something else that clearly marks the outer perimeter of your property. Hamilton v. State, 645 So.2d 555 (Fla. 2DCA 1994). If you own several acres of property that are all within a common fence -- it is not curtilage -- that would probably be interpreted as the "open fields" portion of your property. Curtilage generally refers to

a more immediate area.

203. F.S. 316.003(21) & (22);   F.S. 320.01; F.S. 320.27.

204. Senate Staff Analysis, Judiciary Committee, February 25, 2005. See also, Senate Staff Analysis, Criminal Justice Committee, February 10, 2005.

205. "The presumptions created by the committee substitute, however, appear to be conclusive". Senate Staff Analysis, Judiciary Committee, February 25, 2005, page 6.

206. Bartlett v. State, 993 So.2d 157 (Fla. 1DCA 2008).

207. I would assume that "imminent" in this sense means that the crime, or the "attempt" is already in progress, and is way beyond the planning stages.

208. Let's not get cute, or Rambo here! Throwing a bomb, or something extreme that wipes out half the neighborhood in order to stop your attacker is generally not going to be appreciated.   You will be prosecuted for the excess.

209. "Force" is a term of art, and any force, however slight, should qualify. Thus, an intruder who opens an unlocked door is using "force", although an intruder who walks through an open door is not. Capetta v. State, 162 So. 2d 309 (Fla. 3DCA 1964).

210. The 2005 Senate Committee on Criminal Justice "Summary of Legislation Passed", page 106, states that the actual intent of the intruder is "irrelevant".   Once the intruder "unlawfully and by force" enters or attempts to enter a person's dwelling, residence, or occupied vehicle – there is a conclusive presumption he did so to "commit an unlawful act involving force or violence" regardless of actual intent. F.S. 776.013(4). Moreover, since any such entry or attempted entry is a felony, the element of force or violence automatically elevates it to a "forcible felony".

211.   For you lawyers out there,   since   we're talking about conclusive presumptions and immunity here – the only logical way

to resolve this is by placing the burden of proof on the State that (1) a crime was not in progress, and (2) that the statutory exceptions did not apply. This should first happen on a pre-trial motion to dismiss, and since the burden is on the State, I think all that the courts will have to ignore a strict <u>Rule</u> 3.190(c)(4) motion because the Defendant shouldn't have to swear to anything, it should be the other way around. Remember – we're talking about "immunity" from prosecution! <u>F.S.</u> 776.013(1)(B) requirement of a reasonable belief that a crime is occurring seems to be irrelevant since the State has the burden of disproving that a crime on the structure/vehicle was not happening. This should be the real interesting area on how the courts will interpret the statute. It will be interesting to see if this gets to a civil-like "summary judgment" type of proceeding as it matures.

212. <u>F.S.</u> 776.013(2)

213. Why? Because the immunity section of the law, <u>F.S.</u> 776.032 also includes this requirement.

214. Why else would the Legislature put subsection (b) into <u>F.S.</u> 776.012, in the disjunctive ("or") – unless the retreat rule was out across the board – so long as the "reasonable", "necessary", "imminent", and other predicates were met?

215. Trying to figure out <u>F.S.</u> 776.013(3) will drive you crazy! Why include a subsection that **doesn't apply** to a dwelling, residence, or occupied vehicle (ie: "in any other place") in a section that is really designed to cover only a dwelling, residence, or occupied vehicle? Was it meant to mean that unless you're an occupant or have a right to defend the property like in <u>F.S.</u> 776.031 you must retreat? Heck! That makes no sense if there is imminent fear of death or great bodily harm, or an imminent felony. It also would negate the other amendments and new subsections. Does it mean you must try to retreat if you are engaged in unlawful activity, or are on somebody else's property where you would otherwise need permission to be? I haven't a clue.

216. Yeah, I know I'm not being totally accurate here. There has never been a "retreat" requirement to stop a forcible felony so long as the use of deadly force appeared reasonable and necessary.

217. Kastigar v. United States, 406 US 441, 460 (1972); Zile v. State, 710 So.2d 729 (Fla. 4DCA 1998); State v. Williams, 487 So.2d 1094, 1095 (Fla. 1DCA 1986).

218. Velasquez v. State, 34 Fla. L. Weekly D266 (Fla. 4th DCA Feb. 2, 2009)(motion to dismiss must be denied if facts are disputed); Peterson v. State, 983 So.2d 27 (Fla. 1DCA 2008)(procedure on motion to dismiss is same as for an illegal confession)

219. F.S. 776.07(1)

220. F.S. 782.07, and 782.11

221. If the guy definitely has a gun in hand, a warning may not be the safest thing you could do since he could turn, and shoot you, or a bystander, before you could shoot him. While I'm not saying you should shoot first under these conditions -- it's a very tough judgment call.

222. F.S. 784.011 and 784.0211

223. For instance: an injunction against violence; maybe hiring an off-duty police officer to catch the jerk in the act and arrest him (alot cheaper than spending ten grand on me to defend you); etc. There are lots of ways, if you take the time to think about it.

224. F.S. 782.03

225. Florida Standard Jury Instructions, 603 So.2d 1175 (Fla. 1992). See also, Falco v. State, 407 So.2d 203 (Fla. 1981); and Cobb v. State, 376 So.2d 230 (Fla. 1979), where the Florida Supreme Court stated:

> "Homicides committed while resisting anothers unlawful act are punishable only if not excusable, as provided in section 782.03 . . . or if not justifiable, as provided in section 782.02, or chapter 776, Florida Statutes".

226. F.S. 782.03

227. Florida Standard Jury Instructions, 603 So.2d 1175 (Fla. 1992).

228. Prudential Property & Casualty Ins. Co. v. Swindal, 622 So.2d 467 (Fla. 1993).

229. State Farm v. Marshall, 554 So.2d 504 (Fla. 1989)

230. Stewart v. State, 672 So.2d 865 (Fla. 2DCA 1996)

231. If he was armed -- tell the officer what he had, and where it is now. Hopefully, it does not have your fingerprints on it. More hopefully, it has somebody's fingerprints on it, because if you've wiped it clean, you've tampered with evidence, and screwed your whole case.

232. The Orlando Sentinel, May 7, 1995, Metro Section, editorial by Charley Reese.

233. In today's world people illegally use the police for their own purposes by making false police reports to get someone else in trouble, for whatever reason. Typical are criminals trying to cover their illegal acts, couples involved in a divorce trying to gain leverage against the other partner, people trying to get someone "out of the way" so they can get something they otherwise couldn't, children for all sorts of crazy reasons, and petty "pay-backs" between neighbors and others. A good example of one of these situations is Mabrey v. State, 28 FLW 2576 (Fla. 2DCA 11/03), where the defendant's girlfriend called 911 claiming he had struck her. The police came and arrested him. It turns out she made the whole thing up because he wouldn't let her take his car on a trip. Once he was arrested — you guessed it — she took the car. Typical in today's world.

INDEX